A **FALCON** GUIDE ®

TRAVELING
the
OREGON TRAIL

Second Edition

Julie Fanselow

FALCON ®

Guilford, Connecticut
An imprint of The Globe Pequot Press

A FALCON GUIDE ®

Library of Congress Cataloging-in-Publication Data is available.

ISBN 1-58592-080-0

Manufactured the United States of America
Second Edition/First Printing

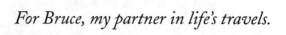

For Bruce, my partner in life's travels.

A re-enactment shows what it must have been like traveling by wagon train along the Oregon Trail in the 1800s. Photo courtesy of Wyoming Division of Tourism.

Contents

ACKNOWLEDGMENTS

Much has happened in the eight years since I researched the first edition of this book, but I must again thank Kyle Chapin and Linda Baird, who hired me to write copy for an Oregon Trail map covering Idaho. That project convinced me of the need for a modern travel guide to the trail. It was my first guidebook, and it set me on a course I've found quite fulfilling.

Many other authors have written about the Oregon Trail, but I owe a particular debt of gratitude to Gregory Franzwa, owner of the Patrice Press. His *The Oregon Trail Revisited and Maps of the Oregon Trail* were invaluable references, and I turned to them countless times while researching and writing both editions of this book.

Mac Bates, Will Harmon, Randall Green, and Bill Schneider welcomed me into the Falcon family. For this edition, thanks to Jessica Solberg and Leeann Drabenstott at Falcon, who helped me work it into a much busier schedule than I had back in 1992.

Many people all along the trail offered advice, book loans, suggestions, and hospitality, in 1992 and 2000. Although there are too many names to mention them all, these people stand out: Helen Anderson Adkins, Julia Anderson and Bill Kelley, Tori Benson, Bruce Berst, Morris Carter, Chuck Coon, Mary Ethel Emanuel, Kevin Howard, Dave Hunsaker, Stephanie Roush, Karen Runkel, Linda Sauer, Georgia Smith, and the Swetye family, with whom I made my first trips out west. A big yahoo to the Casper crew: my sister-in-law, Kay Phillips, and her daughters Risa, Jami, and Bree. Thanks for the Fort Caspar tour way back when, and double thanks for welcoming Natalie and me to your home in July 2000.

Finally, thanks to my family here in Twin Falls—my husband, Bruce Whiting; our daughter, Natalie Fanselow Whiting; and my Dad, Byron Fanselow. Thanks for holding down the fort, for supporting all I do, and for making home the best place along the trail.

FOREWORD

Lured by tales of land, gold, and a new life, more than 300,000 Americans migrated westward on the Oregon Trail system during the mid-nineteenth century. Stretching from Independence, Missouri, to the Willamette River Valley in Oregon, the primitive route promised—and delivered—a difficult journey. Emigrants battled unforgiving terrain, extreme weather, poor equipment, illness, and occasional attacks from Indians, who viewed the wagon trains with increasingly wary eyes. But the travelers pressed on across the plains and mountains, ready to endure the Wild West's risks and rigors, eager to see and settle in Oregon's lush river valleys or find their fortunes in golden California.

Many good books have been written about the trail, and some can guide the modern visitor to the exact routes the pioneers traveled, mile by mile across the continent. But few, if any, books have provided today's traveler with a guide both to the trail's history and present-day attractions nearby. That is what this book aims to do. Whether you have a long weekend, a two-week vacation, or just a favorite armchair, you can use this guide to help you get a taste of the Oregon Trail.

HOW TO USE THIS BOOK

To follow every twist and turn in the primary route of the Oregon Trail would take about a month. There are guidebooks to help the reader do just that—most notably Gregory M. Franzwa's *The Oregon Trail Revisited* and an excellent, spiral-bound atlas, *Maps of the Oregon Trail*, by the same author. But *Traveling the Oregon Trail* assumes a different type of trail traveler.

You are fascinated with the Oregon Trail, its tales of human drama and its meaning in American history, and you'd like to see many of the trail's highlights. But like most people, your vacation time is limited. And you have other interests in addition to exploring history: hiking, camping, fishing, swimming, rodeo, golf, rock climbing, rafting, or just plain sight-seeing and relaxing.

This guidebook provides information on all the major Oregon Trail historic sites as well as places to eat, sleep, and play along the trail of today. The next section of this chapter presents a nine-day trip (suited to those with two-week vacations). This nine-day trip gives a good overview of what life was like along the Oregon Trail. Those who can't spare nine days this trip can always do half the trail this year and half some other time. You could also split the trail into three long weekends, or focus on one particularly intriguing area of trail. The most important thing is to adjust the trip to your own interests, learning about the trail while savoring your favorite leisure activities. We want you to arrive home feeling as if you've had a vacation, after all!

SUGGESTED TRIP

The following is a suggested nine-day trip along the Oregon Trail. Approximate driving times and distances are given, along with major stops en route. More specific instructions to places listed are given in the appropriate later chapters. Please remember this trip plan is only a suggestion and can easily be modified to suit your family's interests and needs.

Day One: From St. Louis to Independence, Missouri.

Start in St. Louis by visiting the **Gateway Arch and Museum of Westward Expansion.** After lunch, drive west on I–70 to **Arrow Rock, Missouri,** where a state historic site and several private businesses preserve what was once an important stop for many settlers on their way to the frontier. Drive on to Independence for the evening.

Approximate driving time/distance: 5 hours, 275 miles

Day Two: From Independence, Missouri, to Manhattan or Marysville, Kansas.

Begin the day with a visit to the **National Frontier Trails Center** in Independence. Drive on into Kansas City to visit **Westport,** a district where emigrants made final preparations for the trip west. After lunch in Kansas City, take I–70 to US 75 at Topeka. Follow US 75 north 2 miles to US 24. Afternoon stops along or near US 24 could include **St. Marys Mission** at the town of St. Marys, which was an Oregon Trail resting stop, and the **Vermillion River Crossing** near Louisville. Overnight at Manhattan or Marysville, Kansas.

Approximate driving time/distance: 3 hours, 180 miles

Day Three: From Manhattan or Marysville, Kansas, to Kearney, Nebraska.

This morning, visit **Alcove Spring** on a back road between Blue Rapids and Marysville, Kansas. At Marysville, turn left (west) on US 36, then watch for the signs at KS 148 for the **Hollenberg Ranch,** a favorite Oregon Trail campsite and Pony Express station. In the afternoon, visit **Rock Creek Station State Historical Park** near Fairbury, Nebraska, then drive on to Kearney. (See the choice of routes detailed in the Nebraska chapter.) End the day with visits to **Fort Kearny State Park** and the **Archway Monument,** and spend the night at Kearney.

Approximate driving time/distance: 5.5 hours, 250 miles

Day Four: From Kearney, Nebraska, to Scottsbluff, Nebraska.

Today's itinerary includes some of the most famous sights along the Oregon Trail. Take I–80 west from Kearney to Ogallala. Take US 30 west to Brule to visit the excellent trail ruts at **California Hill.** Proceed on US 26 to **Ash Hollow State Historical Park,** making sure to stop first to see the steep and dangerous descent wagons faced at **Windlass Hill.** Continue west on US 26 to see **Courthouse and Jail Rocks** near Bridgeport and **Chimney Rock** near Bayard. Spend the night at Scottsbluff.

Approximate driving time/distance: 5 hours, 275 miles (Time zone change from Central to Mountain)

In-Depth Alternative: Break up your tour here for a trip with the Oregon Trail Wagon Train, which offers wagon train adventures ranging from three hours to four days. See the Nebraska chapter for more information.

DAY FIVE: FROM SCOTTSBLUFF, NEBRASKA, TO CASPER, WYOMING.

Before leaving Nebraska, drive to the top of **Scotts Bluff National Monument,** another major trail landmark. The first stop in Wyoming will be **Fort Laramie,** a center of activity for pioneers, military personnel, Indians, and fur traders. Next, visit Guernsey, where emigrants signed their names on **Register Cliff** and left some of the deepest wagon wheel ruts remaining anywhere along the Oregon Trail. Pick up I–25 about 15 miles west of Guernsey and drive to **Ayres Natural Bridge** near Douglas. From there, continue on I–25 to Casper, where Fort Caspar marks a crossing of the North Platte River and the **National Historic Trails Interpretive Center** (opening late 2001) details the many trails that converged in the area. Spend the night in Casper.

Approximate driving time/distance: 3 hours, 175 miles

In-Depth Alternative: Historic Trails West, based in Casper, leads wagon and horseback riding trips ranging from a few hours to five days. See the Wyoming chapter for more details.

DAY SIX: FROM CASPER, WYOMING, TO KEMMERER, WYOMING.

(Special note: Hit the road early for this longest day on the trail. If you have an extra day, split this itinerary in half, overnighting in Lander or Atlantic City.) Drive southwest of Casper on WY 220. Make a brief stop at Bessemer Bend to see the **Red Buttes,** noted in many emigrant diaries. Drive on to **Independence Rock,** where pioneers often spent the Fourth of July. **Devil's Gate,** another landmark, is just a few miles west. Take US 287 heading northwest at Muddy Gap Junction and drive to the intersection with WY 28 south of Lander. Fol-

low WY 28 south and watch for the signs to South Pass City, a restored historical mining town. (The actual South Pass crossing of the Continental Divide is nearby; see the Wyoming chapter for directions.) Take WY 28 and US 191 south to Rock Springs, then travel west on I–80 to **Fort Bridger,** established by the famous mountain man Jim Bridger as an outfitting post. From Fort Bridger, take WY 412 or US 189 north to Kemmerer, where travelers can spend the night before heading into Idaho.

Approximate driving time/distance: 7 hours, 380 miles

Day Seven: From Kemmerer, Wyoming, to Twin Falls, Idaho.

Take US 30 into Idaho. The day's first stop will be at the **National Oregon/California Trail Center** at Montpelier, an interesting interpretive site incorporating live actors. Not far west, stop briefly in **Soda Springs,** where emigrants marveled at one spring with water that tasted like beer and another that sounded like a steamboat. At the junction of I–15, head north to Pocatello and visit the replica of **Fort Hall.** Turn west on I–86 and drive to **Massacre Rocks State Park,** surrounded by the lava fields that characterize this part of Idaho. Continue on I–86 and I–84 to Burley, where US 30 comes in. **The Milner Ruts** Bureau of Land Management Interpretive Area boasts some fine wagon ruts. Approaching Twin Falls, visit the **Stricker Store,** where emigrants often camped, and **Shoshone Falls,** which many pioneers heard but never saw. Overnight in Twin Falls.

Approximate driving time/distance: 5 hours, 280 miles

In-Depth Alternative: Visit the original Fort Hall with a Native American guide. Take a wagon or horseback riding trip on the California Trail (which finally left the Oregon Trail route in Idaho's Raft River Valley) with War Eagle Outfitter & Guides.

Day Eight: From Twin Falls, Idaho, to Baker City, Oregon.

Leave Twin Falls on US 30, which leads through the Hagerman Valley, where emigrants saw water cascading from the Snake River Canyon wall at **Thousand Springs.** Return to I–84 at Bliss and drive west to Glenns Ferry, site of the **Three Island Crossing,** one of the trail's most difficult river fords. **Bonneville Point,** located near exit 64, was where travelers first saw the green Boise River Valley that marked the desert's end. Parma is home to a replica of the Hudson's Bay Company's **Fort Boise.** Continue into Oregon on US 26 and follow the instructions in the Oregon chapter to see **Keeney Pass** and the Oregon Trail murals in Vale, Oregon, before backtracking to nearby Ontario. From Ontario, I–84 parallels the trail past **Farewell Bend** and the **Burnt River Canyon.** Take exit 302 (OR 86) at Baker City to **Flagstaff Hill,** home of the BLM's Oregon Trail Interpretive Center. Visit the center and spend the night in Baker City.

Approximate driving time/distance: 4.5 hours, 250 miles (Time zone change from Mountain to Pacific)

DAY NINE: FROM BAKER CITY, OREGON, TO OREGON CITY, OREGON.

Drive through the Grande Ronde Valley and into the Blue Mountains, stopping at the Blue Mountain Crossing interpretive area. Continue west on I–84 to **The Dalles.** Here, the emigrants had to make a choice and today's travelers will, too: Either continue on down the **Columbia River** (stay on I–84) or take the overland **Barlow Road** south of Mount Hood. Whichever way you pick, trail's end is reached at **Oregon City,** on I–205 southeast of Portland.

Approximate driving time/distance: 5.5 hours, 320 miles (via I–84 instead of the Barlow Road)

In-Depth Alternative: This day's trip could easily be split up into two days, with an overnight in The Dalles or Hood River before continuing on to Oregon City. If you have time for this, be sure to visit the Tamastslikt Cultural Institute at Pendleton for a Native American view on the Oregon Trail and the Columbia Gorge Discovery Center at The Dalles. Also see Touring With a Group—Or on Your Own? on page xx for information on small-ship cruises on the Columbia River.

Some people won't have time to see the entire trail. If you have only a few days to travel, or if you would like to work a short Oregon Trail sojourn into your vacation elsewhere out West, consider the following: Get off I–80 at Ogallala, Nebraska, and follow the directions in this book from there to Guernsey, Wyoming. This 190-mile stretch offers many of the best, most scenic, and most historic Oregon Trail landmarks, including California Hill, Windlass Hill, Ash Hollow, Courthouse Rock, Chimney Rock, Scotts Bluff, Fort Laramie, and the outstanding trail ruts at Guernsey. The terrain is classic American West: broad horizons, strange and beautiful rock formations, miles and miles without a town. What's more, this trip doesn't range too far afield;

travelers can hop on I–25 just 15 miles west of Guernsey and get back on I–80 at Cheyenne a mere hour-and-a-half later.

When to Go

The emigrants started their journey by midspring, aiming to reach Oregon's Blue Mountains before the snow flew in October or November. Today's pioneers should make the trip sometime during the same seasons to best see what the pioneers saw.

June may be the best month to make the journey. Go earlier, and suffer chilly nights, spring rains, and impassable roads; wait until later in the summer, and endure oppressive heat crossing the high, arid stretches of trail through Wyoming, Idaho, and eastern Oregon, where temperatures regularly push the 100°F mark in July and August.

Western weather is unpredictable and sometimes extreme. High winds and sudden heavy rains can occur any time during the spring, summer, and fall. But don't worry if the weather turns nasty—there are excellent museums and plenty of other indoor diversions along the trail route where travelers can pass time until the clouds blow over (or the heat dies down).

How to Travel

Most people will want to start their Oregon Trail trek from either St. Louis or Independence, Missouri, both located on I–70. Although it will add a day to the trip, a start in St. Louis works best for several reasons. First, the city served as a funnel for the pioneers, with many boarding steamboats here for the trip up the Missouri River to Independence and the actual jumping-off points for Oregon. Second, St. Louis is home to the Gateway Arch and Museum of Westward Expansion, which does a great job of interpreting not just the pioneer trails but the whole history of Americans pushing west.

Situated as it is in middle America, Missouri is within two to three long days of driving for anyone in the continental United States. Here's an extreme case: With only two weeks—actually sixteen days, with weekends—for vacation, a determined sightseer could drive from Boston or Miami to St. Louis (about 1,200 miles, either way) in two days, take the suggested nine-day trip to Oregon City, and still be home (after another five-day haul back across the country) in time to return to work. But if time is limited or home is really far from the trailhead, then fly to St. Louis or Kansas City, rent a vehicle, drive to Oregon, and fly home from Portland.

The Oregon-bound pioneers rarely blazed new trails. Most of the route had been used for centuries, first by Native Americans, later by explorers, trappers, and mountain men. These guys knew what they were doing, and the routes they picked—mostly by following rivers—still are used today.

Because much of the Oregon Trail runs either beneath or within several miles of our modern-day highways, any family car in good condition should be able to make the trip without trouble. This book describes several side trips off the beaten path, and these too can all be traversed in a typical two-wheel-drive vehicle. (My pickup truck, with minimal clearance, more than 100,000 miles, and a measly four cylinders, was subjected to all routes described and survived intact.)

To get way off the beaten path, take a four-wheel-drive vehicle. Anyone hoping to follow Gregory Franzwa's detailed route mile by mile would need a four-by-four, as would anyone who wanted to make the trip in early spring, since even the "easy" back roads can prove muddy in April and May.

Air-conditioning serves two purposes in Oregon Trail country: climate control and dust abatement. For those traveling with air-conditioning, make sure to get out of the vehicle often enough to actually feel the hot, dry air and the dust, both constant companions to the westering emigrants. Those without air-conditioning can console themselves with the knowledge that the pioneers didn't have it, either, and today's "covered wagons" make a heck of a lot better time than the prairie schooners did. At any rate, it's wise to wear light-colored, airy clothes and drink plenty of water.

Air-conditioning may be a luxury, but don't forego any of the following: dashboard compass, working odometer, full-size spare tire and jack, gasoline can, shovel (in case the trail's mud claims yet another set of wheels), and some kind of basic emergency kit including flashers. The truth is, although most of the trail follows modern roads, many blacktopped western highways are as lonesome as the most desolate dirt road in the East or Midwest. Make sure your car or truck is in good shape before starting out, paying particular attention to tires, belts, and hoses. And once on the road, keep an eye on the gas gauge—it's 50 miles or more between filling stations in some areas.

A word about side trips: Out West, distances between towns are so much greater that most natives are accustomed to driving vast stretches without thinking much of it. Whereas Easterners may pale at the thought of driving from Pittsburgh to Chicago—a distance of 475 miles, many Westerners regularly cover as many miles just to shop at a larger town. And some folks out West can travel 475 miles in one direction without crossing a state line!

Bear this in mind when a side trip beckons to Yellowstone National Park, Oregon's Wallowa Mountains, or the Badlands of South Dakota. Reckon the additional distances—and days needed—carefully. For those who do decide to stray, this book includes information on many famous western destinations—most within 150 miles of the Oregon Trail.

Finally, just a few rules for traveling in the West. Most of the areas described in this book are open to the public, but a few require permission to enter. If that is the case, please respect the landowner's wishes and consult with the property owner before proceeding. If access is uncertain, the nearest Bureau of Land Management or Forest Service office is often the best place to find out who owns the land in question. Whether on private or public land, treat it with care. Leave gates as you find them, stay on the main trails, and refrain from littering or otherwise spoiling the view for others.

WHERE TO STAY; WHAT TO EAT

Each of the following chapters ends with a list of lodging options, campgrounds, and restaurants for each area along the trail. The listings follow the Oregon Trail from east to west. In most cases, establishments mentioned are simply representative of what is available in each town; listing in this guidebook does not imply endorsement of any kind, nor does space permit listing of all worthy establishments.

Many modern-day pioneers will want to camp at least part of the way. Sleeping outdoors gives a better taste of what pioneer life was like, and it helps save money, too. My favored routine of cross-country travel calls for camping out in a tent two to three nights in a row, followed by one night in a motel or a stay with friends en route. I'm convinced one of life's greatest pleasures is a long, hot shower and nice, soft bed after a few days of "roughing it."

State park facilities are often your best bet along the route. Aside from being plentiful, state park campgrounds usually offer clean and scenic grounds, shower facilities, friendly advice, and easy access. Most are quite reasonable, too, charging from $5.00 to $15.00 per night (although many state parks now charge vehicle admission fees, which can add a few dollars to the tab).

Because the Oregon Trail follows so many major highways, motels are plentiful. And because so much of the route is far from urban America, rates are quite reasonable. The national budget chains are well represented, but even better deals are sometimes found at independent "mom-and-pop" motels tucked away from the interstate in nearly every town. Some motels run as low as $30 to $40 for two people. Hotel, motel, and bed-and-breakfast rates listed in this guidebook typically reflect summertime charges as of 2000.

Driving and sight-seeing take up a lot of time on an Oregon Trail trip, so quick and simple meals are best. Restaurants are plentiful in most regions, but economical lunches and snacks can be carried in a well-stocked cooler.

The restaurants listed in these pages disclose my bias toward locally owned eateries. Many offer regional specialties and down-home cooking unavailable at the national chains, and prices are often in line with those at fast-food joints. Nevertheless, most good-sized towns along the main highways will have several chain restaurants in addition to the locally owned spots.

More complete lists of hotels, motels, campgrounds, and restaurants are available from state and local tourism bureaus, many of which have Web sites and toll-free phone numbers for information. State tourism offices are listed at the end of this chapter, and local offices are listed throughout the book.

WHAT TO PACK

If you're camping with kids and they are old enough, pack along two tents. Most kids love to have a tent of their own, and having separate tents will give the grown-ups some privacy and quiet, too, always prized on a long road trip. As mentioned earlier, skies along the trail can be unpredictable, so make sure the tent is waterproof, pack along a ground cloth, and put up the fly. Wind is another constant on the plains, so remember the tent stakes, too.

Other camp essentials include a simple tool kit with a hammer, ax, and pocket knife; a reliable camp stove and fuel (especially since campfires are prohibited in some locations); cooking and eating utensils; a can opener; insect repellent; a water bucket for hauling water and washing dishes; biodegradable dish soap; rope (for clothesline or other uses); first-aid and snake-bite kits; a camp lantern and flashlights; matches; trash bags; and a bag for dirty laundry.

Starting an Oregon Trail trip with a flight to Missouri doesn't mean camping is out of the question. Some state parks and campgrounds offer either cabins or rent-a-camp sites, and a few are equipped with all the essential gear. One note of caution: Many rental cabins, while slightly cheaper than most motel rooms, offer no motel-type amenities other than a roof over your head. Bring a sleeping bag and cooking and eating utensils . . . even a lantern.

As for clothing, it's best to be prepared. In summer, bring plenty of short-sleeved shirts and shorts. But toss in long pants, sweaters, and a jacket, too, because early mornings and nights can be chilly. Sneakers will suffice for walks around many historic sites, but most travelers will want a pair of hiking boots, too.

Still have room? Toss in a swimsuit and sun block. Remember a camera, and a wide-angle lens for those high, wide horizons. Binoculars might come in handy, as will books and travel games. Finally, don't forget maps—the ones in this book are general and should always be used in conjunction with a more detailed local highway map.

TRAVELING WITH KIDS

A trip along the Oregon Trail makes an ideal family vacation. It's interesting, educational, informal, and can easily be blended in with a more traditional western vacation to the national parks and landmarks. Best of all, it is blessedly easy on the pocketbook, since most historic sites are free or cheap, and since most of the trail winds far from expensive cities and theme parks.

Still, kids can get antsy on long drives, and looking for ways to keep them happy and occupied is always a challenge. Throughout the book, I've made note of free or low-cost recreational activities that can give children a chance to blow off a little steam—playgrounds, parks, and pools are especially good. Some historic sites offer programs just for kids, and these are mentioned, too.

One activity that can be planned in advance is an Oregon Trail scavenger hunt. Before the trip, make a list of things the kids can look for along the way. The list might include such items as a covered wagon, Chimney Rock, Indian teepee, pronghorn antelope, Pony Express station, cactus, sod house, wagon ruts, deer, Independence Rock, fort, and river. For extra fun, give the kids a single-use or other inexpensive camera so they can take photos of the discoveries as they are made. Just as many pioneers kept written journals of their trek, modern children may also enjoy the opportunity to record their journey in their own words. A blank book or even a spiral-bound notebook can be a good place to write, as well as glue postcards, ticket stubs, and other trip mementos.

Kids love to have a little bit of their own money to spend on vacation, and this helps teach them financial responsibility and decision-making. Consider giving each child a special trip allowance. Make sure they know that this allowance should cover any souvenirs they want to buy and it must last the whole trip.

A personal note: I became a parent since the first edition of this book came out, and my daughter has traveled quite a bit of the trail with me. Her favorite memories include a cookout and campfire at Chimney Rock in Nebraska, the very kid-friendly Columbia Gorge Discovery Center in Oregon, and the Bonneville Dam fish ladders in Washington state. But perhaps no other experience beats a summer day in central Wyoming. We started with a climb up Independence Rock—quite a challenge for a child who had just turned six. After a brief stop at Devil's Gate, we picnicked at Sweetwater Station, enjoyed an afternoon of exploration at South Pass City, and topped it off with ice-cream cones (for dinner, no less) at the Farson Merc. It's a day, as mapmaker John Fremont might have said, that will be fixed in our memories for years to come.

TOURING WITH A GROUP—OR ON YOUR OWN?

There aren't many organized tours along the Oregon Trail, but a few exist. See the Nebraska chapter's Chimney Rock section for information on the Bayard-based Oregon Trail Wagon Train and the Wyoming chapter's Casper section for details on Historic Trails West. Both companies run a variety of authentic trail adventures ranging from a few hours to several days, and either could be the centerpiece of your Oregon Trail vacation.

Small-ship cruises on the Columbia River have become popular, and several companies have tours that include Oregon Trail interpretation and stops at historic sites and interpretive centers. The *Queen of the West* sternwheeler, based in Portland, Oregon, offers four-night and seven-night small cruise ship tours on the Columbia, Snake, and Willamette Rivers. For details, write the American West Steamboat Company, 601 Union Street, Suite 4343, Seattle, WA 98101, call (800) 434–1232, or see www.columbiarivercruise.com. The Delta Queen Steamboat Company, famous for its trips on the Mississippi River, has expanded its offerings to include Pacific Northwest cruises on the *Columbia Queen*. For information on its eight-night *Columbia Queen* voyages, call (800) 297–3960 or see www.columbiaqueen.com.

WHAT TO READ

Many travelers want to read more about the Oregon Trail before, during, or after following the route. Especially recommended, in addition to Gregory Franzwa's books mentioned at the beginning of this chapter, are the following volumes: *Historic Sites along the Oregon Trail* by Aubrey L. Haines; *The Way West*, a novel by A. B. Guthrie Jr.; and *The Wake of the Prairie Schooner* by Irene D. Paden, who spent many years tracing the trails with her family. Also interesting are the many trail diaries kept by emigrants during the Oregon Trail era. Most of the major interpretive centers along the trail have a good selection of books. Online, check the Oregon-California Trails Association's virtual bookstore (see following) for many good trail-related titles. If titles are out of print, try a used bookstore or search service, or check your library.

TENDING THE TRAIL

The Oregon National Historic Trail was designated by Congress in 1978 and is managed by the National Park Service in conjunction with the Bureau of Land Management, the USDA Forest Service, state and local governments, and private landowners along the route. The park service's Web site at www.nps.gov/oreg/oreg.htm is one of the best sources of trail information on the Internet.

Trail buffs also may want to consider a membership in the Oregon-California Trails Association, which helps mark, interpret, and preserve the trails. Members receive *Overland Journal* and *News From the Plains* and can take part in local chapter activities. For information write OCTA at P.O.

Wooden oxbows and a yoke like those used by many emigrants on the Oregon Trail are on display at the National Frontier Trails Center in Independence, Missouri. Photo courtesy of the Missouri Division of Tourism.

Box 1019, Independence, MO 64051-1019 or call (816) 252–2276. OCTA also maintains an information-packed Web site at www.octa-trails.org, where you can join online.

STATE TOURISM OFFICES

Every state along the trail offers free vacation-planning information including photo-packed books of attractions, lists of visitor amenities, and detailed road maps. Call or write six weeks or so before your trip to get the information in time.

MISSOURI DIVISION OF TOURISM
Truman Office Building, P.O. Box 1055, Jefferson City, MO 65102
(800) 877–1234
www.missouritourism.org

KANSAS TRAVEL & TOURISM DIVISION
700 Southwest Harrison, Suite 1300, Topeka, KS 66603
(800) 252–6727
www.kansas-travel.com

NEBRASKA TRAVEL & TOURISM DIVISION
P.O. Box 94666, 700 South Sixteenth, Lincoln, NE 68509
(800) 228–4307
www.visitnebraska.org

WYOMING DIVISION OF TOURISM
I–25 at College Drive, Cheyenne, WY 82002
(307) 777–7777 or (800) 225–5996
www.wyomingtourism.org

IDAHO DIVISION OF TOURISM DEVELOPMENT
700 West State Street, Boise, ID 83720
(208) 334–2470 or (800) 635–7820
www.visitid.org

OREGON TOURISM DIVISION
775 Summer Street Northeast, Salem, OR 97310
(800) 547–7842
www.traveloregon.com

State Parks Departments

If you plan to camp for much of your trip, contact each state's parks department for detailed information on campground facilities.

Missouri Department of Natural Resources/Division of Parks
P.O. Box 176, Jefferson City, MO 65102
(800) 334–6946
www.mostateparks.com

Kansas Department of Wildlife and Parks
512 Southeast Twenty-fifth Avenue, Pratt, KS 67124
(316) 672–5911
www.kdwp.state.ks.us/main2.html

Nebraska Game & Parks Commission
2200 North Thirty-third Street, Lincoln, NE 68503
(402) 471–0641
www.ngpc.stat.ne.us

Wyoming Division of State Parks & Historic Sites
6101 Yellowstone Road, Cheyenne, WY 82002
(307) 777–6323
www.commerce.state.wy.us/sphs/index1.htm

Idaho Parks & Recreation Department
Statehouse Mall, Boise, ID 83720-8000
(800) 635–7820
www.idahoparks.org

Oregon Parks and Recreation Department
1115 Commercial Street Northeast, Suite 1, Salem, OR 97301-1002
(800) 551–6949
www.prd.state.or.us

IS THIS BOOK OUT OF DATE?

The first edition of this book was published in 1993, when the United States commemorated the 150th anniversary of the Oregon Trail. Ever since then, interest in historic trails has continued to grow. Several towns along the route have new interpretive centers, and others are expanding or otherwise changing the facilities already in place. I am eager to hear from people involved with these projects or with other Oregon Trail–associated businesses, because your help in keeping me informed will help me keep *Traveling the Oregon Trail* as up to date and complete as possible.

Of course, other things may change, too. Restaurants and motels may change names, and visitor attractions mentioned in these pages may alter operating schedules.

If you spot an error, omission, or change, please write me in care of The Globe Pequot Press, P.O. Box 480, Guilford, CT 06437, or e-mail me at juliewrites@yahoo.com. We will use your input in future editions of *Traveling the Oregon Trail.*

This book will probably be all you need to plan your Oregon Trail vacation, but I am available to provide personal itinerary advice for trips along the route. For more information, write me at P.O. Box 1593, Twin Falls, ID 83303, or go to Guidebookwriters.com and follow the links to the Oregon Trail.

May you have many happy travels!

MAP LEGEND			
Interstate Highway	44	Outward Bound 1804–1805	....
U.S. Highway	71	Homeward Bound 1806	- - - - - - - - - -
State Highway	15	Town	O **KANSAS CITY**
Forest Road	220	Airport	✈
River or Stream	⌇	Trail Landmark	✸
Peak	▲ **Mountain Peak**	Compass	W◆E (N/S)
Boundary	▬ ▬ ▬ ▬		0 5 10 miles
Trail	....	Scale	▰▱▰▱

CHAPTER ONE

THE OREGON TRAIL: A BRIEF HISTORY AND OVERVIEW

*T*o many, the idea seemed preposterous. Why would anyone want to leave the safety of the United States to push into unknown country? Why would anyone willingly choose to endure six months of choking dust, searing heat, and rain-swollen river crossings along a trail lined with grave sites and discarded possessions?

The pioneers had their reasons. Many were fed up with poor eastern soil, which had become overpriced, overcrowded, and worn thin through excessive cultivation. Land in the Oregon country, by contrast, was plentiful and dirt cheap. And what a land it was rumored to be! Why, in Oregon, beets were said to grow 3 feet in diameter and turnips 5 feet around. One trail proponent even told would-be emigrants that, in Oregon, "the pigs are running about under the great acorn trees, round and fat, and already cooked, with knives and forks sticking in them so that you can cut off a slice whenever you are hungry." Who could resist such tales of plenty, even if they were somewhat, ah, exaggerated?

Other emigrants were motivated by pure patriotism and the notion of "manifest destiny." In the early nineteenth century, the Northwest was still shared with the British, but many emigrants felt sure that if enough Americans settled in Oregon, the United States could lay a legitimate sole claim to the area. It worked, too; Oregon was awarded territorial status in 1849 and became a state just one decade later, thirty-one years before either neighboring Idaho or Washington attained statehood.

Finally, many pioneers simply had the urge to push ever westward as their ancestors had done for generations—from Europe to the New World, from Plymouth Rock to Philadelphia, from Pennsylvania across the Alleghenies to Ohio and Kentucky and Missouri and on across the plains. This trip would not disappoint them, for although it was long and potentially dangerous, it boasted the most amazing scenery they had ever viewed. Wide-horizoned plains gave way to jagged mountains and steep canyons, then fragrant pine forests. And at the end, Oregon, promising land enough for everybody and a new start on life.

By the time the first emigrant wagon trains rolled in the 1840s, the Oregon Trail was a well-known route. Native Americans had long ago pioneered the way. Lewis and Clark sparked Euro-American interest in the West after

President Thomas Jefferson dispatched their Corps of Discovery to survey the lands acquired in the Louisiana Purchase. Inspired by the explorers' reports, New York fur dealer John Jacob Astor sent parties to build trading posts along the Columbia River.

The Astorians, as they came to be known, were the first whites to discover the South Pass route through the Rockies. Later, brave mountain men set off to discover firsthand the beaver and buffalo, the mountains and raging rivers, and the curious, self-assured Native Americans.

The real push took place, however, after missionaries Marcus Whitman and Samuel Parker traveled from Liberty, Missouri, to the West in 1835. Convinced by the efforts of earlier missionaries such as Jason Lee that Indians wanted the white man's "medicine"—Christianity—Whitman returned the next year to establish a mission on the Walla Walla River. The trip made history for two reasons. First, Whitman brought along his brand new wife, Narcissa Prentiss Whitman, who—along with Eliza Spalding, wife of missionary Henry Spalding—would become the first white woman to travel the road to Oregon. Together, they proved families could make the trip. Second, the Whitmans traveled by wagon, and although their vehicle didn't last the entire journey, they showed wheeled passage was possible. The missionaries succeeded in establishing the first white settlements in the Pacific Northwest, and by 1840, at least 100 men, women, and children had arrived from the United States.

After that, the tide of emigration swelled. Stories appeared in the national press and exciting letters streamed in from neighbors who had made the journey. In 1843, about 1,000 people left Independence for Oregon. Two years later, more than 3,000 people made the trip, and in 1847, as many as 4,000 folks signed on. But busiest of all were the gold rush years of 1849 through 1852, when tens of thousands of people followed the overland route as far as present-day Idaho before cutting southwest to California.

A typical trip along the 2,000-mile trail took about five months, with emigrants traveling at the rate of just 15 to 20 hard, dusty miles per day. The journey usually started late in April or early in May, as soon as the grass had grown high enough to feed the livestock that would be making the trip.

In the trail's early days, Independence was the main supply post and jumping-off spot. Emigrants often arrived at Independence by steamboat from St. Louis and points east. Once there, they'd organize into wagon trains and make final preparations for the journey.

Most important was the wagon, which most emigrants already had obtained by the time they arrived on the frontier. In his guidebook *The Prairie Traveler: A Handbook for Overland Expedition*, Captain R. B. Marcy said wagons should be simple, strong, and light, made of well-seasoned timber. He recommended that wheels be made of osage orange or white oak to prevent shrinkage in the hot, dry West. The wagon bed—frequently built by the emigrant himself—was 10 to 11 feet long, 4 feet wide, and 2 feet deep. A good wagon cost about $85.

Emigrants often argued over whether to use mules or oxen for the trip. Many favored mules because, with good roads and plenty of grain, they could travel fast and stand up to the heat. But a six-mule team cost $600. Oxen, on the other hand, cost just $200 for eight and had more stamina over the long run. Oxen also were less likely to stampede and could be used for food. In addition to the mules or oxen, most parties brought along a few cows for milk.

With few trading posts on the frontier, the emigrants also needed to stockpile provisions. The following grocery list was typical for a family of four: 824 pounds of flour, 725 pounds of bacon, 75 pounds of coffee, 160 pounds of sugar, 200 pounds of lard and suet, 200 pounds of beans, 135 pounds of peaches and apples, and salt, pepper, and bicarbonate of soda.

Once on the road, the emigrants started each day early, awakened by a trumpet reverie or a gunshot blast at 4:00 A.M. They'd usually hit the trail near dawn, eager to start the day's journey so they could be that much closer to Oregon. Emigrants rarely rode in the wagons, for the vehicles were small, full of possessions, and hardly comfortable for traveling. Instead, they walked alongside. The trains traveled all day except for an hour "nooning" break at midday.

Finally, at about 6:00 P.M., the pioneers would draw their wagons into a circle to ward off intruders and form a corral for the stock. Everyone would wander off to collect buffalo chips for the evening fire. After dinner, the emigrants would often enjoy singing, dancing, and storytelling around the crackling campfire.

The Oregon Trail has sometimes been described as "the world's longest graveyard." Cholera killed thousands. Others died by accidental gunshot or rattlesnake bite. Indian attacks claimed a few lives. In all, about one in seventeen adults died along the trail. For kids, the toll was even higher. Of every five children who started the trip, one would fail to finish. Emigrants who died were often buried right on the trail, where wagon wheels rolling over the fresh plot would help hide the body from coyotes, wolves, and grave-robbers.

Although a mile of trail could contain as many as fifteen graves, most who started the trip survived to see Oregon and tell tales of the great adventure for many years to come. By the time Oregon Trail travel trickled off in the mid-1860s, more than 300,000 people had moved to the West Coast. Propelled by patriotism, driven by a restless spirit, Americans had made the greatest peacetime migration in the history of the world. "Manifest destiny" was secure, for better or for worse. The United States was truly one nation, indivisible, from sea to shining sea.

BOLD BEGINNINGS: MISSOURI AND KANSAS

A multitude of shops had sprung up to furnish the emigrants and Santa Fe travelers with necessaries for their long journey and there was an incessant hammering and banging from a dozen blacksmiths' sheds, where the heavy wagons were being repaired, and the horses and oxen shod.

—Francis Parkman at Independence Square, 1846

ST. LOUIS, MISSOURI, AND THE GATEWAY ARCH

*T*hey came, mostly from Arkansas, Missouri, Kentucky, and Illinois. For months they'd discussed going west to Oregon, and now the time had arrived. Wide-eyed with excitement, they arrived in St. Louis ready to begin the adventure of their lifetimes.

St. Louis has long been known as "Gateway to the West." Today, most people would argue that the West really begins some 500 miles west of St. Louis, where the 100th meridian streaks past such towns as Dodge City, Kansas; Kearney, Nebraska; and Pierre, South Dakota. But St. Louis is where the idea of westward expansion began both in theory and in practice. Nowhere is this better explained than at the **Jefferson National Expansion Memorial** and its centerpiece, the **Gateway Arch.**

One of the nation's greatest monuments, the Gateway Arch is also the tallest at 630 feet. (The Washington Monument, by contrast, is 555 feet tall and the Statue of Liberty reaches a mere 305 feet into the sky.) Finnish-American architect Eero Saarinen's design for the stainless-steel rainbow won a national contest in 1947; unfortunately, he died in 1961, a year before the Arch's construction actually began. The monument was completed in October 1965, and more than 50 million people have visited since its opening.

A ride to the top of the Arch is a thrilling experience. After a four-minute trip up the Arch's innards in a space-capsule-like tram car, visitors reach an observation room with vistas 30 miles both east and west on a clear day. Some of the best sights, however, are spread at the Arch's feet—the Mississippi River and its fancy riverboats, Busch Stadium and the Old Courthouse, the green

The 630-foot-tall Gateway Arch towers above the city of St. Louis, Missouri.
Photo courtesy of the Missouri Division of Tourism.

jewel of the parkland around the Arch, and the bright blue swimming pools atop downtown hotels.

The Museum of Westward Expansion also sits beneath the Arch. In its center is a life-size statue of Thomas Jefferson, who presided over the Louisiana Purchase and sent Meriwether Lewis and William Clark forth from Missouri to survey the new lands. From the statue, museum displays radiate outward in semicircles, each describing a key aspect of westward movement between 1803—the date of the Louisiana Purchase—and 1890, when the frontier was officially declared closed.

TOURING ST. LOUIS

The Gateway Arch symbolizes St. Louis, and it's also the heart of a vibrant riverfront district offering plenty of urban fun.

Riverboats line the levee, ready to treat visitors to a variety of cruises. The biggest company is Gateway Riverboat Cruises, which operates the *Belle of St. Louis, Becky Thatcher, Huck Finn,* and *Tom Sawyer* boats. Even McDonald's has its own riverboat restaurant, complete with a 200-gallon aquarium.

To the north of the Arch, Laclede's Landing marks the spot where Pierre Laclede founded a fur trading post in 1764. Once a decaying industrial district, Laclede's Landing is now one of the most popular spots in St. Louis. Attractions include antiques, rare book, and craft shops and an array of restaurants and nightspots, many featuring live music.

Soulard, 2 miles south of the Arch on Broadway, calls itself "St. Louis' French Quarter" and has one of the city's liveliest music scenes. Check out the great variety of clubs featuring rock, jazz, blues, and even Irish music.

Also near the Arch is Busch Stadium, home of the St. Louis Cardinals. Right next door is the International Bowling Museum and Cardinals Hall of Fame. Dog fanciers may enjoy the American Kennel Club's Museum of the Dog (1721 South Mason Road). The Campbell House (Fifteenth and Locust Streets) offers exhibits on early St. Louis and the city's fur trading days.

The Missouri Botanical Garden spans 79 acres at 4344 Shaw Boulevard and features an English woodland garden, a Japanese garden, and a fragrance garden for the blind. If your botanical tastes run more toward hops and barley, plan a stop at Anheuser-Busch. The brewery at Lynch and Twelfth Streets is listed on the National Register of Historic Places and offers free tours Monday through Saturday.

St. Louis began as a trading post, and shopping continues to play a prominent role in the city's life. Union Station has evolved from a train depot to a popular marketplace with shops, restaurants, and lodging. The St. Louis Centre, also downtown, contains more than 150 stores and restaurants.

If you happen to be in St. Louis on the second Sunday of the month, consider the architectural tour offered by the local chapter of the American Institute of Architects. The group also offers free self-guiding maps of the city's architectural highlights. Call (314) 621–3484 for information.

Sports-minded visitors should head over to Forest Park. This 1,293-acre preserve in the city's West End offers bicycle rentals, jogging paths, fishing, boating, two public golf courses, and tennis courts. It's also home to the St. Louis Zoo, the St. Louis Art Museum, and the Missouri Historical Society's museum. The St. Louis Science Center, filled with interactive exhibits, is just across I–64 from the park.

No description of attractions near St. Louis would be complete without mention of Six Flags Over Mid-America. The mega-amusement park is about 30 miles southwest of downtown, near the Allenton exit off I–44. Water-park fans will enjoy Raging Rivers, located at the opposite end of the St. Louis metro area in Grafton, Illinois.

For more information on St. Louis, stop by the visitor center at Seventh and Washington Avenues or at Lambert Airport, call (800) 916–0092, or see the Web site at www.st-louis-cvc.com. ◢

National Park Service rangers lead guided tours through the museum on a regular basis. Visitors can also wander through on their own. Displays include an overland wagon, a pioneer sod house, and exhibits on mountain men, buffalo hunters, miners, and cowboys, all interspersed with historical quotations such as this one from President James Polk's 1845 inaugural address: "Our title to the country of the Oregon is clear and unquestionable and already are our people preparing to perfect that title by occupying it with their wives and children."

The museum is open daily from 8:00 A.M. to 10:00 P.M. Memorial Day weekend through Labor Day and 9:00 A.M. to 6:00 P.M. the rest of the year. Admission to the Arch tram and museum is $7.00 per person ages seventeen and up, $5.00 for students ages thirteen through sixteen, and $3.00 for children ages three through twelve. All facilities at the Arch are closed Thanksgiving, Christmas, and New Year's Day.

To learn more about the Arch and how it was built, see "Monument to the Dream," a thirty-five-minute documentary shown in a theater beneath the Arch. Films also are shown in the Odyssey Theatre with its four-story-high screen. Each film carries a separate charge, or you can buy museum and tram admission plus movies in a package; call (877) 982–1410 or see the Web site at www.stlouisarch.com for details.

The Old Courthouse, also on the national monument grounds, dates from 1826 and was the setting for many cases involving slavery, the fur trade, and equal rights, including the 1857 Dred Scott decision. Courthouse admission is free, but you can rent an audio tour for $3.00 per adult and $1.50 for children ages three to twelve.

ST. LOUIS TRAVEL TIPS

Lambert-St. Louis International Airport (STL) is served by most major and Midwest regional airlines. The airport will be undergoing a major expansion starting in 2001. Rental cars are available from numerous companies. The Amtrak station is at 550 South Sixteenth Street, and the Greyhound terminal is at 1450 North Thirteenth Street.

St. Louis' MetroLink light-rail system is an easy way to get around town. Although parking is plentiful and fairly cheap at the riverfront, savvy travelers will hop the MetroLink at Laclede's Landing to explore other area sites such as Union Station and Forest Park. It's also possible to take the train from several convenient stops near the airport and I–70 (though you'll want to leave early if it's the night of a Cardinals' home game, when the park-and-ride lots are jammed). Look for a MetroLink route map at your hotel, or call (314) 231–2345 from 6:00 A.M. to 8:00 P.M. weekdays or 8:00 A.M. to 5:00 P.M. weekends. ♠

The Jefferson National Expansion Monument is located along the Mississippi River on Memorial Drive. Several parking garages are located nearby, including the reasonably priced Arch Garage on the park's north side. Avoid rush hour, particularly during the construction-intensive spring and summer seasons.

The Missouri and Mississippi Rivers meet north of St. Louis, and IL 3 leads to a view of the confluence. Narcissa Whitman, one of the first white women to travel to the Oregon country, described her 1836 visit to the spot like this: "Twilight had nearly gone when we entered the waters of the great Missouri, but the moon shone in her brightness. It was a beautiful evening. My husband and I went up on the top of the boat to get a more commanding view of the scenery. How majestic, how grand was the scene, the meeting of two such great waters."

Just west of St. Louis on the Missouri River and along I–70, the city of **St. Charles** dates from 1769, when French-Canadians founded it. It later served as Missouri's first capital from 1821 to 1826. But it is possibly most famous for its ties to westward expansion. The Lewis & Clark Center (701 Riverside Drive) is a hands-on museum that traces the explorers' expedition and its discoveries. It is open daily except holidays from 10:30 A.M. to 4:30 P.M. A re-enactment of the Lewis and Clark encampment takes place in St. Charles every third weekend in May. St. Charles' other big annual shindig is Fete des Petites Cotes ("Festival of the Little Hills"), which draws about 300,000 people annually in mid-August.

From St. Charles, continue west on I–70 to Arrow Rock. This small settlement in the middle of Missouri has long been a stopover for people heading west.

ARROW ROCK

To the harried city-dweller or suburbanite making this tour, Arrow Rock serves as the first indication that life in some places along the old emigrant trail continues today pretty much as it has for generations. Located 13 miles northwest of I–70 (take exit 98 to MS 41), this town was once home to about 1,000 people. These days, about eighty folks remain.

Settled early in the 1800s, Arrow Rock was originally called New Philadelphia. The town got its current name when two men were vying for the love of a local Indian chief's daughter. The chief said whichever man could shoot an arrow the farthest could marry the young woman. One arrow shot from a sandbar in the Missouri River stuck in the crevice of a bluff above the river, and thus the town was named Arrow Rock.

Throughout the mid-nineteenth century, Arrow Rock played host to a steady stream of emigrants passing through on their way to the trailheads farther west. The town's population peaked about 1860 but began to dwindle after the Civil War and the decline of traffic on the nearby Missouri River.

Today, Arrow Rock looks much like it did in the mid-1800s. A state interpretive center explains the town's history, and visitors can see the past up close by walking through town. Historic buildings include the tavern, the old seminary, and a home occupied by frontier artist George Caleb Bingham from 1837 to 1845. John P. Sites, considered one of the most skilled gunsmiths in the nation, moved here in 1844 and catered extensively to the emigrant trade. His restored shop may still be seen.

A tiny one-room jailhouse—or calaboose—is another point of interest. According to local legend, the only prisoner ever placed in the cell found it so cold that he decided to build a fire. The fire warmed him, but it also woke up several snakes that had been hibernating in the stone building. This understandably unnerved the prisoner, who reportedly raised quite a racket. He was transferred to another jail in nearby Marshall, and the one-room jail was never used again.

About two dozen merchants and innkeepers are doing their best to keep Arrow Rock alive, and the town enjoys thriving tourism, especially in the summer. Shop for everything from antiques and pottery to cast iron cookware and

The "calaboose," or one-man jail, is an attraction at Arrow Rock, Missouri.

Native American art. The Lyceum Theatre presents professional drama June through August, and village tours are offered daily in summer and weekends in spring and fall. Stop by the Friends of Arrow Rock office on Main Street or call (660) 837–3231. The Arrow Rock State Historic Site interpretive center is open from 10:00 A.M. to 5:00 P.M. daily June through August, from 10:00 A.M. to 4:00 P.M. in spring and fall, and from 10:00 A.M. to 4:00 P.M. Friday through Sunday in winter. For more information on Arrow Rock, see the town's Web site at www.arrowrock.org.

INDEPENDENCE, MISSOURI

The "Queen City of the Trails," Independence today is a somewhat sleepy little city swallowed up by the Kansas City metropolitan area. Aside from the choking traffic on the town's major thoroughfares, it's difficult to believe more than 115,000 people live within the Independence city limits.

But in the mid-nineteenth century, Independence was one brawling, boisterous town. Located just 12 miles from the frontier, the city served as the major supply depot for travelers heading out on the Oregon, California, and Santa Fe Trails. Steamboats from St. Louis docked at Independence Landing to unload people, animals, and wagons. The emigrants would then climb a steep road to the town itself.

During the day, Independence rang with the sounds of people eager to be on the move. Blacksmiths, wagon builders, and other merchants worked fever-

LAKE OF THE OZARKS

When Missourians play, they frequently head for the Lake of the Ozarks region, located about 75 miles southwest of Columbia via US 63 and US 54.

Lake of the Ozarks was created in 1931 with the completion of Bagnell Dam. With 58,000 acres of water surface and 1,375 miles of twisting shoreline, the "Big Dragon"—as Lake of the Ozarks is known—has more shoreline than the California coast, all set against the rolling green Ozark hills.

Lake of the Ozarks State Park near Osage Beach is Missouri's largest state park at 17,087 acres. It offers two swim-ming beaches, boat rentals, horseback riding, fishing, hiking, and 172 campsites. More than 200 resorts are located elsewhere on the lakeshore.

The Ozarks continue on south into Arkansas. Branson, a town near the border, is best known for its dozens of country music theaters, but it also boasts such family attractions as the Silver Dollar City theme park and the Branson Scenic Railway. For more information on these regions, call the Lake of the Ozarks Visitors Bureau at (800) 325–0213 or the Branson Chamber of Commerce at (417) 334–4136. ▲

ishly all spring to supply the emigrants. By night, the town continued to bustle as men met in the saloons to talk about Oregon and the coming trip. Campsites dotted the outlying meadows, and in the spring, there would be at least 10,000 oxen grazing in the fields, waiting to move west with the wagon trains.

Independence served as the main jumping-off spot for the Oregon Trail until the late 1840s and early 1850s. After that, the Missouri River shifted its course and Westport, St. Joseph, Weston, and Council Bluffs eclipsed Independence as major trailheads. But during the 1840s, at the height of excitement over westward emigration, Independence truly was the "last rest stop in the United States"!

Plenty of Oregon Trail history lives on in Independence, including one of the best trail interpretive sites to be found anywhere: the **National Frontier Trails Center** at 318 West Pacific Avenue, built near "Lot 143," where emigrants topped off their water barrels before heading west.

The center offers a seventeen-minute film that details the origins of all three major trails, the Oregon, California, and Santa Fe. The exhibits allow visitors to both read and hear pioneer diary excerpts and examine artifacts. These halls are filled with human drama, giving names and faces to some of the emigrants and conveying the terrible hardships they endured.

The trails center also is home to an archives and research library containing rare books, letters, and emigrant diaries. Visitors can try to trace their own ancestors' movements across the plains. A statue by Juan Lombardo Rivera commemorates women's roles in westward expansion, and a Lewis and Clark exhibit explains how that expedition paved the way for the fur trade and emigrant travel.

The National Frontier Trails Center is open from 9:00 A.M. to 4:30 P.M. Monday through Saturday and from 12:30 to 4:30 P.M. on Sunday. Admission is $3.50 for adults, $3.00 for senior citizens, and $2.00 for students ages six to seventeen. Children ages five and under are admitted free. For more information, call (816) 325–7575. While at the center, pick up a copy of the locally produced *Trailside Travelers* leaflet, which points the way to nine identified trail sites in the Kansas City metro area.

Among them, **Independence Courthouse Square** was the closest thing to an official starting point the Oregon Trail ever had. It is bordered by Main, Maple, Lexington, and Liberty Streets. Nearby, at the corner of Noland and Truman Roads, is the **Brady Cabin and Spring,** site of the free-flowing springs that first attracted settlers to Independence.

Every Labor Day weekend, Independence stages Santa-Cali-Gon Days, a festival marking the city's role as "Queen City of the Trails." The event on Independence Square typically offers Old West foods, carnival rides, staged shoot-outs, entertainment, and arts and crafts exhibits.

Pioneer Trail Adventures, stationed on the Main Street side of Courthouse Square, gives horse-drawn carriage rides from 9:00 A.M. to 9:00 P.M. Tuesday through Saturday. A variety of tours are offered, from a $5.00 per person fifteen-minute ride around Independence Courthouse Square to an hour-long excursion along the Santa Fe Trail route and to several Civil War sites. The same company can also arrange pioneer-style dinners and entertainment for families and groups at its campsite near the National Frontier Trails Center. Call (816) 254–2466 for details.

Most folks here say that the remains of Jim Bridger, the famous mountain man and western guide, are buried in Mount Washington Cemetery, west of Brookside Avenue between Truman Road and US 24. Because

The historic Brady Cabin stands near the beginning of the Oregon Trail in Independence, Missouri.

Bridger was originally buried in Dallas, Missouri, which is now part of Kansas City, some historians believe the remains at Mount Washington aren't actually those of Bridger. Nevertheless, a monument on the site notes his role in opening the West.

Independence is perhaps most famous as the hometown of President Harry S Truman, and anyone interested in his life and career can choose from a wealth of informative attractions. Truman's courtroom and office are located in the Jackson County Courthouse on the square, where visitors can see a multimedia presentation titled "The Man from Independence." The Truman Library and Museum, at US 24 and Delaware Street, includes a replica of Truman's office in the White House.

When not in Washington, D.C., Harry and Bess lived at 219 North Delaware Street from their marriage in 1919 to his death in 1972, and the home is now designated the Harry S Truman National Historic Site. Tours are available, but space is limited and tickets must be obtained at the Truman Home Ticket and Information Center at Truman Road and Main Street. Truman held down his first job at Clinton's Soda Fountain & Gifts (100 West Maple Street, on the square).

Other Independence attractions include the unusual spiral-topped temple built by the Reorganized Church of Jesus Christ of Latter-day Saints (River Boulevard and Walnut Street); the RLDS' Auditorium complex, which includes a Children's Peace Pavilion museum; a Mormon Visitors Center run by the regular Church of Jesus Christ of Latter-day Saints (937 West Walnut Street); the 1859 Jail & Marshal's Home (217 North Main Street); and the fabulous Victorian-style Vaile Mansion (1500 North Liberty Street). Missouri Town 1855, a restored nineteenth-century community, is located in Fleming Park south of Independence in the city of Blue Springs. For more information on area attractions, contact Independence Tourism at (800) 748–7323 or see the Web site at www.ci.independence.mo.us.

KANSAS CITY AND WESTPORT

Eager to save time and head out across the prairie as soon as possible, some emigrants bypassed Independence in favor of **Westport Landing,** 8 miles farther up the Missouri River. The original landing was situated between the present-day Broadway and Heart of America bridges over the Missouri River.

The Westport district, south of downtown via Broadway Avenue, is where Kansas City began and where many emigrants outfitted their wagons before heading west. Today's Westport combines history with a wealth of restaurants, nightclubs, art galleries, and unusual stores.

Begin a tour of Westport at **Pioneer Park** on the corner of Westport Road and Broadway. Here stands the "Three Trails West" terrazzo mosaic and a statue of three key players in Westport history: freighting magnate Alexander Majors, John Calvin McCoy (who laid out the town in 1834 and was considered the "Father of Kansas City"), and mountain man/frontier scout Jim Bridger.

From the park, head southwest down Westport Road to see two of Kansas City's oldest buildings. The old **Ewing-Boone Store** at 500 Westport Road was operated as an outfitting store from 1851 through 1854. Albert Gallatin Boone (Daniel's grandson) bought out the Ewings and ran a general store on the site until 1859. Like any good businessman, Boone knew the value of "location, location, location"—wagon trains bound for Santa Fe and Oregon passed right by his front door!

The Ewing-Boone building survived several Civil War–era fires. Daniel Meriwether, who ran a grocery and hardware store, then remodeled it. A one-story addition was built in 1892. Today, the building houses Kelly's Westport Inn, a friendly, neighborhood-style tavern (and site of Kansas City's premier St. Patrick's Day party). Right next door at 504 Westport Road, Cyprien Choteau and Price Keller built a two-story brick building in 1850. In 1866, Jim Bridger bought the store for $1,000 and had his son-in-law, Albert

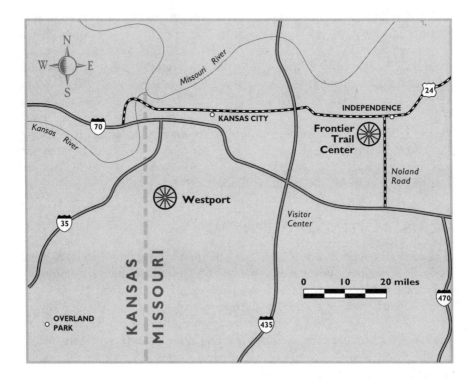

Wachsmann, run the business. The building is now Stanford & Sons Comedy Club and Restaurant, where they serve a Jim Bridger Burger and a cheesecake once voted the best in Kansas City.

Westport also played a role in Civil War history. The Battle of Westport was fought here in October 1864, marking the end of Major General Sterling Price's attempt to seize Missouri from Union control. That explains the Confederate and Union "soldiers" still standing watch in the second-floor windows at Kelly's Westport Inn.

Because the emigrants followed different routes out of Kansas City, the wagons rolled in many areas. Few actual ruts remain, but swales may be seen in several locations, including the grounds of the Bingham-Waggoner Estate in Independence (ask at the National Frontier Trails Center) and at Minor Park along Red Bridge Road south of I–435 in Kansas City. Minor Park's Santa Fe Trail Historic Site, 0.4 mile east of Holmes Road, features an interpretive panel overlooking several deep swales.

You could spend many days in Kansas City and not see all its museums. The **Kansas City Museum** at 3218 Gladstone Boulevard has a display and video on westward expansion. It's open from 9:30 A.M. to 4:30 P.M. Tuesday

The statue of Alexander Majors, John Calvin McCoy, and Jim Bridger at Westport in Kansas City, Missouri, is a reminder of some of the trail's early pioneers.

through Saturday and noon to 4:30 P.M. on Sunday; admission is $2.50 for adults and $2.00 for seniors and children.

The brick Greek Revival **Wornall House,** at 61st Terrace and Wornall Road, was built by John Wornall in 1858. It served as a hospital for both Union and Confederate casualties during the Civil War. Now fully restored and full of nineteenth-century textiles, glass, silver, and ironware, Wornall House also offers summer programs for children. It is open from 10:00 A.M. to 4:00 P.M. Tuesday through Saturday and 1:00 to 4:00 P.M. on Sunday. Admission is $3.00 for adults, $2.50 for senior citizens over sixty-two, and $2.00 for children under twelve.

The **Alexander Majors House** also invites visitors at 8201 State Line Road. Majors began hauling freight from Independence to Santa Fe in 1848. In later years he joined forces with William H. Russell and William B. Waddell to become the top freighting firm on the American frontier. At one point, the company owned 3,400 wagons and 40,000 oxen and employed 4,000 people. The trio also were responsible for starting the short-lived but famous Pony Express overland mail service. The Majors House may be toured for $3.00 ($1.50 for children) from 1:00 to 4:00 P.M. Saturday and Sunday, April through December. The last tour starts at 3:30 P.M.

KANSAS CITY ATTRACTIONS

You wouldn't expect a city in America's heartland to have a decidedly European feel with fountains, broad boulevards, and fine architecture. But Kansas City has long thrived on defying expectations and delighting anyone who pictured it as an overgrown cow town.

Kansas City is, of course, really two geographically and politically separate cities. Kansas City, Missouri (often referred to as KCMO), has a population of about 435,000, while its smaller counterpart in Kansas is home to about 150,000. The seven-county metro area adds nearly a million more people.

Kansas City, Missouri, welcomes travelers with a great visitor center right off I-70 at the Harry S Truman Sports Complex. The friendly people are full of good advice and will even draw a detailed map to help visitors find their way around the area. The Blue Ridge Cutoff heading south of this area was a major route for Santa Fe–bound emigrants.

The Truman Sports Complex dominates the view of anyone entering Kansas City from the east. Two huge stadiums with a total of 118,000 seats give a big home-field advantage to baseball's Royals and football's Chiefs. College sports fans won't want to miss the NCAA Visitors Center at 6201 College Boulevard in Overland Park, Kansas, where photos and videos pay tribute to great collegiate athletes.

Recreation enthusiasts can choose from an embarrassment of riches, too. Swope Park's 1,772 acres offer swimming, tennis, golf, fishing, and boating, plus summer concerts by popular entertainers.

Culture plays an equally strong role in Kansas City's life. The Nelson-Atkins Museum of Art (Forty-fifth and Oak Streets) includes fifty-eight galleries and the largest collection of Henry Moore sculptures in the United States. Kansas City was home to artist Thomas Hart Benton, whose home may be toured at 3616 Belleview Avenue. The city is also known as one of the world's great jazz capitals. The American Jazz Museum (1616 East Eighteenth Street) has excellent exhibits detailing the genre's history, including many interactive stations that help visitors understand how to "think in jazz." The Negro Leagues Baseball Museum is in the same complex.

History enthusiasts won't want to miss the terrific new statue of Meriwether Lewis, William Clark, York, and Sacagawea and her baby Jean Baptiste. The tribute to the Corps of Discovery by sculptor Eugene Daub is at a small park at the north end of Jefferson Street just west of downtown.

Travelers who don't get their fill of shopping and entertainment in Westport can check out Country Club Plaza to the south at Forty-seventh Street and J.C. Nichols Parkway. Built in 1922, it was the first planned shopping center in the United States. Antiques collectors flock to Forty-fifth Street and State Line Road, a district with more than fifty antiques, arts, and crafts dealers. The open-air City Market at Fifth and Walnut Streets near the river is a good place to stock up on fresh fruit. The River Market area also includes the Arabia Steamboat Museum, featuring more than 200 tons of goods salvaged from a steamboat that sank in the Missouri River in 1856.

Crown Center just south of downtown is yet another place to eat, party, and shop. Hallmark Cards has its headquarters here, and a free visitor center demonstrates the art and business of greeting cards. Kids will enjoy a stop at the Crayola Store and Café to see how crayons are made. Worlds of Fun, a major amusement park 13 miles north of town off I–435, is another family-pleasing place.

Kansas City International Airport (KCI), 17 miles north of downtown, is served by most major and Midwest regional airlines. Rental cars are available from numerous companies. The Amtrak station is at Twenty-third and Main Streets, and the Greyhound terminal is at 1101 Troost Street. The Metro is the local bus system.

For more information on Kansas City, write or visit the Convention & Visitors Bureau of Greater Kansas City at 1100 Main Street, Suite 2550, Kansas City, MO 64105; call (800) 767–7700; or see the Web site at www.experiencekc.com. ▲

Emigrants sometimes spent their first night on the trail camping at **Cave Spring**, now part of William M. Klein Park at the southwest corner of Gregory and Blue Ridge Boulevards just west of the suburb of Raytown. New Santa Fe, located near where State Line and Santa Fe Roads intersect, was the last "civilized" settlement Oregon-bound emigrants would see before the frontier. From here, about 18 miles from the starting point in Independence, the pioneers pressed on into what is now Kansas—and what was then the great unknown.

Barely a mile into Indian territory, wagon trains passed the **Shawnee Indian Mission**, at Mission Road and West Fifty-third Street in the present-day town of Fairway, Kansas. The Reverand Thomas Johnson established the mission in 1839, and emigrants on their way to Oregon or Santa Fe often stopped to camp in the vicinity. Now a state historic site, the mission is open from 10:00 A.M. to 5:00 P.M. Tuesday through Saturday and 1:00 to 5:00 P.M. Sunday. Admission is by donation.

Another stretch of trail ruts is visible at Harmon Park, at Seventy-eighth Street and Mission Road in the suburb of Prairie Village, Kansas. This was part of the Olathe Cutoff, used by many early emigrants from Westport. Another Olathe Cutoff landmark, **Mahaffie House** at 1100 Kansas City Road in Olathe, served as a wagon and stagecoach stop toward the end of the Oregon Trail's existence.

Emigrants often stayed at **Lone Elm Campground,** at 167th and Elm Streets in Olathe. Another possible campsite, simply called Elm Grove, was located about 2.5 miles northwest.

The Oregon and Santa Fe Trails split near what is now Gardner. A lone sign on the right fork pointed the way, stating simply, ROAD TO OREGON. A historical marker about 2 miles west of town on US 56 notes the parting of the ways, but historians believe the actual split was in Gardner proper, possibly where the elementary school now stands.

This point marks the end of the trail's route through what is now the Kansas City metropolitan area. From here, the Oregon Trail runs north and west near DeSoto and Eudora and on into what is now Lawrence.

LAWRENCE AND TOPEKA

As the wagon trains rolled on toward present-day Lawrence, Kansas, the emigrants saw Blue Mound, the first significant landmark on the trail. Although it couldn't compare with the mountains they'd see later, the Blue Mound (today called Mount Bleu) was quite a spectacle to the former flatland farmers, and many climbed it to see the view.

Today, Mount Bleu and the plains are heavily wooded and sure to smash many misconceptions about Kansas. In the Oregon Trail days, however, eastern Kansas conformed more to its barren stereotype. The best view of the Blue Mound is from KS 10, which leads into Lawrence as Twenty-third Street. The rise is about 6 miles southeast of town.

Many pioneers who passed through the area sent favorable reports back home, and settlement of eastern Kansas started in earnest by the early 1850s. By 1854, Congress had enacted the Kansas-Nebraska Act organizing the Kansas and Nebraska territories and giving them self-determination on the red-hot issue of slavery. The New England Emigrant Aid Company, a group organized to lead Northern resistance against pro-slavery powers, established the town of Lawrence in September 1854, giving it strong abolitionist sentiment from the start.

But the pro-slavery faction wasn't ready to concede. In August 1863, Confederate guerrilla William Quantrill led between 300 and 450 western Missourians into Lawrence, where they sacked and burned homes and businesses, left 150 citizens dead, and caused some $1.5 million in damage. The renegades no doubt thought they'd had the last word, but Lawrence residents quickly rallied to rebuild their town, and its population more than doubled within the next two years, from 2,000 to 5,400. The University of Kansas was founded here in 1866.

Lawrence now has a population of about 85,000 people, and while things are a lot calmer today than during the "Bleeding Kansas" era, the city revels in its youthful population, active cultural scene, and abundant recreational opportunities. (The Civil War–era hasn't been forgotten, though; Lawrence holds a "Civil War on the Western Frontier" event each August, with several weeks of performances, lectures, living history, and re-enactments.) Stop at the handsome visitor center in the renovated train depot at North Second and Locust

The Blue Mound was a navigational landmark near Lawrence, Kansas.

Streets; here, you can view a thirty-minute film about Lawrence history and pick up a brochure detailing a two-hour self-guided driving tour of the Oregon Trail through Douglas County. Or head straight downtown to Massachusetts Street for excellent restaurants and nightlife. The KU campus is southwest of downtown; its most popular attraction, aside from Jayhawk sporting events, is probably the Dyche Museum of Natural History. Its many interesting exhibits include Comanche, a mounted horse who was the only Seventh Cavalry survivor of Custer's Last Stand.

Lawrence has a strong, varied arts scene that is the envy of cities many times its size. Galleries abound, and the community enjoys a full slate of festivals and performances. The Bottleneck at 737 New Hampshire Street is particularly renowned for its eclectic selection of live music seven nights a week. First-run art and independent films show nightly at Liberty Hall, 642 Massachusetts Street.

Lawrence takes its recreation seriously, too. Much of it centers around Clinton Lake, 4 miles southwest of the city via US 40 (which parallels the Oregon Trail). Boating, fishing, swimming, horseback riding, hiking, and camping are all enjoyed on or around the 7,000-acre lake. Clinton Lake and Tuttle Creek near Manhattan are two Kansas state parks that offer "Rent-A-Camp" sites to visitors. For about $15 per night, a family of four gets use of a

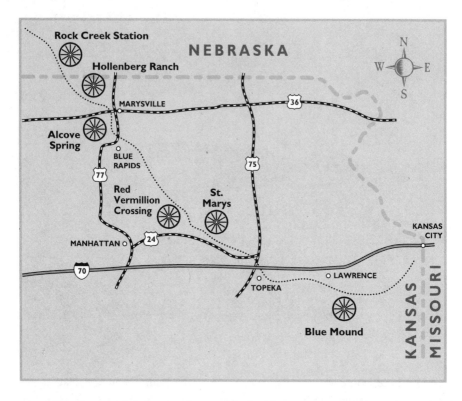

tent (already set up) and campsite outfitted with propane stove, lantern, cooler, propane fuel, and cots or sleeping pads. Reservations may be made by mail or by telephone with a major credit card; see the camping section at the end of this chapter for telephone numbers.

Alvamar Golf and Country Club at 1800 Crossgate Drive has a public eighteen-hole course that has been dubbed one of the nation's fifty best. Lawrence has thirty parks, many of which have plenty of playground gear to keep the kids entertained.

For more information on Lawrence, stop by the visitor center, call (785) 865-4499 or (888) LAWKANS, or see the Web site at www.visitlawrence.com.

From Lawrence, the Oregon Trail wandered west near present-day I-70 and US 40. At what is now the little town of Big Springs, the trail split, with some wagons rolling southwest on the Union Ferry Branch and most staying on the main stem straight into present-day downtown Topeka. The branches met again near what is now Rossville. The Oregon Trail Adventure Company offers history tours in the Big Springs area, but only by reservation for groups of twenty-five or more. Call (785) 887-6660 for more information.

Although they had already crossed a few small streams with steep banks that made the going difficult, it was in Topeka—after about eight days on the trail—that the emigrants encountered their first real river crossing. Explorer John Fremont, who mapped and described the trail in 1842, described the Kansas River ford as 230 yards wide, with a "swollen, angry yellow turbid current." Sometime that year or soon after, Joseph and Lewis Papan established a ferry to help emigrants across at the price of $1.00 per wagon.

By the time they'd reached the Kansas River, the emigrants had gotten to know one another pretty well. It was at this point most wagon trains reorganized, electing a new captain if necessary and cracking down on discipline for the long trip ahead. Jesse Applegate, who made the trip in 1843, described the election process in his journal *A Day with the Cow Column*. At a signal, all would-be captains marched across the prairie. Their fellow emigrants would then run after the candidate of their choice, and the man with the longest "tail" of people would win the job.

Topeka is justly proud of its **Kansas Museum of History,** located at 6425 Southwest Sixth Street near the Kansas River. Here, visitors can see displays telling the natural and human history of the Kansas plains. The "Overland Commerce and Migration" exhibit details travel on the Oregon and Santa Fe Trails. Other notable galleries focus on railroad history and the recent past via artifacts from the 1960s, 1970s, and 1980s. The museum shop sells gifts with Kansas motifs like sunflowers and "The Wizard of Oz." Also on the grounds are the Center for Historical Research, hiking trails, and a playground behind the Koch Industries Education Center (which was built in 1848 as a mission to the Pottawatomie Indians). The museum is open from 9:00 A.M. to 4:30 P.M. Monday through Saturday and 12:30 to 4:30 P.M. on Sunday. There's a suggested donation of $2.00 per adult and $1.00 per child.

Like Lawrence, Topeka was founded as a free-state stronghold in 1854, and it became the state capital in 1861. Although Topeka saw a few clashes between abolitionists and pro-slavery forces, the city is more famous for a battle fought 100 years later, when the U.S. Supreme Court ruled in favor of school desegregation in Brown versus The Topeka Board of Education. Topeka is also famous for being home to the Menninger Foundation, considered the pre-eminent neuropsychiatric center in the United States.

While in Topeka, tour the state house, which boasts some fine art (including John Steuart Curry's "The Settlement of Kansas" featuring abolitionist John Brown). The Topeka Zoological Park, with its domed tropical rain forest exhibit, is another popular draw. It's located in Gage Park, which sits along Gage Boulevard between Sixth and Tenth streets. The Combat Air Museum, located at Forbes Field south of the city, has examples of aeronautical technology from all twentieth-century U.S. military conflicts.

For more information, call the Topeka Convention and Visitors Bureau at (800) 235–1030 or see its Web site at www.topekacvb.com.

St. Marys Mission was established in 1848 at St. Marys, Kansas.

ST. MARYS

From Topeka, take US 75 north 2 miles to US 24, and head west. Again, the highway parallels the old trail right through the small towns of Silver Lake (which bills itself "The Fastest Growing City in the Country"), Rossville, and St. Marys. Watch your speed on this stretch, particularly in Silver Lake.

St. Marys is an interesting little gem of a town rarely mentioned in guidebooks. Many Oregon Trail emigrants camped here since fresh horses and oxen were available. But the town's main claim to fame was the **St. Marys Mission,** established in 1848 among the Pottawatomie Indians. The Jesuit missionaries had lived with the tribe in eastern Kansas for a decade and followed the Indians here when the federal government forced the tribe's relocation. The Indian Pay Station Museum, at First and Mission Streets, has exhibits on Pottawatomie history.

On the north side of US 24, you'll find St. Marys College, which still operates as a preparatory school for boys. A boulder on campus marks the site of the mission's log cabin cathedral, the first erected between the Missouri River and the Rocky Mountains. A chapel of more recent vintage remains on campus, but it was seriously damaged by fire in 1978. You can still see the outline of a once-beautiful stained-glass window.

West of St. Marys, watch on your right-hand side for a sign pointing to the **Oregon Trail Nature Park.** It's a good place to take a short hike, or simply stop to see the silo murals painted by area artist Cindy Martin. One mural depicts the Oregon Trail, while the others pay tribute to Kansas wildlife and Native American history.

RED VERMILLION RIVER CROSSING

Continue west from the Oregon Trail Nature Park on the gravel (but well maintained) Oregon Trail Road. In 5 miles, you'll come to Onaga Road (No. 509). Drive west another mile to the **Louis Vieux Gravesite,** in a cemetery high on a hill.

Vieux, of mixed French and Pottawatomie ancestry, ultimately became chief of the Pottawatomie tribe. He moved to the area in 1847 or 1848 and established a toll bridge over the river. Many Oregon Trail emigrants used the bridge, which cost $1.00, and Vieux made as much as $300.00 a day during the peak travel season. He added to that income by selling hay and grain to the pioneers.

A bit farther west, look for a farm gate on the north side of the road. Pull over without blocking the gate and walk 300 feet down the farm road. This is a cholera cemetery from the spring of 1849, when an outbreak of Asiatic cholera choked the emigrant camps, killing dozens of travelers. More than

Silo paintings at the Oregon Trail Nature Park near St. Marys, Kansas.

Some emigrants forded the turbulent Red Vermillion River, but many travelers paid to cross a toll bridge instead.

fifty people in one train died and were buried near the river. A small, fenced-in plot preserves three headstones, and one still bears the faint inscription T.S. PRATHER, MAY 27, 1849.

Nearby, visitors can see the beautiful Red Vermillion River. Birds swoop down its canyon as wind rushes through the trees on the riverbank. Well off the beaten path, the crossing gives the modern traveler a chance to breathe deeply and forget the urban rush, for it will be a long time before next encountering anything that could be called a traffic jam.

Emigrants liked this area, too, for it offered plenty of water, wood, and grass, which all would be in short supply in the months ahead. The famous Louis Vieux elm, once among the largest of its species at 99 feet high, is just west of the Vermillion bridge. The tree was severely damaged in a 1994 storm, but it remains quite a sight, hollowed out in the back and still sprouting leafy branches. This is an excellent spot for a picnic.

From the Vermillion, follow the back road 4 miles southwest to KS 99 at Louisville. At this point, travelers can stay closest to the original trail by taking KS 99 north for 33 miles to Frankfort. Stop en route at Westmoreland's Oregon Trail Park to see an overland wagon and oxen team fashioned by metal smith/sculptor Ernest White. Pick up KS 9 at Frankfort and drive 14 miles west to Blue Rapids. Or, from Louisville, drive 3 miles south on KS 99 to

The Louis Vieux elm near the Vermillion River crossing.

Wamego on US 24, and take US 24 to Manhattan, a good alternative overnight stop.

Manhattan, a town of some 37,000 folks, is home to Kansas State University. Tuttle Creek State Park, a popular and productive fishing spot with hundreds of campsites, is just north of town. **Fort Riley** is also nearby. Established in 1852, the outpost was situated midway between the Oregon and Santa Fe Trails and was designed to provide protection to travelers on both routes.

Travelers taking the route through Manhattan will find the intersection of US 24 and US 77 about 15 miles northwest of the city. US 77 runs north to Blue Rapids and Alcove Spring, the next major site along the Oregon Trail.

SIDE TRIP: OTHER TRAILHEADS

Independence and Westport were the best-known jumping-off spots for the Oregon Trail. But other settlements along the Missouri River—notably Weston and St. Joseph, Missouri, and Council Bluffs, Iowa—rose to prominence as trailheads, too.

Weston, Missouri, no longer sits on the river, but in 1853 it was the state's second-largest river port and a major embarkation point for Oregon Trail travelers. Today, this town 20 miles south of St. Joe is best known for its many pre–Civil War homes and for the nation's oldest and smallest distillery, the McCormick Distilling Company, founded in 1856 by stagecoach magnate Benjamin Holladay. The facility is located southeast of Weston on County Road JJ, and tours are available.

Joel Palmer recommended St. Joseph highly in his emigrant guidebook, writing "For those emigrating from Ohio, Indiana, Illinois, and Northern Missouri, Iowa, and Michigan, I think St. Joseph the best point; as by taking that route the crossing of several streams (which at the early season we travel are sometimes very high) is avoided." By 1849, about twenty steamboats visited St. Joseph each day, and most of the boats were filled with people bound for the West.

An exhibit titled "Wagons West" at the **St. Joseph Museum** tells of the city's role in the westward migration. It explains how travelers often waited two or three days to have their wagons ferried across the Missouri River so they could roll west. The museum, located at Eleventh and Charles Streets, is in the 1879 Wyeth-Toole Mansion. While in St. Joe, also pay a visit to the **Pony Express National Memorial** at 914 Penn Street, where you'll find a museum dedicated to the "lightning mail" service of 1860 to 1861.

What is now known as Council Bluffs, Iowa, was a major Mormon community called Kanesville in the 1840s. Members of the Church of Jesus Christ of Latter-day Saints built the town in 1846, only to abandon it a few years

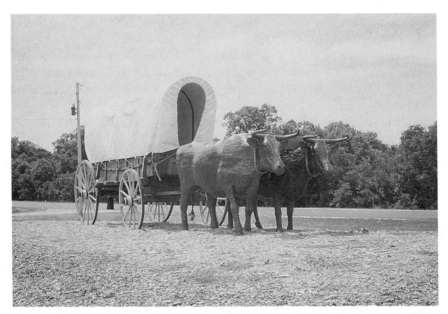

Oregon Trail sculpture at Westmoreland, Kansas.

later at the behest of church president Brigham Young, who summoned them to the new Mormon settlement near Utah's Great Salt Lake. When the Mormons left, Kanesville's population dropped abruptly from 8,000 to 1,000. But the city soon became a key rail center, and it continued its importance to overland emigrants as a natural gateway to the Platte River Valley, pathway across the plains. Today, it's home to the excellent **Western Historic Trails Center,** which offers good overviews of the Mormon, Oregon, and California Trails as well as the Lewis and Clark Expedition, which also passed this way.

Leavenworth, Kansas, was not on the main Oregon Trail, but the town still played a role in westward expansion. **Fort Leavenworth** was established in 1827 to protect traffic on the Santa Fe Trail. In later years, other emigrants passed through the area, and in 1856 the freighting firm of Majors, Russell, and Waddell made Leavenworth its headquarters. The Frontier Army Museum at Fort Leavenworth explains the military's role in opening the West.

ALCOVE SPRING

Long one of the most celebrated stops on the Oregon Trail, **Alcove Spring** is located north of Blue Rapids along River Road west of US 77. To get there, turn west just south of the Georgia-Pacific plant 1.5 miles north of Blue Rapids, then follow the signs about 6 miles north. You can also backtrack about the same distance via East River Road just south of Marysville.

Emigrants typically arrived at Alcove Spring in late spring and often had to camp several days to wait for the Big Blue River's early season runoff to subside so they could ford safely at Independence Crossing, just a quarter-mile away. But it was a fine place to be delayed for a while. Many emigrant diaries noted the cold, clear rushing water, the tall green grass, and the beautiful wildflowers blooming in profusion near the spring. The only problem was the mosquitoes, which some emigrants insisted were as big as turkeys. But mountain man Joe Meek tried to put that rumor to rest by reporting that "the biggest one I saw was no larger than a crow." Alas, the pesky critters still throng around the spring today, and insect repellent is a must.

Among those who camped here were the Donner Party of 1846, which would later be trapped by an early blizzard in the High Sierra of California. Edwin Bryant, a Donner Party member, is said to have named Alcove Spring, and he and fellow traveler Byron McKinstry carved that name on the rock surrounding the spring.

James Frazier Reed also was traveling with the Donner Party. Reed, who survived the Donner trek, carved his initials in a boulder at the spring. His mother-in-law, "Grandma" Sarah Keyes, was seventy years old, blind and deaf.

The obscure Alcove Spring was a pleasant rest spot before crossing the Big Blue River.

THE PONY EXPRESS

The histories of the Oregon Trail and the Pony Express are closely intertwined. Each took place during the same era in American history, following roughly the same route across the plains of Kansas and Nebraska. Each involved elements of excitement, romance, and danger. And many road ranches built to serve the emigrant trade later became Pony Express stations.

The Pony Express was founded in April 1860 by William H. Russell, Alexander Majors, and William B. Waddell, the same trio who ran the Overland Stage Freighting Company. Their new corporation, the Central Overland and Pike's Peak Express, promised mail delivery between St. Joseph, Missouri, and Sacramento, California, in a mere ten days, about half the time of the fastest stagecoaches.

The entrepreneurs advertised for courageous young men to ride the mail across the 1,800-mile route and back again. The Pony Express recruiting poster specified the company's preferences: YOUNG SKINNY WIRY FELLOWS NOT OVER 18. MUST BE EXPERT RIDERS WILLING TO RISK DEATH DAILY. ORPHANS PREFERRED. Eighty such young men rode the Pony Express at a time, forty going west, forty going east. Their pay was $50 each month, plus meals.

A series of way stations, where riders changed horses, was established about every 10 miles along the route. "Home" stations, where riders could sleep, were set up about every 50 miles.

The first ride from St. Joseph to Sacramento took nine days and twenty-three hours. The fastest run—carrying President Lincoln's inaugural address to an eager Western audience—took just seven days and seventeen hours. At first, the Pony Express run was made just once weekly, but that quickly grew to twice weekly and then daily.

In his book *Roughing It,* Mark Twain described the delight of seeing a Pony Express rider from his stagecoach: "We had a consuming desire, from the beginning, to see a pony-rider, but somehow or other all that passed us and all that met us managed to streak by us in the night, and so we heard only a whiz and a hail, and the swift phantom of the desert was gone before we would see him in broad daylight."

Finally, however, the stage party spotted a rider in time. "Every neck is stretched further, and every eye is strained wider. Away across the endless dead level of the prairie a black speck appears across the sky, and it is plain that it moves. Well, I should think so! In a second or two it becomes a horse and rider, rising nearer—growing more and more defined—nearer and nearer, and the flutter of the hoofs comes faintly to the ear. Another instant a whoop and hurrah from our own upper deck, a wave of the rider's hand, but no reply, and man and horse burst past our excited faces, and go winging away like a belated fragment of a storm."

Although popular, the Pony Express was expensive. Initially, it cost $5.00 to send a letter weighing a half-ounce, but the price was later reduced to $1.00. Operational expenses, however, did not diminish. In all, the service required 500 horses, 200 men to care for the animals en route, and vast amounts of grain to feed the animals. Russell, Majors, and Waddell lost $100,000 during the "lightning mail" system's eighteen months of operation.

The Express' history was fraught with physical as well as economic peril. Indians frequently burned and looted Pony Express stations, which were highly visible reminders of the white man's increasing presence in the West. Riders also had to contend with blizzards, stream crossings, and hot desert sand. Despite these dangers and discomforts, only one rider was killed and no deliveries were ever lost.

The Pony Express ended in October 1861 when completion of a transcontinental telegraph system made it possible to deliver messages in seconds, not days. A service that only months before had seemed new, exciting, and incredibly fast had been rendered obsolete. But the Pony Express lives on in the American imagination and at a few well-preserved landmark stations strung out across the nation. ♠

She was traveling west in hopes of rejoining her son, who had emigrated to Oregon two years earlier. But she died at Alcove Spring, a merciful thing considering the horrors the Donner Party would face farther west. The Daughters of the American Revolution marker commemorating her journey reads: GOD IN HIS LOVE AND CHARITY HAS CALLED IN THIS BEAUTIFUL VALLEY A PIONEER MOTHER.

Grandma Keyes was buried here, but not before relatives clipped and saved a lock of her hair. Amazingly, the lock survived the whole trip, even the Donner Party's trek across the Sierras. When eight-year-old Patty Reed was rescued from a snow cave in California, she was found clutching her grandma's lock of hair in her small hand.

Kansas storms are legendary, and it was near here that Francis Parkman encountered one of the worst he would see along the trail in 1846. "Scarcely had night set in when the tumult broke forth anew," he wrote. "The thunder here is not like the tame thunder of the Atlantic coast. Bursting with a terrific crash directly over our heads, it roared over the boundless waste of prairie, seeming to roll around the whole circle of the firmament with a peculiar and awful reverberation. The lightning flashed all night, playing with its livid glare upon the neighboring trees, revealing the vast expanse of the plain, and then leaving us shut in as if by a palpable wall of darkness."

The Alcove Spring Historical Trust is now working to preserve the spring and 223 surrounding acres. For more information on Alcove Spring, stop by Iles Pharamacy in Blue Rapids or call the city clerk at (785) 363–7736.

From Alcove Spring, River Road continues north until it rejoins US 77 just south of Marysville. Like Blue Rapids, Marysville is a cordial little town offering free RV camping in its city park. Marysville also has a small selection of motels and restaurants.

Marysville got its name from the wife of frontier merchant Frank Marshall, who ran an emigrant ferry across the Big Blue River. Marysville was also a major town along the Pony Express route. An original Pony Express home station and museum may be visited at 106 South Eighth Street, and a sculpture on US 36 leading out of Marysville tells more about the mail service. Follow US 36 west to KS 148. Turn north and drive 4.5 miles to KS 243. Turn right. The Hollenberg Ranch is 1 mile east.

HOLLENBERG RANCH

Set on a prairie miles from the nearest town, the **Hollenberg Ranch** is a key spot for Pony Express and Oregon Trail history. This was where travel along the original Independence Road and the later St. Joseph Road converged. A woman whose name was lost to history offered this description of the scene near Hollenberg Ranch: "It was a grand spectacle when we came for the first time, in view of the vast migration, slowly winding its way westward over the broad plain. The country was so level we could see the long trains of white-topped wagons for many miles . . . it appeared to me that none of the population had been left behind. It seemed to me that I had never seen so many human beings before in all my life."

German native Gerat H. Hollenberg had traveled the Oregon Trail as a gold miner in 1849. He later moved to Kansas and ran a general store in Marshall County before moving west to Washington County in 1858, where he and his wife Sofia established a business a few hundred yards northwest of Cottonwood Creek. The Hollenberg Ranch Station, as it was named, included a general store, post office, and tavern, as well as the Hollenberg home.

Hollenberg knew what he was doing when it came to locating his business. Countless emigrants passed through the valley, camping at Cottonwood Creek and relying on Hollenberg Ranch—sometimes called Cottonwood Station—for meals, lodging, food, clothing, and livestock. In 1860, Hollenberg Ranch became a station for the Pony Express, and it is today the only remaining unaltered Pony Express station standing on its original site in the entire United States. In 1991, repairs were made to stabilize the building without altering its historical character, and everything was put back to within an .08 inch of where it had been. In the meantime, an archaeological dig unearthed many souvenirs of the ranch's heyday.

Stop first at the site's visitor center. Highlights here include a beautiful Oregon Trail mural by Charles Goslin and many artifacts from the archaeological dig, as well as an 1849 emigrant tombstone from a grave in the Frankfort area. Visitors can also play a few rounds of The Oregon Trail computer game or try sending a telegraph. A short trail leads from the visitor center to

The Hollenberg Ranch, sometimes called the Cottonwood Station, provided meals, lodging, and livestock for emigrants.

the original station, a National Historic Landmark. The surrounding grounds are planted in native grasses, as well as wildflowers that typically bloom in midsummer. Visitors can also picnic out on the lawn overlooking the Cottonwood Creek valley, where it's easy to imagine the hundreds of white-topped wagons that crowded the area 150 years ago.

Hollenberg Ranch is open from 10:00 A.M. to 5:00 P.M. Wednesday through Saturday and from 1:00 to 5:00 P.M. on Sunday. Admission is by donation. On the last Sunday each August, Hollenberg Ranch holds a Pony Express Festival featuring Oregon Trail and Pony Express re-enactments, barbecues, living-history demonstrations, and a circuit-rider church service.

Hollenberg Ranch is just a few miles from the Nebraska border. Return to KS 148 and head north into the Cornhusker State.

Lodgings, campgrounds, and restaurants listed on the following pages are a representative sampling of what is available. Listing in these pages does not imply endorsement, nor is this a complete listing of all reputable businesses. For more complete listings, contact the visitor information bureau or chamber of commerce in each town. Room rates were accurate as of summer 2000, but are subject to change.

LODGING

GREATER ST. LOUIS, MISSOURI

Baymont Inn & Suites, (636) 946–6936, I–70 exit 229B (St Charles), $60.

Best Western Camelot Inn, (618) 931–2262, I–270 and IL 111 North (Pontoon Beach, Illinois), $50–$70.

Drury Inn Union Station, (314) 231–3900, 201 South Twentieth Street, $115–$135.

Embassy Suites, (314) 241–4200, 901 North First Street at Laclede's Landing, $110–$210.

Hampton Inn–St. Louis Northwest, (314) 839–2200, I–270 exit 26B (Florissant), $75–$85.

Regal Riverfront Hotel, (314) 241–9500, 200 South Fourth Street, $120.

COLUMBIA, MISSOURI

Comfort Inn, (573) 443–4141, I–70 Exit 128A, $60–$90.

Drury Inn, (573) 445–1800, 1000 Knipp Street, $74–$84.

Eastwood Motel, (573) 443–8793, 2518 Business Loop 70E, $45.

University Ave Bed & Breakfast, (573) 499–1920, 1315 University Avenue, $80–$90.

BOONVILLE, MISSOURI

Days Inn, (660) 882–8624, 2401 Pioneer, $60–$75.

The Homestead Motel, (660) 882–6568, MO 5, $30.

ARROW ROCK, MISSOURI

Borgman's Bed & Breakfast, (660) 837–3350, $55–$60.

Cedar Grove Bed & Breakfast, (660) 837–3441, $50–$60.

Down Over Inn Bed & Breakfast, (660) 837–3268, $60–$95.

Miss Nelle's Bed & Breakfast, (660) 837–3280, $50.

Westward Trails B&B, (660) 837–3335, $60–$65.

INDEPENDENCE, MISSOURI

American Inn East, (816) 795–1682, I–70 and Noland Road, $55–$85.

Howard Johnson Hotel, (816) 373–8856, 4200 South Noland Road, $80–$130.

The Inn at Ophelia's, (816) 461–4525, 201 North Main Street, $75–$125.

Red Roof Inn, (816) 373–2800, I–70 exit 12, $56–$60.

Serendipity Bed & Breakfast, (816) 833–4719, 403 North Delaware, $45–$100.

Super 8, (816) 833–1888, I–70 and Noland Road, $45–$57.

Woodstock Inn Bed & Breakfast, (816) 833–2233, 1212 West Lexington Avenue, $70–$190.

GREATER KANSAS CITY, MISSOURI/KANSAS

Adam's Mark Hotel, (816) 737–0200, 9103 East Thirty-ninth Street, $110–$170.

Best Western Seville Plaza, (816) 561–9600, 4309 Main Street, $80–$90.

Fairfield Inn–KCI Airport, (816) 464–2424, I–29 exit 13, $80.

Hampton Inn, (913) 393–1111, 12081 South Strang Line Road (Olathe, Kansas), $65–$72.

Holiday Inn–Mission/Overland Park, (913) 262–3010, 7240 Shawnee Mission Parkway, $76.

Microtel Inn & Suites, (816) 224–1122, 3120 Northwest Jefferson Street (Blue Springs), $60.

The Quarterage Hotel, (816) 931–0001, 560 Westport Road, $110.

LAWRENCE, KANSAS

Best Western Hallmark Inn, (785) 841–6500, 730 Iowa Street, $50–$90.

Circle S Guest Ranch & Country Inn, (785) 843–4124, 3325 Circle S Lane, $140 and up.

Eldridge Hotel, (785) 749–5011, 701 Massachusetts Street, $75 and up.

Holiday Inn, (785) 841–7077, I–70 West Lawrence exit, $100–$130.

Westminster Inn, (785) 841–8410, 2525 West Sixth Street, $40–$70.

TOPEKA, KANSAS

Comfort Inn, (785) 273–5365, 1518 Southwest Wanamaker Road, $70–$110.

Days Inn Capital Centre, (785) 232–7721, 91 Southeast Madison, $55–$70.

Heritage House Bed & Breakfast, (785) 233–3800, 3535 Southwest Sixth, $65–$140.

Quality Inn, (785) 273–6969, 1240 Southwest Wanamaker Road, $65–$90.

Senate Luxury Suites, (785) 233–5050, 900 Southwest Tyler, $70–$90.

WAMEGO, KANSAS

Eagle View Inn, (785) 456–9053, 520 Lincoln Street, $55–$75.

MANHATTAN, KANSAS

Guest Haus, (785) 776–6543, 1724 Sheffield Circle, $60.

Hampton Inn, (785) 539–5000, 501 East Poyntz Avenue, $65–$80.

Motel 6, (785) 537–1022, 510 Tuttle Creek Boulevard, $45–$55.

Ramada Plaza Hotel, (785) 539–7531, Seventeenth and Anderson, $85–$95.

Super 8 Motel, (785) 537–8468, 200 Tuttle Creek Boulevard, $60–$80.

MARYSVILLE, KANSAS

Best Western Surf Motel, (785) 562–2354, 2105 Center Street, $55.

Gloria's Coffee & Quilts Bed & Breakfast, (785) 763–4569, KS 9 (Barnes, Kansas), $35–$65.

Oak Tree Inn, (785) 562–1234, 1127 Pony Express Highway (US 36), $50 and up.

Super 8 Motel, (785) 562–5588, 1155 Pony Express Highway, $45 and up.

Thunderbird Motel, (785) 562–2373, US 36 West, $38 and up.

BARNES, KANSAS

Gloria's Coffee & Quilts (B&B), (785) 763–4569, KS 9 near Hollenberg Ranch.

CAMPING

GREATER ST. LOUIS
Babler Memorial State Park, (636) 458–3813, Chesterfield.

North Greater St. Louis KOA, (618) 931–5160, 3157 West Chain of Rocks Road, Granite City, Illinois.

St. Louis West KOA, (314) 257–3018, I–44 Business Loop, Allenton, Missouri.

WENTZVILLE, MISSOURI
Pinewoods Camping & Fishing Park, (636) 327–8248, I–70 exit 208.

JONESBURG, MISSOURI
Jonesburg KOA, (636) 488–5630, I–70 exit 183.

DANVILLE, MISSOURI
Graham Cave State Park, (573) 564–3476, I–70 exit 170 to County Road TT.

Kan-Do Kampground, (573) 564–7993, I–70 exit 170 to Service Road TT.

BOONVILLE, MISSOURI
Bobber Campground, (660) 882–6334, I–70 and Highway B.

ARROW ROCK, MISSOURI
Arrow Rock State Historic Site, (660) 837–3330, MO 41.

GREATER KANSAS CITY, MISSOURI
Basswood Country Inn & RV Park, (816) 858–5556, 15880 Interurban Road, Platte City.

Campus RV Park, (816) 254–1815, 406 South Pleasant, Independence. One block west of Trails Center.

Kansas City East KOA, (816) 690–6660, I–70 exit 28, Oak Grove.

LAWRENCE, KANSAS
Clinton State Park, (785) 842–8562, US 40 West. Rent-A-Camp sites available; call for information.

Lawrence KOA, (785) 842–3877, northeast of town on US 40.

TOPEKA, KANSAS
Capital City RV Park, (785) 862–5267, 1949 Southwest Forty-ninth Street.

KOA of Topeka, (785) 246–3419, US 24, Grantville.

Lake Shawnee Campground, (785) 267–1859, 3435 Southeast Eastedge Road.

Perry State Park, (785) 289–3449, 16 miles northeast on KS 237.

MANHATTAN, KANSAS
Tuttle Creek State Park, (785) 539–7941, US 24 North. Rent-A-Camp sites available; call for information.

MARYSVILLE, KANSAS

City Park, (785) 562–3101, Tenth and Walnut.

WASHINGTON, KANSAS

Rose Garden RV Camp, (785) 325–2411, 127 East Ninth Street.

RESTAURANTS

GREATER ST. LOUIS, MISSOURI

Casa Gallardo, several locations in St. Louis area, including 12380 St. Charles Rock Road, (314) 739–5700. Mexican food, Sunday brunch.

Charlie Gitto's Pasta House, (314) 436–2828, 207 North Sixth. Popular restaurant for the budget-conscious.

Kennedy's 2nd Street Company, (314) 421–3655, 612 North Second Street. Casual dining with live music. Children welcome.

Norton's Cafe, (314) 436–0828, 808 Geyer. Cajun and Creole specialties.

Old Spaghetti Factory, (314) 621–0276, 727 North First Street. Italian food in converted 1874 factory building.

ST. CHARLES, MISSOURI

Madison's Cafe, (636) 928–7355, 73 Charleston Square. Italian and American dishes.

Old Country Buffet, (636) 947–0122, 2867 I–70 Service Road.

COLUMBIA, MISSOURI

Carlos Garcia's, (573) 442–1184, 909 Business Loop 70 East. Northern Mexican food.

Heritage House Smorgasbord, (573) 443–4567, 1010 I–70 Drive Southwest.

Katy Station, (573) 449–0835, 402 East Broadway. Dine in converted boxcars and train station.

Old Plantation House, (573) 443–6212, 4515 Highway 763 North. Rural setting with steak and seafood.

The Original Bobby Buford Restaurant, (573) 445–8647, I–70 and Stadium Boulevard. Steak and seafood.

BOONVILLE, MISSOURI

Bobber Cafe, (660) 882–6334, I–70 and Highway B. Open twenty-four hours.

ARROW ROCK, MISSOURI

Arrow Rock Ice Cream Emporium, (660) 837–3337. Sandwiches, desserts.

The Evergreen Restaurant, (660) 837–3251, MO 41. Fine dining in restored 1840s home. Call for reservations.

Grandma D's Café, (660) 837–3335. Home cooking for lunch and dinner.

The Old Schoolhouse Cafe, (660) 837–3331. Breakfast and lunch.

The Old Tavern, (660) 837–3200, Main Street. Country-style cooking.

INDEPENDENCE, MISSOURI

Applebee's Neighborhood Grill and Bar, (816) 795–7799, 2035 Independence Center. Family-style food.

Courthouse Exchange, (816) 252–0344, 113 West Lexington. Midwest cuisine.

Ophelia's, (816) 461–4525, 201 North Main Street. Regional American cuisine.

The Rheinland Restaurant, (816) 461–5383, 208 North Main Street. German cuisine.

Winstead's, (816) 252–9363, 1428 South Noland Road. Steakburgers, fountain specialties.

GREATER KANSAS CITY, MISSOURI/KANSAS

Corner Restaurant, (816) 931–6630, 4059 Broadway. Westport's favorite breakfast spot.

D'Bronx, (816) 531–0550, 3904 Bell Street. New York–style deli fare.

Frontier Restaurant, (913) 788–9159, 9338 State Avenue (Kansas City, Kansas).

Gates Bar-B-Q, (816) 921–0409, 4621 Paseo Boulevard. Often voted Kansas City's best.

Jumpin' Catfish, (913) 829–3474, 1861 South Ridgeview (Olathe, Kansas).

Papagallo, (816) 756–3227, 3535 Broadway. Italian, Mediterranean, and vegetarian cuisine.

Remington's, (816) 737–4760, in the Adam's Mark Hotel, I–70 at Sports Complex. Steaks, seafood, wild game.

Westport Flea Market, (816) 931–1986, 817 Westport Road. Famous burgers.

LAWRENCE, KANSAS

Don's Steak House, (785) 843–1110, 2176 East Twenty-third Street.

Free State Brewing Co., (785) 843–4555, 636 Massachusetts Street. Microbrewery and restaurant, all ages welcome.

Pachamama's, (785) 841–0990, 2161 Quail Creek Drive. World cuisine.

Paradise Cafe, (785) 842–5199, 728 Massachusetts Street. Creative menu, fresh fish, bakery.

Plum Tree, (785) 841–6222, 2620 Iowa Street. Oriental food.

Teller's, (785) 843–4111, 746 Massachusetts Street. Pizza, Italian food featuring organic ingredients.

TOPEKA, KANSAS

Annie's Place, (785) 273–0848, 4014 Southwest Gage Center Drive. Casual dining featuring fresh-baked breads and desserts.

Casa Authentic Mexican Food, (785) 266–4503, 3320 Southwest Topeka Boulevard.

Carlos O'Kelly's, (785) 266–3457, 3425 South Kansas Avenue. Mexican-American cafe.

Old Country Buffet, (785) 273–3165, 1801 Southwest Wanamaker Road (in the West Ridge Mall). Wide selection of food.

Por'e Richard's, (785) 233–4276, 705–707 South Kansas Avenue. Casual dining downtown.

WAMEGO, KANSAS

The Friendly Cooker, (785) 456–8460, 520 Lincoln Street.

MANHATTAN, KANSAS

Country Kitchen, (785) 776–6301, 420 Tuttle Creek Boulevard. Reliable family fare.

Harry's Uptown, (785) 537–1300, 418 Poyntz Avenue. Causual dining in historic building.

Sirloin Stockade, (785) 776–0516, 325 East Poyntz Avenue.

MARYSVILLE, KANSAS

Fiesta La Grande, (785) 562–5395, 308 Center.

Koester House Restaurant, (785) 562–1075, 908 Elm.

Wagon Wheel Cafe, (785) 562–3784, 703 Broadway.

HANOVER, KANSAS

Pony Express Cafe, (785) 337–2697, US 36 and KS 15 East.

THE PLATTE RIVER ROAD: NEBRASKA

"As we wended our way up the valley of the Platte, one could look back for miles and miles on a line of wagons . . . with vari-colored wagon covers, resembling a great serpent crawling and wriggling up the valley."

—William Thompson, overlander

ROCK CREEK STATION

It is true the Platte River accompanied the emigrants most of their way across what is now Nebraska. But to reach the Platte, the travelers stayed close to the Little Blue River, moving northwest across what is still a sparsely settled area of American plains.

The first stop in Nebraska on today's trail is **Rock Creek Station State Historical Park,** and although it is somewhat off the beaten path, it is well worth a visit. The Nebraska Game and Parks Commission has done a great job of interpreting this site, and there's something to capture everyone's interest.

KS 148 becomes NE 112 and meets NE 8 at a T intersection. Turn west (left) and drive 13 miles. Just before the town of Endicott, watch for a sign pointing the way to Rock Creek Park. From here, it's 2.75 miles north then 1 mile east to the park.

Rock Creek was a popular camping spot for trappers, traders, and emigrants even before a station was officially established. Although Rock Creek's steep-sloped crossing was difficult, the area offered good spring water, fuel, and grass for grazing. Among the most notable early visitors to the area were John Fremont and his scout, Kit Carson, who camped in the area in 1842.

The first recorded settlers came to the area in 1856, and S. C. and Newton Glenn built Rock Creek Station on the west side of the creek in 1857, operating the stage station and trading post for several years until David McCanles took over. Deciding the West Ranch lacked sufficient water, McCanles built a new ranch on the creek's east side and enlarged it a few years later. McCanles also built the toll bridge that saved travelers from having to make the difficult creek crossing. He charged from 10 cents to 50 cents per wagon, depending on ability to pay and the size of the wagon load.

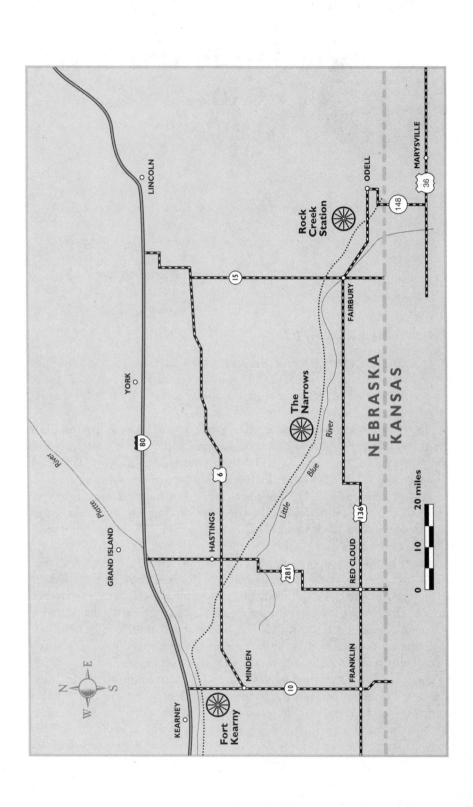

At the Rock Creek Station, visitors can see wagon replicas and other historical reconstructions.

Although Rock Creek Station was a major stopping point on the Oregon Trail, the Overland Stage route, and the Pony Express, it is perhaps best known as the place where James Butler "Wild Bill" Hickok launched his gunfighting career by killing McCanles and two hired men on July 12, 1861, in a gruesome incident witnessed by McCanles' twelve-year-old son, Monroe. Hickok had been on the ranch since the spring of that year, working as a hand; McCanles had nicknamed him "Duck Bill" because of Hickok's nose and prominent upper lip. The shootings took place when McCanles attempted to collect a long-overdue payment on the East Rock Creek Station from Horace Wellman, who managed the site for Russell, Majors, and Waddell's Pony Express. Early in July 1861, Wellman said he would travel to Nebraska City to attempt to get the money from the stage company. He arrived back at the ranch July 12. A Nebraska state pamphlet on the incident relates the day's events like this:

"When Mrs. Wellman came to the door, McCanles asked if her husband was there. When she replied that he was, McCanles demanded that he come out. She informed him that he would not, adding to McCanles' anger and suspicion. He then told Mrs. Wellman that if her husband would not come out, he would come in and drag him out. With that, Hickok stepped to the door.

"Hickok's sudden appearance disconcerted McCanles and heightened his anger. He figured that either the company was bankrupt and could not pay the money due or Wellman had collected it and planned to cheat him out of it. He had mentioned these suspicions to his family many times during the preceding month.

"Being a former sheriff and with no law close at hand, McCanles determined on quick action. Powerfully built and unafraid of any man, he would repossess the station by simply throwing the occupants off the premises by physical force.

"Having no quarrel with Hickok, McCanles asked him if they hadn't always been friends. Hickok assured him this was so. Evidently sensing that something was amiss and in a play for time, McCanles asked Hickok for a drink of water. While drinking he apparently saw something, and, handing the dipper back to Hickok, hurried to the other door. While he was crossing the room, Hickok ducked behind the calico curtain that divided the room.

"Although his quarrel was with Wellman, McCanles now had Hickok to contend with as well. At the same time, Hickok must have realized that both he and Wellman were no match for the powerful McCanles. As he reached the other door, McCanles called for Hickok to come out and fight it out fair if he had anything against him.

"In reply to McCanles' challenge, Hickok, from his hiding place behind the curtain, took aim with the very rifle McCanles had left behind to defend the station. Deliberately and in cold blood, he shot McCanles through the heart. It was a tactic that he would use successfully throughout his gunfighting career."

Hearing the commotion, McCanles' cousin, James Woods, and his friend, James Gordon, ran toward the cabin. They, too, were shot dead by Hickok, who later tried to claim the killings were in self-defense. His account gained credibility through publication in dime-novels and magazines. Hickok was acquitted of the killings when young Monroe McCanles was not allowed to testify at Hickok's trial in Beatrice. He went on to become one of the West's most notorious characters, before meeting his demise at age thirty-nine in a Deadwood, South Dakota, saloon.

Before exploring Rock Creek State Historical Park, take a good look at the land here. Much of it has never been tilled. The grasses grow high, and many species of birds and flowers thrive. This is an excellent example of basically unaltered prairie, and it is as beautiful in its own way as the Rocky Mountains or the desert Southwest.

Rock Creek Station State Historical Park took shape only in recent years. During the 1960s, the Nebraska Game and Parks Commission set about purchasing the land that encompassed the two old road ranches. At that time, no traces could be seen of the East Ranch, the West Ranch, or the toll bridge that connected the two. By the early 1980s, archaeological teams arrived to

HOMESTEAD NATIONAL MONUMENT

A 30-mile round-trip detour east on NE 4 (11 miles north of Fairbury) leads to the Homestead National Monument near Beatrice. This 160-acre claim was filed by Daniel Freeman, who settled on it during the Civil War under the provisions of the Homestead Act of 1862. He was one of more than a million homesteaders who settled the Great Plains beginning about the same time that travel on the Oregon Trail was slowing to a trickle. The site includes a century-old log cabin, a restored country school, and a pioneer farm equipment display, as well as trails through the tall grass prairie. August and September are the best months to see the grasses reach their peak heights of 8 feet or more.

Homestead National Monument is open daily from Memorial Day through Labor Day and weekends the rest of the year. It's closed Thanksgiving, Christmas, and New Year's Day. Call (402) 223–3514 for more information. ▲

unearth clues on the whereabouts of the ranch buildings and how life had been lived there. Since then, several ranch buildings and the toll bridge have been reconstructed.

At the visitor center, exhibits tell of the Oregon Trail, the Pony Express, and the Hickok connection. Don't miss the aerial photo showing scars left by wagon wheels. Other interesting items include some artifacts found on the site by archaeologists and a set of overland wagon blueprints. Kids may want to get a copy of the park scavenger hunt list at the front desk.

A path from the visitor center to the West and East Ranches parallels some of the wagon ruts. Faint spur trails exist in a few spots; take one and walk to the rim of the wagon swales to marvel at how deep they are. The main path is lined with dozens of native grasses in individually planted plots, all identified and labeled. Wagon replicas are on view at both the West and East ranches. A 3-mile hiking/horseback trail from the East Ranch affords another opportunity to see ruts and prairie.

Rock Creek Station's visitor center is open from 9:00 A.M. to 5:00 P.M. daily during the summer and from 1:00 to 5:00 P.M. weekends during May, September, and October. Admission is by a $2.50 daily permit, which is good until noon after the day of issue. Annual permits that cost $14 also are available. A campground with showers and horse camping facilities are on the grounds, too. For more information, call (402) 729–5777.

Fairbury, about 6 miles west of Rock Creek, is a pleasant town of 4,300 people. Its beautiful city park includes a playground, pool, and lots of shade. For information on Fairbury, call (402) 729–3000 or see www.oregontrail.org on the Internet.

George Winslow's grave near Fairbury, Nebraska.

An average of fifteen people died each mile along the Oregon Trail, and most of their graves were quickly lost to history. But some may still be seen. A Massachusetts native, George Winslow was on his way to the California gold-fields in 1849 when he came down with cholera near present-day Topeka, Kansas. Unlike many cholera victims, he actually started getting better for a spell until a violent storm hit the high plains. Winslow took a turn for the worse and died near what is now Fairbury. To see his resting place—probably the only marked emigrant's grave in Nebraska dating before 1850—drive about 4 miles north of Fairbury on state NE 15 and take the first left after the historical marker (which commemorates the Pony Express). Drive west for 1.5 miles and park at the farm gate on the north (right) side of the road. You needn't seek permission to enter, but the landowner asks visitors to leave the gate as they find it, open or closed. Winslow's monument is visible on the skyline a short hike away; placed in 1912, it's embedded with Winslow's original headstone.

From Rock Creek the trail cuts northwest to the Platte River, meeting it near Fort Kearny, your next stop. No main roads parallel the Oregon Trail through this region. The pioneers followed the Little Blue River, which today still winds its way northwest from Fairbury past the small towns of Powell, Hebron, Oak, Angus, and Deweese. West of Oak, the emigrants traveled through a stretch known as The Narrows, where the space between the river-bank and surrounding bluffs left only enough room for a single wagon.

There are several ways to get to Fort Kearny from Fairbury; the one you take will depend on your time and interest. One good option is staying on US 136 west to Red Cloud, where you can see the girlhood home of Pulitzer Prize–winning author Willa Cather. Tours of the town's notable Cather sites are available daily except Sunday; stop at the Willa Cather State Historic Site at 326 North Webster Street or call (402) 746–2653 for details. From Red Cloud, continue 24 miles west on US 136 to NE 10, which heads north toward Minden and Kearney.

Or take US 81 north from Fairbury to US 6, the route to Hastings. Attractions along this route include short detours to the Hastings Museum or the Stuhr Museum of the Prairie Pioneer in Grand Island. Situated on an is-land in a man-made lake, the latter is considered one of the best museums in the region. Its exhibits include a re-created nineteenth-century railroad town and the birthplace of actor Henry Fonda. Two popular state recreation areas—Mormon Island and Windmill—also lie along this route. Each offers camping, picnicking, swimming, and non-motorized boating.

FORT KEARNY

Fort Kearny was built in 1848 to protect travelers on the Oregon Trail. It was the first of six major forts the pioneers would pass on their way west, and the

Fort Kearny, Nebraska.

only one built specifically for their safety. Fort Kearny also served as a Pony Express and Overland Stage station, an outfitting post for many Indian campaigns, and the seat of military and civil government in the area. The fort was named for Colonel Stephen Watts Kearny, who was the first to suggest that a chain of military posts be built from the Missouri River to the Rocky Mountains to protect the Oregon migration.

Congress agreed. In addition to authorizing the forts, it created an Oregon battalion of mounted volunteers to help patrol the route. The first Fort Kearny was established at Table Creek (present-day Nebraska City, near the banks of the Missouri River in the state's southeast corner), but the location was later shifted 197 miles west.

Fort Kearny was a busy place, particularly during the peak years of California gold rush migration. One traveler who visited Fort Kearny described its impact like this: "The emigrant . . . sees once more the evidence of civilization and refinement, the neat and comfortable tenements of the officers, the offices and stores, all remind him of home, and as he looks aloft at the masthead, where the stars and stripes are proudly waving to the breeze, he fully realizes he is still protected, still inhabits America."

War Department records show that 30,000 people passed through the fort during one 18-month period in the late 1840s. A decade later, the march was still on: One report indicated that 800 wagons rolled through on a single day just before the Civil War. Business slacked off after the war, and Fort

Kearny was abandoned as a military post in 1871.

After the fort closed, its buildings were torn down to make way for home-steaders. Soon, the earthworks of the fortifications and the big cottonwood trees, still visible around the old parade grounds, were all that remained. In 1928, the Fort Kearny Memorial Association was formed. It purchased the 40 acres where most of the old buildings stood. But it wasn't until 1960 that the Nebraska Game and Parks Commission set about interpreting the site.

Today, **Fort Kearny State Historical Park** boasts beautiful tree-shaded grounds. A stockade replica has been erected, but visitors may be surprised to learn that the original wasn't even in place until 1864, a time when Oregon Trail traffic was tapering off but Indian "depredations" were on the rise.

Elsewhere on the grounds, the outlines of many fort buildings are still vis-ible. A self-guided walk offers a glimpse of what life was like at the facility. Especially interesting are the posted excerpts from an 1864 inspection. Offi-cials were praised, for example, for planting cedar, cottonwood, and elm trees near the hospital for the pleasure of convalescing patients.

Modern-day Fort Kearny also includes a re-created blacksmith's shop (with demonstrations on summer holidays) and an interpretive center with fort artifacts and a slide show. Kids may enjoy trying on pioneer clothing from a rack in the visitor center, then going out to take photos near the covered wagons. The center is open from 9:00 A.M. to 5:00 P.M. daily all summer and 1:00 to 5:00 P.M. weekends only in May, September, and occasionally October; it also opens daily during the sandhill crane migration from mid-March through late April. The fort grounds stay open from 8:00 A.M. to 8:00 P.M. year-round. Admission is $2.50 for a daily permit and $14 for an annual pass. For more information on park activities, call (308) 865–5305.

Two settlements near Fort Kearny—Doby Town 2 miles west and Dog Town 8 miles east—catered to soldiers at the post and sold them goods and services that were banned or otherwise unavailable at the fort. Civilians too sometimes visited these frontier tourist traps. Of Doby Town, one writer of the era said: "The townspeople are mostly frontiersmen who settled there for the sole purpose of preying on those who traveled the Oregon Trail. The pop-ulation consisted chiefly of men; about two dozen permanent inhabitants, mostly gamblers and saloon keepers, some loafers . . . and a few women of well-known reputation."

Fort Kearny State Recreation Area is next door to Fort Kearny Historical Site. This pleasant park features a 1.8-mile hike-bike trail that crosses several channels of the Platte River; there's also camping, fishing, swimming, boating (non-motorized), and picnicking. It's a popular spot, so expect crowds and ar-rive early in the evening to get a campsite.

Just a few miles from Fort Kearny, the city of Kearney is one of the most interesting towns in Nebraska. Home to about 25,000 people and a 10,000-

The Archway Monument spans all four lanes of I–80 near Kearney, Nebraska.

student University of Nebraska branch campus, the town has more than its share of culture, recreation, and other diversions, not to mention a wide range of motels and restaurants. The Kearney Visitors Bureau has an office at 1007 Second Avenue; you can also get information by calling (800) 652–9435 or visiting www.kearneycoc.org on the Internet.

Kearney's biggest attraction is the Archway Monument (see sidebar), but there are many other interesting sites. Railroad buffs will enjoy the Trails and Rails Museum at 710 West Eleventh Street, and motorheads will thrill to Chevyland U.S.A., located west of town at I–80's exit 257. Cabela's, the outdoor outfitting catalog company, has a showroom store on US 30 east of Kearney featuring one of the state's largest aquariums and trophy game and fish displays, and a "bargain corner" full of discontinued catalog merchandise. Cooks will probably want to pay a visit to Morris Press on east US 30, which has published fund-raising cookbooks for groups in all fifty states. They offer one free cookbook per visitor; additional books are $2.00 to $5.00 each.

Eight of Nebraska's I–80 rest areas feature sculptures that were put in place during the state's celebration of the U.S. Bicentennial in 1976. One of the most interesting installations is located just west of Kearney. George Baker's 7,200-pound stainless-steel "Nebraska Wind Sculpture" floats lazily on a lake, reflecting the blue sky and golds and greens of the surrounding plains.

PIONEER VILLAGE AND THE ARCHWAY MONUMENT

For miles away in every direction, travelers see the signs: VISIT PIONEER VILLAGE, NEBRASKA'S NO. 1 ATTRACTION, SEE HOW AMERICA GREW. Minden, Nebraska, is indeed synonymous with Harold Warp's **Pioneer Village.** Warp, who made big money as the inventor of Flex-O-Glass and other plastics, got the idea for Pioneer Village when the old country school he had attended as a child in Minden went up for sale in 1948. Practically a city unto itself, Pioneer Village (with more than two dozen buildings and its own RV park, motel, and airstrip) boasts 50,000 historical items that depict America's progress since 1830. The collection includes 350 antique autos, 100 antique tractors, 20 historic "flying machines," original art by the likes of John James Audubon and William H. Jackson, toys, trolleys, bicycles, buttons, golf clubs, bath tubs, and the list goes on and on.

Poring over the massive collections at Pioneer Village can easily eat up several days, but visitors can enjoy a stop at the site even if with only an hour or two to spare. Pioneer Village is open daily except Christmas from 8:00 A.M.; closing hours vary. Admission, $7.00 for adults and $3.50 for kids ages six to twelve, is good for any number of consecutive days. For more information, call (800) 445–4447 or (308) 832–1181 in Nebraska.

While Pioneer Village is strictly a tribute to the past, the new **Great Platte River Road Archway Monument** is an attraction powered by modern technology, and plenty of it. The seven-story Archway spans all four lanes of I–80 east of Kearney; inside, the high-tech exhibits take a sweeping look at the forces that fueled America's westward expansion, from the pioneer trails to the transcontinental railroad to fiber-optic cable. It pounds home the point that almost all these developments took place right here along the Great Platte River Road.

Once inside the monument, visitors are given headphones before ascending an escalator into the past. The headphones pick up signals as you move from room to room; be aware you have to stand very still once the stories are in progress to keep the sound from cutting out. Other multimedia effects range from simulated storms to films of stampeding bison and Pony Express riders. Toward the end, two windows facing I–80 allow you to clock the speeds of the traffic passing underneath. It's all quite a spectacle, well worth the $7.50 admission ($6.00 for children under twelve and seniors sixty-five and older). The Archway is open from 8:00 A.M. to 10:00 P.M. daily May through September. The rest of the year, it's open 8:00 A.M. to 10:00 P.M. weekends and 11:00 A.M. to 6:00 P.M. weekdays. There's a small food court and gift shop. Take exit 272 at Kearney. Call (877) 511–ARCH for more information. ◆

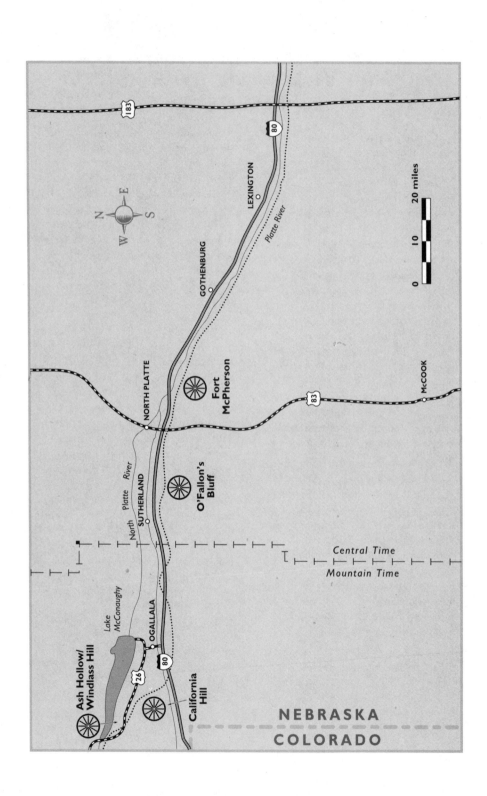

Speaking of landscape, Kearney is in Nebraska's famous sandhills region, which runs north of the Platte River roughly from Grand Island west to Lewellen. The sandhills are still covered with rich native grass and act as natural reservoirs for irrigation water. The rises at the south edge of the Platte River valley are clay hills, not sandhills, and they are primarily used for grazing.

This also was the area in which the pioneers first caught up with the Platte, which would guide them for hundreds of miles into present-day Wyoming. A natural thoroughfare for travelers, the Platte offered good supplies of grass and water. Emigrants marveled at the shallow, muddy waterway, calling it "a mile wide and an inch deep" or "too thick to drink and too thin to plow." One traveler said it appeared to be flowing bottom-side up. However it is described, the Platte certainly is one of the most distinctive-looking rivers in North America.

Oregon Trail pioneers weren't the only travelers who passed through the Platte River valley. Even today, about a half-million birds—80 percent of the world's sandhill crane population—rest and feed in central Nebraska during their annual migration north to Canada and Alaska. Popular places to watch the cranes include Fort Kearny and Mormon Island State Recreation Areas. The birds are usually seen only during a six-week span in March and April.

GOTHENBURG AREA

Travelers along I-80 will see signs encouraging them to stop and see the Pony Express station in Gothenburg (exit 211). The station was built in 1854, 4 miles east of Fort McPherson along the Oregon Trail, and moved to its present location in 1931. It's open daily from 8:00 A.M. to 9:00 P.M. during the summer and from 9:00 A.M. to 6:00 P.M. during May and September. Horse-drawn carriage rides are offered about every twenty minutes. For more fun, stop by Lake Helen on the north edge of town. Rent a paddleboat or canoe, do some fishing, picnic, and see what is possibly Nebraska's only covered bridge. Camping is available in adjacent Lafayette Park.

Fort McPherson National Cemetery is between Gothenburg and North Platte, 4 miles south of the Maxwell interchange (exit 190). The cemetery sits near the site of Cottonwood Springs, which was a major Oregon Trail campsite, trading post, and Pony Express station. A fort was established nearby in 1863 to protect the final waves of traffic along the Oregon Trail during a period of increased Indian hostilities. Emigrant wagon trains sometimes banded together here so that they could face the rest of the way west with increased strength and safety in numbers.

Southeast of the cemetery, a monument on the right side of the road marks the site of the fort's flagstaff. The monument also pays tribute to the Seventh Iowa Cavalry, Civil War veterans who were the first troops stationed

NORTH PLATTE AND THE
BUFFALO BILL RANCH

The Oregon Trail stayed south of present-day I–80 through what is now Lincoln County, but North Platte—the county seat and one of the region's largest cities—still proves fascinating to anyone interested in the lore of the American West.

North Platte's main attraction is probably Buffalo Bill State Historical Park. Located 3.5 miles northwest of town via US 30, the park preserves the home of William F. "Buffalo Bill" Cody, one of the West's most colorful characters.

Born in 1846 in Iowa, Cody moved to Kansas with his family in 1853. By age eleven he was driving oxen for 50 cents a day; later, he supposedly joined the Pony Express as one of its youngest riders. Legend has it he once rode 322 miles in twenty-one hours and forty minutes, exhausting twenty horses along the way—although some historians now dispute whether he rode in the ranks at all.

Cody was too young to enlist when the Civil War began, but he did serve the Union as a ranger, dispatch bearer, and scout. In 1864, he enlisted in the Kansas Volunteer Infantry and served until the end of the war. He later was employed to kill buffalo to feed workers on the Kansas Pacific Railroad.

Cody settled in the North Platte area in 1878 and built the home at his Scout's Rest ranch in 1886. This was the heyday of his Wild West Show, which traveled across North America and even into Europe. All of Cody's many exploits are described in detail at the park, and visitors can even see the Wild West Show via rare film footage shot by Thomas Edison in 1898. Horseback riding is another ranch attraction.

The Cody home is open from 10:00 A.M. to 8:00 P.M. daily Memorial Day through Labor Day, as well as from 9:00 A.M. to noon and 1:00 to 5:00 P.M. weekdays only in April, May, September, and October. The park grounds are open year-round. Admission is $2.50 for a daily vehicle permit or $14.00 for an annual state parks permit. Call (308) 535–8035 for more information.

The four-day Buffalo Bill Rodeo kicks off each year's celebration of Nebraskaland Days, one of the state's largest festivals. Typically held the third week in June, Nebraskaland Days also features parades, top-name country music entertainment, barbecues, dances, and old-style shootouts. Other rodeos are held throughout the summer. Check with the visitors bureau (following) for dates and details.

Bailey Yard, focal point of the Union Pacific system, is a must for railroad fans. Three miles west of North Platte on Front Street, the yard is the largest rail classification center in the United States. A railroad museum at the city's Cody Park is home to Union Pacific's Challenger 3977, the world's largest steam locomotive and the only one in its class on display anywhere. Other Cody Park attractions include swimming, tennis, picnic grounds, and summer carnival rides for the kids.

For more information on North Platte, stop by the Convention & Visitors Bureau at 219 South Dewey, call (800) 955-4528, or see the Web site at www.northplatte-tourism.com.

It's about 130 miles north of North Platte via US 83, but canoeists will not want to miss the Niobrara River. Ranked as one of the nation's best paddling streams, the Niobrara features pine-dotted canyons and waterfalls accessed via the Fort Niobrara National Wildlife Refuge area east of Valentine. Call the Valentine Visitor Center at (800) 658–4024 for more information. ♠

at Fort Cottonwood, which was renamed Fort McPherson in 1866. The fort was disbanded in 1880, but its headquarters building may still be seen at the Lincoln County Historical Museum in North Platte.

Valley View Guest Ranch near Maxwell offers swimming, guided trail rides, hayrides, fishing, campsites, and housekeeping cabins. The ranch sits 2 miles south of the Maxwell exit, then 0.5 mile west and another 0.5 mile south. Call (308) 582–4320 for more information.

Travelers interested in Native American life may want to take a side trip to the Dancing Leaf Earth Lodge south of North Platte. Hosts Les and Jan Hosick offer a variety of programs ranging from two-hour tours to overnight stays, all by appointment. For more information, write 6100 East Opal Springs Road, Wellfleet, NE 69170, or call (308) 963–4233.

O'FALLON'S BLUFF

The truth is, a modern traveler could get a fairly good idea of what the Oregon Trail was all about without ever leaving the interstate highway. Many rest areas along the route have excellent displays interpreting the great emigration. One of the best is along I–80 in Nebraska at **O'Fallon's Bluff,** about twenty minutes west of North Platte.

Iron hoops resembling wagon wheels mark the trail at O'Fallon's Bluff.

Ogallala and Lake McConaughy

Sitting at the gateway to Nebraska's "panhandle," Ogallala is the jumping-off spot for western Nebraska's Oregon Trail landmarks: Courthouse Rock, Chimney Rock, and Scotts Bluff. Aside from that, Ogallala and its neighbor to the north, Lake McConaughy, combine to offer a region full of activities and recreation.

Named for the Oglala Tribe of the Dakota Sioux, Ogallala nonetheless is more famous for cowboys than for Indians. From 1875 to 1885, Ogallala reigned as "Queen of the Cowtowns," the end of the Texas Trail. From here, cattle driven north from Texas were shipped via the Union Pacific to ranges all over the northern Plains.

Ogallala had another nickname, too: "Gomorrah of the Plains." Much of the town's rowdy reputation came courtesy of cowboys, who flooded Ogallala's saloons and gambling parlors to celebrate the end of their cattle drive. Attracted by all the commerce and commotion, Ogallala soon became a haven for unsavory characters, many of whom are now buried in Boot Hill at Tenth and West C Streets.

A historical marker at the cemetery confirms that many buried there "came by running afoul of the law—some for stealing another man's horse. Others were killed by re-fighting the Civil War or for questioning the gambler's winning hand. In July of 1879, three cowhands were buried in a single day, victims of the sheriff's guns. Another man, 'Rattlesnake Ed,' was buried here after he was shot down over a $9.00 bet in a Monte game in the Cowboy's Rest, a local saloon."

Today's Ogallala—a community of about 5,000 people—is considerably more tame than the town of yore. But touches of the frontier live on. Front Street is the hub of activity, offering such attractions as the family-style Crystal Palace Revue, a free Cowboy Museum, and nightly "shoot-outs" all summer long. Ogallala also has a good selection of restaurants and recreational attractions including golf, miniature golf, bowling, roller skating, and swimming.

Lake McConaughy sprawls 9 miles north of Ogallala via NE 61, and it must be seen to be believed. With 105 miles of sandy beach, the 35,000-acre "Big Mac"—Nebraska's largest reservoir—caters to boaters, water and jet skiers, sailboarders, anglers, swimmers, campers, and sunbathers. As with all Nebraska state parks, a $2.50 vehicle entry permit is required and may be purchased from the state game commission or from lake-area concessionaires (who charge 25 cents extra). Stop by any local business for an orientation map.

Lake McConaughy is famous for its fish, and its waters have yielded state-record salmon, trout, striped bass, walleye, and tiger muskie. All anglers ages sixteen and over need a license; three-day non-resident permits cost $10.75.

Several full-service campgrounds dot the area around Lake McConaughy and its small neighbor to the east, Lake Ogallala. But visitors can also camp free in many areas around both lakes. Among the choicest locations: Spring Park/Otter Creek, located at Gate 12; Martin Bay, at Gate 1; and the west side of Lake Ogallala. Cabins are available in several locations, too, as are services including boat and diving equipment rentals, showers (there are no shower facilities in the state park camping areas), and guide services for anglers and hunters.

"Big Mac" was created in 1941 with the completion of the Kingsley Dam, which impounded the North Platte for irrigation and power generation. When completed, it was the world's second-largest hydraulic dam, and it produces nearly 100 million kilowatt hours of electricity each year, the equivalent of 175,000 barrels of oil.

This is a great place to view bald eagles during their annual migration from late December through late February. The eagle-viewing center is open during those months from 8:00 A.M. until noon on Thursday and Friday and 8:00 A.M. to 4:00 P.M. on Saturday and Sunday. While you're there, ask for a copy of the area bird checklist, which lists the 300 or so species that have been seen in the area.

For more information on Ogallala or Lake McConaughy, stop by the Ogallala/Keith County Chamber of Commerce at 204 East A Street, call (800) 658–4390, or see the Web site at www.ci.ogallala.ne.us. The Nebraska National Trails Museum Foundation hopes to build a major trails interpretive facility near Ogallala. For more information, write P.O. Box 268, Ogallala, NE 69153; or call (308) 284–2000, or see the group's Web site at www.megavision. net/nntm. ♠

There's only one minor problem: The bluff is located on the eastbound side of the interstate. If you're traveling west, as most folks tracing the Oregon Trail will do, you will need to backtrack slightly to get there. Leave I–80 at exit 158, the Sutherland interchange. Get back on the highway eastbound; the rest area is just 2 miles away.

Although it isn't officially part of Nebraska's I–80 "sculpture garden without walls," the O'Fallon's Bluff deserves honorary membership. Walk to the east edge of the rest area to see several historical markers describing the Oregon Trail. Nearby are several sets of large iron hoops resembling wagon wheels, all poised to roll off across the prairie. Very faint ruts are visible along the ground below.

O'Fallon's Bluff was a landmark to mountain men and pioneers alike. The bluff came so close to the Platte River that emigrant wagons were forced to travel single-file over the route.

From here, the emigrants continued along the south side of the Platte to the Lower California Crossing near present-day Brule, Nebraska. Modern westbound travelers should backtrack 3 miles east to the Hershey interchange (exit 164), then continue west on I–80 to Ogallala.

There are a few other sites of interest along or near the Platte in south-central Nebraska. Sutherland State Recreation Area, south of exit 159 on NE 25, is popular with anglers, boaters, and swimmers. For a break from the interstate, take US 30, which parallels I–80 through some of the finest sandhills country and through small towns including Hershey, Sutherland, Paxton, and Roscoe.

If the family's fixin' for a meal at this point, consider stopping in Paxton at Ole's Big Game Steakhouse. Established by Rosser O. "Ole" Herstedt one minute after Prohibition ended on August 9, 1933, Ole's is most famous for its collection of trophy game, all taken by Ole himself during five decades of hunting on every continent. More than 200 mounts are on display, including a 1,500-pound, 11-foot polar bear taken by Ole in 1969 in the Chukchi Sea off Sibera. He once turned down an offer of $50,000 for the bear.

Ole's menu features steaks, buffalo burgers, seafood, and chicken. What with its decor, Ole's—even more so than most places in cattle country—is probably not the best rest stop for ardent vegetarians and animal-rights activists. But for everyone else, it's a Nebraska institution.

One additional note: Don't forget to set watches back one hour at the Lincoln-Keith County line, where the mountain time zone begins. This is the first of two time zones that give westbound Oregon Trail travelers an extra hour for exploration and fun! It's also another sure sign of officially having passed from the Midwest into the West.

CALIFORNIA HILL

Ready for another adventure? This fact isn't mentioned on many maps or tourist information leaflets, but western Keith County, Nebraska, is home to some of the finest Oregon Trail ruts to be seen anywhere along the route. At **California Hill,** visitors can walk where the wagons rolled and see the emigrant caravans' impact on the land—traces that haven't vanished more than 150 years later. To get to California Hill, drive west on US 30 from Ogallala to Brule. Before continuing, take a look at the South Platte River, which may be seen from the road bridge leading to the I–80 interchange south of town. It was in this general location that the emigrants crossed the Platte and started northwest, ultimately following the North Platte's course after a trek of about 25 miles across the high plains. The ford here was known as the "Lower California Crossing," taking its name because it was one of the two most popular crossings for those on their way to seek gold in California. (The other, used mostly after 1860, is the Upper California Crossing near Julesburg, Colorado, about 35 miles west.)

Continue west on US 30. About 4.5 miles west of Brule, watch for a historical marker on the right side of the road. It relates that California Hill now sits on land owned by the Oregon-California Trail Association, and that the site is dedicated to the memory of Irene D. Paden, who wrote *The Wake of the Prairie Schooner,* a vivid account of her own family's Oregon Trail explorations early in the twentieth century. Malcolm Smith, a Paden fan from New York State, donated the money for the land purchase.

Wagon ruts cut deep into California Hill near Brule, Nebraska.

To reach the ruts, drive north up the dirt road about 0.5 mile. On the left, look for a white-paneled passageway through the barbed wire fence. Park and walk through the gateway. Start walking northwest, looking for the Oregon Trail marker on the horizon. Keep an eye out for cattle—this is a grazing area—and for prickly pear cactus and the occasional rattlesnake.

Unlike a lot of faint remnants along the Oregon Trail, there is no mistaking these ruts. The swale up the hill, started by wagon wheels, has been helped along by 150 years of erosion. Along this stretch, wood for fires was scarce. Tires popped off wagon wheels that had first expanded with the Platte's water, then shrunk in the dry air.

By the time the emigrants reached California Hill, they were about thirty-five days and 450 miles from Independence, Missouri. More than three-quarters of their journey remained. They were tired, and this land was hot and windy, but they knew this was no place to turn back. If they had come this far, they could press on.

Modern-day visitors to this area will find it easy to understand what the emigrants endured. Yet from up on this rise, you also can see (and even hear) I-80, US 30, and the Union Pacific Railroad, with trains, trucks, and automobiles rushing east and west—proof once again that our nation's earliest transportation corridors usually proved to be the best.

From here, travelers can continue on the dirt roads, following the same general route of the Oregon Trail. In late spring or during wet weather, two-wheel-drive vehicles should backtrack to the highway due to the possibility of mud bogs on the back roads. But those traveling after Memorial Day or in a four-wheel-drive vehicle should have no problem getting through the back way.

To do so, continue north 0.5 mile to a corner, where the road bears left. Drive west for 3 miles, then north for 4 miles, then west again for 2 more miles. Turn north (right) again; this paved road leads 5 miles to US 26. Turn left at the highway intersection and proceed to Windlass Hill, about 3 miles to the west on the left.

WINDLASS HILL AND ASH HOLLOW

Judging from emigrant diaries, **Ash Hollow** was among the most favored spots along the Oregon Trail. Here, the travelers found welcome shade trees and firewood, abundant grass for their animals, and water that one pioneer called "the best and purest ever drank . . . a beverage prepared by God himself." Indeed, many nineteen-century guidebooks pronounced the water at Ash Hollow the very best along the whole Oregon Trail, and most emigrants rested a day or two at this camp. But before they could enjoy these treasures, the emigrants had to make their way down the dreaded **Windlass Hill,** the steepest descent yet encountered. Today, the incline offers a superb look at the power of natural forces over landscape, humans, and history.

Here, travelers tied ropes to their wagons, locked the wheels, and hoped for the best. One pioneer wrote that the drop was so terrifying that no one spoke the entire time; another noted that the hill was so steep that it seemed to hang "a little past the perpendicular." Diaries also told of broken wagons and broken bones among the animals and the emigrants themselves. Some travelers decided to avoid the hill altogether, keeping to the bluffs another 16 or 17 miles out of their way just to bypass the steep grade.

Despite the name "Windlass Hill," the pioneers apparently did not use windlasses (machines consisting of a cylinder wound with rope and turned by a crank) to ease the descent. A video at the Ash Hollow visitor center explains that such devices were never mentioned in emigrant diaries; if they were used at all, it must have been in later days.

To experience Windlass Hill, turn into the parking lot and walk up the path to a footbridge. Look up and down the steep ravine on either side of the bridge; this was the Oregon Trail. A concrete path continues to the top of the hill, past a 1912 State of Nebraska Oregon Trail marker. Keep to the

Oregon Trail monument atop Windlass Hill in Nebraska.

This sod house replica of a homesteader's cabin marks the entrance to Windlass Hill.

path, but where spurs allow, stray far enough from it toward the top to see Windlass Hill as the emigrants saw it, steep and foreboding.

Before leaving the area, check out the sod house replica near the Windlass Hill entrance. The stones surrounding the historical marker near the house are all that remain of the original dwelling built in the late nineteenth century by Dennis B. Clary, a Methodist minister who was born in Maryland in 1822 and migrated to Nebraska in 1885. Clary's humble home was reconstructed during the Ash Hollow Centennial Pageant in 1967.

Once they'd conquered Windlass Hill, the pioneers were free to frolic at Ash Hollow, which is actually a 6-mile-long plain stretching to the North Platte River. Today, visitors can enjoy a picnic, watch the excellent video presentation at the visitor center, or hike a trail to either Ash Hollow Cave, used by prehistoric people as many as 6,000 years ago, or the site of Ash Hollow Spring. The latter still flows, but modern-day visitors are asked not to drink the water.

Ash Hollow is interesting for reasons other than the Oregon Trail. Scientists have found evidence of prehistoric use dating back 7,000 to 10,000 years and of prehistoric animals including mammoths and mastodons. The area also figured prominently in the beginning of hostilities between Native Americans and whites. It was the site of a major battle between the Sioux and Pawnee in 1835. Later, eighty-six Sioux were killed during a 1855 battle with whites at nearby Blue Water Creek. Although General Harney was initially hailed as a hero following this encounter, the battle later became known as the "Harney Massacre." The Blue Water Battle is considered one of the twelve largest engagements between Indians and whites in the United States, and it is the incident most often cited as precipitating the Indian Wars.

A Nebraska park permit is required for entry into Ash Hollow and Windlass Hill. Permits are available at the park office, which is open from 8:00 A.M. to 6:00 P.M. (mountain time) daily Memorial Day through Labor Day. The grounds are open 8:00 A.M. to sundown year-round. Call (308) 778–5651 for more information, or to get details on the annual Oregon Trail pageant usually held at the park around Father's Day weekend in June.

A small cemetery on the left side of US 26 just past the Ash Hollow park exit is notable as the final resting place of Rachel E. Pattison, who died June 19, 1849, at the age of eighteen. Like so many other emigrants, she woke up one morning in fine health, fell ill by noon, and was dead by sundown. The dreaded cholera had struck again, this time claiming a bride of just two months. Pattison's original headstone may still be seen encased behind glass at the grave, and an accompanying interpretive marker tells what became of her husband.

Once past the cemetery, cross the Platte (the emigrants stayed on the river's south banks), and arrive in Lewellen, a small town with a few cafes and a gas station. Oshkosh, 12 miles west, has a bit more commerce, a couple of small museums, campgrounds, free swimming, and a nine-hole golf course.

North of Oshkosh, Crescent Lake National Wildlife Refuge is popular for hiking, fishing, and bird-watching. Past Oshkosh, it's a scenic fifty-minute drive along US 26 to Bridgeport, home of the trail's next major landmarks, Courthouse Rock and Jail Rock. As always, the North Platte River and the Union Pacific Railroad accompany the roadway. NE 92, which runs 16 miles from Broadwater to Bridgeport, actually parallels the Oregon Trail more closely than does US 26.

COURTHOUSE ROCK AND JAIL ROCK

After several weeks on the Oregon Trail, the boredom could be intense. Emigrants sought to relieve it in a variety of ways: through music and dancing, card games, or conversation. But in what is now western Nebraska, the emigrants found a new source of entertainment in the strange, high rock formations that lined the route, serving as landmarks. Most of the pioneers were former Midwestern flatlanders, and they had never seen anything like these monolithic masses of stone.

Two of the best-known formations, **Courthouse Rock and Jail Rock,** are about 5 miles south of Bridgeport via NE 88. Although the Oregon Trail ran just south of what is now Bridgeport, few emigrants could resist the urge to trek farther south and see the formations up close. Or as Gregory Franzwa put it in *The Oregon Trail Revisited,* "After moving some 500 miles from Independence, another 4 miles was nothing, especially when it could be negotiated either on horseback or afoot, without wagons." Once they reached the rocks, many emigrants climbed them, which visitors can still do today.

As Franzwa also pointed out, Courthouse Rock (sometimes called Courthouse Block) may have gotten its name because it reminded emigrants of the courthouse in St. Louis, which at the time didn't yet have its tall, Italianate dome. Many pioneers probably carved their names on the sandstone and clay rocks, but these have long since worn away.

Enoch W. Conyers, who traveled the trail in 1852, had this to say as his party approached the area on June 16: "We came in view of Courthouse Block and Chimney Rock about noon today while crossing the ruins of the 'ancient bluffs.' We have a splendid view of those noted rocks from our camp tonight which brings to mind some verses composed by 'The Platte River Poet,' one of which runs thus:

The naming of landmarks such as Courthouse and Jail Rocks provided emigrants with a source of entertainment along the trail.

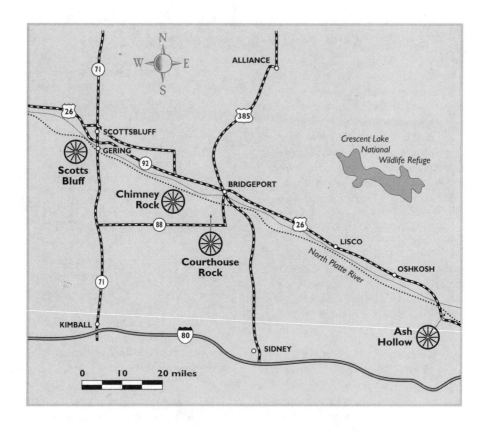

'The next we came to was Platte River
Great sights were there to see.
There was Courthouse Block and Chimney Rock
And, next, Fort Laramie.'"

    Courthouse and Jail Rocks are at the eastern edge of a region known as the
Wildcat Hills. Scenic NE 88 traverses the area, dead-ending at NE 71. A right
turn there leads past Wildcat Hills State Recreation Area and Game Reserve,
where visitors can view buffalo, elk, and longhorn steers. People who visit in
May or June may catch sight of a baby buffalo or elk, and coyotes and bobcats
live in the area, too. The Wildcats offer abundant recreation and are popular
with mountain bikers, campers, horseback riders, and hikers. Those who decide
to take NE 88 around to Scottsbluff Gering may want to first visit Chimney
Rock, which is best accessed via NE 92. It's slightly closer to Bridgeport than
to Scottsbluff, though you can easily backtrack from the latter.

BLACK HILLS AND BADLANDS

Few areas of the West have as motley a mixture of natural and man-made attractions as does South Dakota's southwest corner. A three- to four-hour drive north of Bridgeport, Nebraska, will put travelers within reach of such sights as Mount Rushmore, Badlands and Wind Cave National Parks, the world-famous Wall Drug, and the Pine Ridge Indian Reservation, one of the poorest and most storied in the United States.

Weed through the tourist traps and there's plenty to like about the region. Badlands National Park boasts a raw, rugged landscape and some of the world's finest fossil beds, formed about 37 million years ago during the Oligocene Epoch.

The Badlands offer backcountry adventure for those with time to explore. The Castle Trail is particularly acclaimed for its varied prairie topography and wealth of wildlife, including pronghorn antelope, bison, badgers, coyotes, and prairie dogs.

Those in a hurry can drive the 40-mile loop road (SD 240) between Wall and Cactus Flat. Primitive camping is available, as are cabins, at the Sioux-run Cedar Pass Lodge, located south of Cactus Flat. The White River Visitor Center, on the Pine Ridge Indian Reservation in the park's South Unit, features displays and programs on Sioux history.

Wind Cave National Park, adjacent to Custer State Park on SD 87, offers daily subterranean tours during the summer. The excursions range from short candlelight walks to more strenuous spelunking expeditions. Jewel Cave National Monument, 14 miles west of Custer, South Dakota, on US 16A, is one of the longest caves in the world. It too offers tours, as do a number of privately held caves scattered throughout the area.

The Black Hills were named by the Lakota Sioux for the dark appearance of their coniferous forests. The Sioux considered the land sacred, and their rights to it

Bridgeport also was the home of Paul C. Henderson, who spent fifty-two years researching the emigrant trail. His grave in the cemetery west of town has been marked by the Oregon-California Trails Association. The Morrill County Fair takes place in Bridgeport in late August.

The area north of Bridgeport includes the Bridgeport State Recreation Area, just a mile north of town, and a most unusual roadside attraction 38 miles north in Alliance. "Carhenge," featuring some three dozen vehicles planted in the ground, is the Automobile Age's version of the mysterious Stonehenge monument near Salisbury, England. Alliance celebrates each year's summer solstice at the site with a parade, picnic, pageant, and bonfire. (No one should ever accuse Nebraskans of lacking a good sense of humor.) Bridgeport also is the jumping-off spot for the Black Hills and Badlands of South Dakota.

were ensured in a treaty signed in 1868. But the U.S. government broke the pact during the gold rush of the late 1870s. Today's Black Hills are heavily commercialized, but their beauty remains mostly intact. Check with the Forest Service office in Custer for maps and information on the area's many scenic byways (and for restrictions on motor homes and trailers, which may have trouble negotiating the region's roads).

Mount Rushmore is probably the best-known Black Hills attraction. Created under the direction of Gutzon Borglum, it features the 60-foot-high heads of Presidents George Washington, Thomas Jefferson, Abraham Lincoln, and Theodore Roosevelt. The sculpture is bathed in floodlights each night at dusk.

The Crazy Horse Memorial near Custer was started in 1947 by sculptor Korczak Ziolkowski to honor Chief Crazy Horse and the Native Americans. When completed, it will measure 563 feet high and 641 feet long, which would make it the largest statue in the world. It too is lit nightly at dusk.

Other Black Hills sights include Custer State Park, known for its 18-mile wildlife loop drive and abundant recreation, and Deadwood, which retains much of its old Wild West atmosphere (including small-stakes gambling). It was here that Wild Bill Hickok was shot in the back while playing poker in 1876. He's buried alongside Calamity Jane (who claimed she was his secret bride) in Mount Moriah Cemetery overlooking the city.

Nearby, the town of Lead (rhymes with greed) is famous for its Homestake Gold Mine, largest in the western hemisphere. And in early August, Sturgis attracts hordes of Harley Davidson enthusiasts for the Black Hills Motorcycle Classic. Spearfish is home to the Black Hills Passion Play, presented Sunday, Tuesday, and Thursday June through August.

For more information on South Dakota, write the state Department of Tourism, Capital Lake Plaza, Pierre, SD 57501, or call (800) 843–1930 or (800) 952–2217 in South Dakota. ▲

CHIMNEY ROCK

Of all the natural landmarks along the Oregon Trail, **Chimney Rock** is probably the most famous, mentioned in more emigrant diaries than any other. Rising almost 500 feet above the North Platte River, Chimney Rock can be seen from 30 miles away. The emigrants watched it, entranced, for two to three days as their wagons rolled ever closer. Landmarks such as these eased travelers' minds, for they could tell they were making progress. They could see for themselves that what they'd heard from friends and neighbors was true: The West was a strange and wondrous land, and—although much hard travel lay ahead—the best was yet to come.

"At this place was a singular phenomenon, which is among the curiosities of the country," Captain Benjamin Bonneville wrote in 1832. "It is called the

Chimney Rock is another distinct landmark along the trail in Nebraska.

Chimney. The lower part is a conical mound rising up from the naked plain; from the summit shoots up a shaft or column, about 120 feet in height, from which it derives its name."

Chimney Rock was a popular camping spot with good, dependable water. Thousands of pioneers climbed up the cone to carve their names, although these have long since worn away. There is no record, however, of anyone ever scaling the soft Brule clay spire, although some folks apparently tried—one emigrant noted a name etched in the chimney 30 feet up, and another may have died trying to beat that feat. There also are tales that some emigrants fired guns at the spire, claiming as souvenirs any chips they managed to knock off. Another story holds that later in the nineteenth-century, the U.S. military used Chimney Rock for target practice. More recently, lightning bolts zapped off pieces of the rock in 1972 and 1993.

Every emigrant who kept a diary had something to say about Chimney Rock. Some gave it alternate nicknames: "lightning rod," "elk penis," and "potato hill" were among the most descriptive. "The column that represents the chimney is crumbling away and fast disappearing," James Abbey wrote in 1850. In fact, the monument has probably eroded somewhat over the past 150 years, but not as much as the emigrants thought it would. In 1849, Joseph

The Missouri River
meanders past La
Benite Park, Missouri,
about three miles
upstream from
Independence Landing
where emigrants began
their trek west along
the Oregon Trail.
Photo by Gary Ladd.

A visitor admires one of the displays inside the
National Frontier Trails Center in Independence,
Missouri. Photo courtesy of the Missouri Division
of Tourism.

Alcove Springs near Marysville, Kansas, was a favorite rest stop along the trail. Photo by Julie Fanselow.

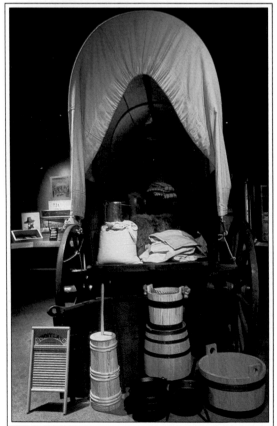

On display at the Kansas Museum of History in Topeka is a covered wagon full of supplies that visitors can unpack and repack, simulating the daily routine of families on the Oregon Trail. Photo courtesy of the Topeka Convention and Visitors Bureau.

Chimney Rock, Nebraska, is now a national historic site and was once a navigational landmark along the trail. Photo by Gary Ladd.

Ruins of old Fort Laramie, Wyoming, (not to be confused with the town of the same name) sit atop a hill. The fort was an important military post on the Oregon Trail. Photo by Joe Bensen.

The Sweetwater River slices through a ridge of granite at Devil's Gate, Wyoming, near the Oregon Trail. Photo by Gary Ladd.

Many emigrants on their way to the California gold fields began their westward trek on the Oregon Trail and took a branch trail through the City of Rocks to connect up with the California Trail. Photo by Randall Green.

Today, the City of Rocks is a popular destination for rock climbers, hikers and sightseers. Photo by Randall Green.

Multnomah Falls cascades into the Columbia River near the trail.
Photo by Julie Fanselow.

Old wagon ruts of the Oregon Trail descend a hill toward Virtue Flat near Baker City, Oregon. Photo by Gary Ladd.

Hackney wrote that Chimney Rock was "the most remarkable object that I ever saw" and added that if it was situated in "the states," it would be visited by people from all over the world. Today, of course, it is.

Long the least interpreted major landmark along the Oregon Trail, Chimney Rock now has a handsome visitor center. The facility is located about a mile off NE 92, 0.75 mile dead east of the monument. The phone number is (308) 586–2581.

In addition to a great view of the landmark, Chimney Rock Interpretive Center offers visitors exhibits and an original fifteen-minute film that describes the rock's role in the overland migration. Children especially are entranced with Chimney Rock, and—like the nineteenth-century emigrants—visitors of all ages are invited to draw a picture and record their thoughts of the monument; many get posted in a display case. The Chimney Rock visitor center is open from 9:00 A.M. to 6:00 P.M. April through October; it closes at 5:00 P.M. the rest of the year. Admission is $2.00 for adults; accompanied children get in free. There are no picnic grounds here, but you can have a picnic at the city park in nearby Bayard. Chimney Rock is lit at dusk each night and remains illuminated until 12:30 A.M. in summer and 11:30 P.M. the rest of the year.

Chimney Rock also serves as backdrop for the Oregon Trail Wagon Train, a family-run tour company offering a variety of pioneer-style adventures. The nightly chuck wagon cookout includes a twenty-minute wagon ride and ribeye steak, followed by a campfire and songfest. Travelers who opt for the three- or four-day wagon trips live much like the emigrants did. Activities on these trips include everything from prairie square dancing and muzzle loading instruction to Pony Express mail deliveries and artifact searches. Twenty-four-hour trips are available, too, for those who think that one night without a soft bed and one morning without a shower is quite enough, thank you.

The Oregon Trail Wagon Train also offers Sunday morning all-you-can-eat breakfasts, three-hour covered wagon tours to the Chimney Rock area, canoe rentals and shuttle service, and campsites. Reservations are needed for all activities. Call (308) 586–1850 or write the Oregon Trail Wagon Train at P.O. Box 502, Bayard, NE 69334. The town of Bayard, just a few miles north of Chimney Rock, has one motel and a few restaurants and service stations. Its annual homegrown celebration, Chimney Rock Pioneer Days, takes place early in September with a Western art sale, parade, kidnappings by "outlaws," entertainment, and a pig roast.

From Chimney Rock, it's on to Scotts Bluff, another famous landmark, and Scottsbluff-Gering, western Nebraska's largest cities. The towns and the monument may be reached either by continuing west on NE 92, or by driving north through Bayard and west through Minatare on US 26. Minatare is near Lake Minatare State Recreation Area, home of some of the area's best camping and fishing. Lake Minatare also boasts Nebraska's only lighthouse, built between 1934 and 1936 by the Civilian Conservation Corps. The 60-foot-high lighthouse can be ascended inside via a narrow spiral staircase.

SCOTTS BLUFF NATIONAL MONUMENT

One of the finest views on the Oregon Trail can be found atop **Scotts Bluff National Monument.** From here, visitors can see Chimney Rock and the Wildcat Hills to the east and even Wyoming's Laramie Peak, 90 air miles to the west. This fortress-like landform is equally fascinating from the ground, looming over the twin towns of Scottsbluff and Gering like a "Nebraska Gibraltar."

The Cheyenne, Sioux, and Arapaho wandered through this area as many as 10,000 years ago, following the Platte River to places where buffalo herds would stop to drink. Native peoples called the monolith "Me-a-pa-te," which meant "hill that is hard to go around." The first whites to see the bluff were probably a party of John Jacob Astor's men heading back east from the Pacific coast in 1812. Soon, the formation became a familiar sight to fur traders and mountain men who traversed the North Platte route while heading to rendezvous and, later, trading posts in the Rockies and beyond.

The story goes that Hiram Scott was leading a trapping expedition through here in 1828 when he was left to die near Laramie Fork. (Stories are inconclusive as to why he was abandoned.) The following spring, his remains were found at the base of Me-a-pa-te. Friends and fellow trappers recalled Scott's wish to someday be buried at the bluffs. How he got there is still a mystery, but the great Western landmark has been known as Scotts Bluff ever since.

Scotts Bluff offers an interesting geology lesson. Much of the monolith is being eroded away by wind and water, just as most of the surrounding Great Plains were worn down over the past 14 million years. But Scotts Bluff is topped by an isolated patch of durable material known as "cap rock," which has served to protect the underlying sandstone, volcanic ash, and siltstone from the natural forces that have wiped out other nearby badlands.

The terrain around Scotts Bluff so intimidated early wagon trains that they went well out of their way to avoid it, traveling through Robidoux Pass (named for a Missourian of French ancestry who set up several trading posts in the area) several miles to the south. Around 1850, the Mitchell Pass route through the bluff opened up and quickly gained favor. Mitchell Pass is right along present-day NE 92; in fact, it is easily visible as you approach the monument from the east as the formidable gash that appears to split the bluff in two.

The monument visitor center is open from 8:00 A.M. to 5:00 P.M. daily with extended hours in the summer. It has displays on the area's natural and

Atop Scotts Bluff National Monument.

Scotts Bluff stands sentinel-like above the trail.

human history, but the real highlight is the Oregon Trail Museum, which boasts a great collection of photos, sketches, and paintings by William Henry Jackson, who first traveled west in 1866 after a broken engagement. (The museum has many Jackson originals; the works on view are mainly reproductions, though at least one original is usually on view, too.)

A short trail leads to Jackson's campsite and to deep ruts left by emigrant wagons. Park rangers present Oregon Trail living-history programs at Scotts Bluff each summer weekend. The visitor center also includes a very good selection of Oregon Trail interpretive material including maps, posters, slides, books, and post cards.

No Scotts Bluff visit would be complete without a trip to the top. A hike to the top and back takes about two hours, which allows time for explorations on the summit. Or drive up in minutes and spend time on the overlook trails. Watch for cottontail rabbits, rattlesnakes, mule deer, and assorted other little critters. The bird kingdom is represented by swifts, cliff swallows, magpies, and meadowlarks. It's important to stay on the trails to help prevent further erosion; rock along the Summit Trail is soft and crumbly, and leaving the trail could be dangerous. The Saddle Rock hiking trail is just over 1.5 miles long, one-way. It includes some fairly steep sections and a few steps. Few emigrants

Prairie scene, Scotts Bluff National Monument.

Robidoux Trading Post replica near Scottsbluff, Nebraska.

had time to make the climb, but modern visitors should make every effort to do so. No one leaves disappointed.

The summit road is open from 8:00 A.M. to 4:30 P.M. with extended hours in the summer. Trailers and motor homes more than 25 feet long are not permitted on the summit road, but a free shuttle service is generally available June through Labor Day for people who want to leave their vehicles at the bottom. The park grounds are open from dawn to dusk all year. Admission to Scotts Bluff National Monument is $5.00 per car, good for seven days. For more information, call (308) 436–4340.

Gering history and tourism officials have built a handsome replica of the second Robidoux trading post. To get there, follow NE 71 south from its intersection with NE 92 and turn right on Carter Canyon Road. After about 6 miles, the road turns to gravel; at that point, it's 2 miles to the replica, which was built in 1993 but could pass for the 1851 model. Either backtrack from here or continue on the gravel and dirt road to Robidoux Pass. A few pioneer graves are in the area, as is a sign marking the first Robidoux trading post. From the graves, it's about 8 miles back to NE 71. You can also do the route in reverse.

Rebecca Winters was a Mormon pioneer who traveled the Oregon Trail with her family in 1852. They were on their way to Utah when cholera hit the wagon train somewhere west of Fort Kearny, and Rebecca died August 15. She was buried and the grave was marked by an extra wagon wheel on which a family friend, William Reynolds, inscribed the words: REBECCA WINTERS. AGED 50 YEARS.

As time went by, Winters' grave became one of the most famous along the emigrant trail. It's even said that when Burlington Railroad surveyors laid a new route through the area, they found the grave, still marked by the wheel, and asked their supervisors for permission to slightly alter the route so the grave would remain undisturbed. But in 1995, railroad officials—concerned that someone would eventually be hit by one of the dozens of trains traveling through the area daily—sought the Winters family's permission to relocate the grave about 900 feet east. More than 125 of Rebecca Winters descendants gathered to see their ancestor reburied. To visit the Winters grave, turn east on Beltline Highway, which intersects with NE 71 just north of the Platte River. Follow Beltline about 2.25 miles southeast, and look for the state historical marker near the railroad crossing.

Those with any doubt that they're in the heart of Oregon Trail country can simply take a glance through the Scottsbluff/Gering phone book. Included are listings for the Oregon Trail Barber Shop, the Oregon Trail Church of the Nazarene, the Oregon Trail Eye Clinic, Oregon Trail Travel, Oregon Trail Hobbies, even Oregon Trail Plumbing, Heating, and Cooling. Each July, Gering holds its Oregon Trail Days bash. The event is one of Nebraska's oldest community celebrations, and it features an old settlers' reunion plus a parade, chili cook-off, athletic competitions, and big-name entertainment.

There's still plenty to see and do for those who can't make it during mid-July. The North Platte Valley Museum at 11th and J in Gering has an 8-foot-square relief map of the various trails from Ogallala, Nebraska, to Douglas, Wyoming, as well as a fur trapper's bull boat, an 1895 sod house, and a settler's log cabin. Wildlife World, also in Gering at 950 U Street, displays more than 250 mounted animals inside a renovated Union Pacific Depot. On a hot day, Gering's Oregon Trail Park is the place to be with its cool pool and 150-foot waterslide.

Scottsbluff is home to Riverside Park and Zoo, located at 1600 South Beltline Highway West. An unusually large facility for a city of Scottsbluff's size, the zoo features lions, tigers, zebras, monkeys, mountain lions, leopards, and a river otter waterslide. Special exhibits geared especially for kids include a prairie dog town, petting zoo, and playground.

Scottsbluff/Gering is the trade center of Nebraska's panhandle, so it offers plenty of choices for restaurants, lodging, and shopping, plus a little bit of nightlife: Check out the Oregon Trail Lounge on east NE 92 in Gering for lively country music and dancing. Annual activities include summer repertory theater, the nation's second-largest antique-car race (the "Sugar Valley Rally," held early each June), the Scotts Bluff County Fair in mid-August, and a hot-air balloon festival in mid-October. For more information, contact the Scottsbluff/Gering United Chamber of Commerce at 1517 Broadway, Scottsbluff, NE 69361, call (308) 632–2133, or see the Web site at www.scottsbluff.net/chamber.

From Scottsbluff, get back on US 26 and head west. Fort Laramie, the first major Oregon Trail attraction in Wyoming, is about an hour's drive away.

Lodgings, campgrounds, and restaurants listed below are a representative sampling of what is available. Listing in these pages does not imply endorsement, nor is this a complete listing of all reputable businesses. For more complete listings, contact the visitor information bureau or chamber of commerce in each town. Room rates were accurate as of summer 2000, but are subject to change.

LODGING

FAIRBURY, NEBRASKA
Capri Motel, (402) 729–3317, Junction of US 136 and NE 15, $30–$40.

HEBRON, NEBRASKA
Rosewood Villa Motel, (402) 768–6524, 140 South US 81, $40–$55.
Wayfarer Motel, (402) 768–7226, 104 North Thirteenth Street at US 81, $30.

RED CLOUD, NEBRASKA
Green Acres Motel, (402) 746–2201, North US 281, $35.

HASTINGS, NEBRASKA
Grand Motel, (402) 463–1369, 201 East "J" Street, $40–$50.
Holiday Inn, (402) 463–6721, 2205 Osborne Drive East, $70–$80.
Rainbow Motel, (402) 463–2989, 1000 West "J" Street, $35–$40.
X-L Motel, (402) 463–3148, 1400 West "J" Street, $40–$50.

GRAND ISLAND, NEBRASKA
Best Western Riverside Inn, (308) 384–5150, 3333 Ramada Road, $70–$76.
Conoco Motel, (308) 384–2700, 2107 West Second Street, $35.
Holiday Inn–I-80, (308) 384–7770, I-80 exit 312, $55–$85.
Kirschke House Bed & Breakfast, (308) 381–6851, 1124 West Third Street, $55–$145.
USA Inns of America, (308) 381–0111, I-80 exit 312, $45–$50.

MINDEN, NEBRASKA
Pioneer Village Motel, (800) 445–4447, US 6 and 34 and NE 10, $45.

KEARNEY, NEBRASKA

Best Western Inn of Kearney, (308) 237–5185, 1010 Third Avenue, $60–$80.
Budget Host Western Inn, (308) 237–3153, 1401 Second Avenue, $42–$56.
Comfort Inn, (308) 237–5858, 903 Second Avenue, $55–$75.
Country Inn & Suites, (308) 236–7500, I–80 exit 272, $70–$90.
First Interstate Inn, (308) 237–2671, 709 Second Avenue East, $40.

LEXINGTON, NEBRASKA

Budget Host Minute Man Motel, (308) 324–5544, 801 South Plum Creek Parkway,
    $38–$48.
Lexington Super 8 Motel, (308) 324–7434, 104 East River Road, $58–$68.

COZAD, NEBRASKA

Budget Host Circle S Motel, (308) 784–2290, 440 South Meridian, $38.
Motel 6–Cozad, (308) 784–4900, 809 South Meridian, $40–$45.

GOTHENBURG, NEBRASKA

Gothenburg Super 8, (308) 537–2684, $55–$70.
Travel Inn, (308) 537–3638, I–80 exit 211, $49.

MAXWELL, NEBRASKA

Valley View Guest Ranch, (308) 582–4320, south of I–80 exit 190.

NORTH PLATTE, NEBRASKA

Best Western Chalet Lodge, (308) 532–2313, 920 North Jeffers Street, $62–$70.
Budget Inn Park Motel, (308) 532–6834, 1302 North Jeffers Street, $42.
1st Interstate Inn, (308) 532–6980, I–80 exit 177, $45.
Motel 6, (308) 534–6200, I–80 exit 177, $52.
Ramada Limited, (308) 534–3120, 3201 South Jeffers Street, $65–$100.
Travelers Inn, (308) 534–4020, 602 East Fourth Street, $32–$38.

SUTHERLAND, NEBRASKA

Park Motel, (308) 386–4384, I–80 Exit 158, $30–$32.

PAXTON, NEBRASKA

Paxton Days Inn, (308) 239–4510, 851 Paxton Road, $50–$65.

OGALLALA, NEBRASKA

Best Western Stagecoach Inn, (308) 284–3656, 201 Stagecoach Trail, $80–$90.
Econolodge, (308) 284–2056, 108 Prospector Drive, $45–$50.
Kingsley Lodge, (308) 284–2775, on Lake McConaughy, cabins for $55–$115.
Ogallala Comfort Inn, (308) 284–4028, $65–$70.

Oregon Trail Motel, (308) 284–3705, 214 East First Street, $38.

Ramada Limited, (308) 284–3623, 201 Chuckwagon Road, $65–$75.

OSHKOSH, NEBRASKA

Oshkosh Inn, (308) 772–3066, 207 West Avenue "A," $30.

Shady Rest Motel, (308) 772–4115, US 26 and Main Street, $36–$40.

BRIDGEPORT, NEBRASKA

Bell Motor Inn, (308) 262–0557, US 385, $45.

Bridgeport Inn, (308) 262–0290, 517 Main Street, $47.

BAYARD, NEBRASKA

Landmark Inn, (308) 586–1375, 246 Main Street, $42.

GERING, NEBRASKA

Circle S Lodge, (308) 436–2157, 400 "M" Street, $34.

Microtel Inn & Suites, (308) 436–1950, 1130 "M" Street, $50.

SCOTTSBLUFF, NEBRASKA

Best Western Scottsbluff Inn, (308) 635–3111, 1901 Twenty-first Avenue, $57–$72.

Capri Motel, (308) 635–2057, 2424 Avenue "I" $36–$40.

Fontenelle Inn Bed & Breakfast, (308) 632–6257, 1424 Fourth Avenue, $60–$125.

Lamplighter American Inn, (308) 632–7108, 606 East Twenty-seventh Street, $45

Sands Motel, (308) 632–6191, 814 West Twenty-seventh Street, $38.

Scottsbluff Super 8, (308) 635–1600, 2202 Delta Drive, $60.

MITCHELL, NEBRASKA

Barn Anew Bed & Breakfast, (308) 632–8647, 170549 County Road L, $75–$80.

CAMPING

FAIRBURY, NEBRASKA

Rock Creek Station State Historical Park, (402) 729–5777, 6 miles southeast of town.

ALEXANDRIA, NEBRASKA

Alexandria Lakes, (402) 749–7410.

HEBRON, NEBRASKA

Hebron Riverside Park Campgrounds, Tenth and Holdredge.

GRAND ISLAND, NEBRASKA

Mormon Island State Recreation Area, (308) 381–5649, I–80 exit 312.

MINDEN, NEBRASKA
Pioneer Village Campground, (308) 832–2750, at Pioneer Village.

GIBBON, NEBRASKA
Windmill State Recreation Area, (308) 468–5700, I–80 exit 285.

KEARNEY, NEBRASKA
Betty's I–80 RV Park, (308) 234–1072, I–80 exit 263 (Odessa).

Clyde & Vi's Campground, (308) 234–1532, I–80 exit 272.

Fort Kearny State Recreation Area, (308) 234–9513, adjacent to Fort Kearny State Historical Park.

LEXINGTON, NEBRASKA
Johnson Lake State Recreation Area, (308) 785–2685, 7 miles south on US 283.

GOTHENBURG, NEBRASKA
Lafayette Park, (308) 537–3867, I mile north of US 30 and NE 47.

Stage Stop Inn KOA, (308) 537–7387, I–80 exit 211.

MAXWELL, NEBRASKA
Fort McPherson Campground, (308) 582–4320, 2 miles south of I–80 exit 190, then 0.5 mile west and 0.5 mile south.

NORTH PLATTE, NEBRASKA
Holiday Trav-L-Park, (308) 534–2265, I–80 exit 177, 0.25 mile north, then 0.5 mile east.

Lake Maloney State Recreation Area, (308) 532–6225, 5 miles south on US 83, then I mile west. Primitive sites.

OGALLALA, NEBRASKA
Lake McConaughy State Recreation Area, (308) 284–3542, 9 miles north of Ogallala.

Lake Ogallala State Recreation Area, 9 miles north of Ogallala.

Meyer Camper Court, (308) 284–2415, south of I–80 exit 126.

Open Corral Camper Court, (308) 284–4327, I–80 exit 126.

Van's Lakeview Fishing Camp, (308) 284–4965, on the south shore of Lake McConaughy at Gate 18.

BRIDGEPORT, NEBRASKA
Bridgeport State Recreation Area, I mile north of town on US 26. Primitive sites.

Golden Acres RV Park, (308) 262–0410, 3 miles north on US 385.

BAYARD, NEBRASKA
Chimney Rock Pioneer Crossing RV Park, (308) 586–1988.

Oregon Trail Wagon Train, (308) 586–1850.

GERING, NEBRASKA

Wildcat Hills State Recreation Area, (308) 436–2383, 10 miles south on NE 71. Primitive sites.

SCOTTSBLUFF, NEBRASKA

Lake Minatare State Recreation Area, (308) 783–2911, 5 miles east, then 4 miles north of Scottsbluff.

Riverside Park Campground, (308) 632–4136, southwest edge of city on Beltline Highway.

Scottsbluff/Chimney Rock KOA, (308) 635–3760, 3.5 miles west on US 26.

RESTAURANTS

FAIRBURY, NEBRASKA

TrailBlazers, (402) 729–5205, 500 Fourth Street. American cuisine. Steaks, pasta, salad bar. Closed Monday.

HEBRON, NEBRASKA

Ortman's Highway Cafe, (402) 768–6174, US 81. Open twenty-four hours.

MINDEN, NEBRASKA

Pioneer Village Restaurant, (308) 832–1550, in Pioneer Village Motel. Casual dining, smorgasbord.

KEARNEY, NEBRASKA

Amigo's, (308) 234–6991, 4207 Second Avenue. Mexican food.

Captain's Table, (308) 237–5971, I–80 exit 272 in the Holiday Inn. Seafood specialties.

The Lodge, (308) 234–2729, 1401 Second Avenue in Budget Host Western Inn. Steak and seafood.

Tex's Cafe, (308) 234–3949, 23 East Twenty-first Street.

Valentino's Ristorante, (308) 234–5545, 815 South Second Avenue. Italian food, pizza.

LEXINGTON, NEBRASKA

Kirk's Nebraskaland Restaurant, (308) 324–6641, I–80 exit 237.

GOTHENBURG, NEBRASKA

Farmer's Wife, (308) 537–7763, 516 South Lake Avenue.

Homestead Restaurant, (308) 537–7422, I–80 and NE 47. Salad bar, cinnamon rolls.

NORTH PLATTE, NEBRASKA

The Airport Inn, (308) 534–4340, at Lee Bird Field. Breakfast, lunch, and dinner at the airport.

Brick Wall, (308) 532–7545, 507 North Dewey. Dining amid antiques displays.

Hunan Chinese Restaurant, (308) 532–8145, I–80 and US 83. Mandarin, Hunan, Szechuan, and Cantonese cuisine.

Village Inn, (308) 534–7944, 111 Halligan Drive. Wide menu, good breakfasts.

Whiskey Creek Steakhouse, (308) 379–7896, 1021 South Thirteenth Street. Steaks and more in casual setting.

PAXTON, NEBRASKA

Ole's Big Game Steakhouse, (308) 239–4500, I–80 exit 145. Steaks, seafood, chicken, buffalo burgers.

OGALLALA, NEBRASKA

Front Street Steakhouse, (308) 284–6000, downtown on US 30. Steaks, salad bar, kids' menu.

Hill Top Inn, (308) 284–4534, at Kingsley Dam 9 miles north of Ogallala. Scenic view of Lake McConaughy, daily specials.

Hokes Cafe, (308) 284–4654, 302 East First. Home cooking featuring chicken-fried steak, fried chicken, steaks.

The Paddock Restaurant, (308) 284–3656, in the Best Western Stagecoach Inn. Sunday champagne brunch, weekly ethnic specialties.

Peking Chinese Restaurant, (308) 284–8300, 112 East "A" St. Szechuan, Peking, and Cantonese cuisine.

Pioneer Trails Restaurant, (308) 284–2388, in Pioneer Trails Mall (55 East River Road). Informal dining featuring steaks and prime rib.

Prokop's Blazin BBQ, (308) 284–3411, 3 North Spruce Street.

BRIDGEPORT, NEBRASKA

Aunt Bee's, (308) 262–0234, 1024 Main Street.

Bell Restaurant, (308) 262–0557, north on US 385 in Bell Motor Inn. Informal dining featuring steaks.

GERING, NEBRASKA

Country Kitchen, (308) 635–3800, 3485 North Tenth. Open twenty-four hours.

Gering Coffee Shop & Luncheonette, (308) 436–5632, 1437 Tenth Street. Homemade breakfast and lunch.

Pasta Villa, (308) 436–5900, 1455 Tenth Street. Creative Italian food.

SCOTTSBLUFF, NEBRASKA

Applebees, (308) 635–7750, 2621 Fifth Avenue.

Bush's Gaslight Restaurant & Lounge, (308) 632–7315, 3315 North Tenth (Terrytown). Casual dining. Steaks, seafood, chicken.

Grampy's Pancake House & Restaurant, (308) 632–6906, 1802 East Twentieth Place. Large menu, breakfast served anytime.

Rose Garden, (308) 635–3111, 1901 Twenty-first Avenue. Varied menu in the Best Western Scottsbluff Inn.

Rosita's Restaurant, (308) 632–2429, 1205 East Overland. Mexican food.

Wonderful House, (308) 632–1668, US 26 and Avenue "I." Chinese food

CHAPTER FOUR

HALFWAY TO HEAVEN: WYOMING

"We have crossed the great divide . . . the valley or gateway is 10 to 20 miles wide . . . the ascent so gradual that we were scarcely aware that the culmination was reached and passed."
—Emigrant David R. Leeper at South Pass, 1849

FORT LARAMIE

*I*t's tempting to think of the Oregon Trail as a lonely route, with a few huddled wagons traveling together across the vast, empty plains. But during the peak years of travel, the trail was in fact quite crowded, with one wagon company after another rolling westward. Nowhere was the congestion more evident than near the six major forts along the route.

The forts were crucibles of humanity, full of emigrants from the Midwest mingling with fur traders, military men, trappers, and Indians. Here the pioneers gathered to rest, repair their wagons, replenish supplies, and swap advice and stories with their fellow travelers. Until Fort Kearny was built in 1848, **Fort Laramie** was the first such outpost along the Oregon Trail.

Fort Laramie—then known as Fort William—was built by fur trader William Sublette in 1834. He sent word to the nearby Sioux and Cheyenne chiefs that he wished to do business with them, but it wasn't until the American Fur Company bought the post two years later that it became a major trading post—at least until 1841, when a competing post, Fort Platte, was built just a mile away. The American Fur Company responded by replacing the rotting, wooden Fort William with a larger adobe structure that they then named Fort John. Later, the fort became known as Fort Laramie after an obscure French-Canadian trapper, Jacques LaRamee, who may have been the first white man to see the area. Despite his low profile, LaRamee ended up giving his name to many of the most prominent features in eastern Wyoming, including Laramie Peak, the Laramie River, and the city of Laramie.

Fort Laramie was always a popular stop along the trail. But as emigrant traffic increased, relations between the whites and the Indians deteriorated rapidly, leading to calls for protection. The Army bought the post in 1849 and converted it to a military outpost. After Oregon Trail traffic trickled off in the

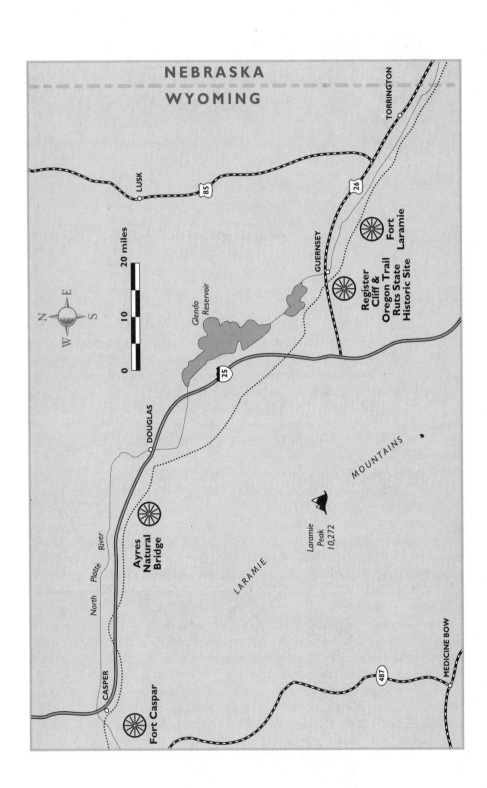

The officers' quarters are some of the remains of old Fort Laramie, Wyoming.

1860s, the site became a major staging area for campaigns against the Indians and later, a buffer between whites and the few Indians who refused to submit to life on the reservations. It also served as a stopping place for prospectors on their way to the goldfields of South Dakota's Black Hills. Finally, with the end of Indian hostilities, the Army abandoned the post in 1890.

Fort Laramie is now a National Historic Site run by the National Park Service. It is located 3 miles southwest of the town of Fort Laramie (250 GOOD PEOPLE AND 6 SORE HEADS, the sign says) off US 26. Begin with a stop in the visitor center, located in the old Commissary Storehouse. Here, travelers can see exhibits on the fort's history and view an 18-minute orientation video. The center's bookstore has an excellent selection of books, maps, posters, and emigrant diaries from the trails era.

During the summer, two-hour ranger-led tours take place twice daily; call ahead for times. Visitors can also tour Fort Laramie with the help of a self-guiding brochure or with an audio tour that can be rented for $3.00. Children ages six through twelve are invited to take part in Fort Laramie's "Junior Ranger" program by asking for an activity packet at the visitor center before touring the fort.

Several sites are of special interest. Old Bedlam, built in 1849, housed bachelor officers and is the oldest military building in Wyoming. The structure was almost ninety years old and near collapse when the federal government re-acquired it and started a stabilization and reconstruction program. The hospital ruins were built on the site of an old Army cemetery used until 1868. The site of the original Fort John may be seen on the banks of the Laramie River behind the Captain's Quarters. It's worth noting that all the buildings at Fort Laramie are restored originals. None are reproductions.

Travelers can take a break after their tour with a root beer or sarsaparilla at the Soldier's Bar, located at the Post Trader's Store, or with a picnic on the grounds near the parking lot. There is no food, lodging, or camping at Fort Laramie, but all are available in nearby towns. Fort Laramie National Historic Site is open from dawn until dusk every day except Thanksgiving, Christmas, and New Year's Day. The visitor center is open from 8:00 A.M. to 4:30 P.M., with extended hours from early June through Labor Day. Admission is $2.00 for people seventeen and older; anyone sixteen and under is admitted free. Special annual events include an Old-Fashioned Fourth of July and moonlight tours. For more information, call (307) 837–2221.

A few miles east of Fort Laramie on US 26, the **Western History Center** is a small museum that focuses on the natural and human history of eastern Wyoming. There are exhibits on several local archaeological dig sites that have yielded everything from mammoth skeletons to projectile points. Other displays feature Native American artifacts and cowboy gear. It's open seven days a week from 8:00 A.M. to 5:00 P.M. Admission is $1.50; children twelve and under get in free. Call ahead at (307) 837–3052 to learn of special events, which include talks and field trips to dig sites.

Continue driving west on US 26. It's only 13 miles from Fort Laramie to Guernsey, home to Register Cliff and some of the best ruts on the Oregon Trail.

REGISTER CLIFF AND THE GUERNSEY RUTS

Just east of Guernsey, a Wyoming state rest stop offers a panoramic viewing area where visitors can look through a series of posts drilled with peepholes at landmarks including Mexican Hill, which emigrants traversed to regain the Platte River route after visiting Fort Laramie; Sand Point, a popular pioneer campsite; and Laramie Peak, which was the travelers' first evidence that they'd successfully crossed the high plains and made it to the mountains.

Once you reach Guernsey, follow the signs through town to **Register Cliff.** This popular campsite was about a day's travel west of Fort Laramie, and the sandstone cliff is covered with the names of people who passed through the area en route to Oregon or other points west. Unfortunately, many of the old signatures have either eroded away or been covered by those of more recent vintage. A good number of names from the nineteenth centu-

Signatures at Register Cliff, Guernsey, Wyoming (above and below).

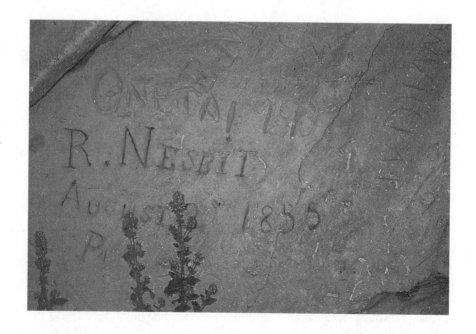

Register Cliff is covered with names of people who traveled through Wyoming along the Oregon Trail.

ry are still visible, however, especially behind the fenced area that begins about 150 feet from the parking lot. Trail remnants can also be seen at Register Cliff, as can the graves of several unknown pioneers.

Alva Unthank of Wayne County, Indiana, traveled the trail in 1850 and was one of the many emigrants who signed his name on the cliff. He didn't last much longer; his grave, dated July 2, 1850, is located near present-day Glenrock. Historians believe he died of cholera or dysentery. In later years, Unthank's nephew, O. N. Unthank, and great-grandson, O. B. Unthank, added their names. Their autographs can be seen across from the last large boulder at the east end of the walking path, about 3 feet off the ground.

From Register Cliff, return to the road and head back toward Guernsey, but turn left into the **Oregon Trail Ruts State Historic Site.** Park and climb the 400-foot trail to the ruts. Many trail remnants along the Oregon Trail are faint or visible only to those with active imaginations. Not so here. Rugged terrain forced the wagons to travel across a narrow ridge of sandstone, wearing ruts that are up to 5 feet deep in some places! These are probably the most famous ruts along the entire Oregon Trail. When leaving the site, note the grave of Lucinda Rollins, who died here in June 1849. A white monument marks the grave, just across the road from the ruts parking area and slightly to the west.

The passage of wagons over the soft sandstone near Guernsey, Wyoming, left ruts nearly 5 feet deep. Photo courtesy of the Wyoming Division of Tourism.

Just outside town, Guernsey State Park is a popular recreation area with hiking, picnicking, water sports, and a museum. Bluffs surrounding the reservoir block the wind, creating scenic campgrounds and prime conditions for boating and swimming—but not for sailboating or sailboarding. For that, try Glendo State Park about 35 miles northwest via I–15. Some Wyoming state parks charge entrance fees, which in 2000 were $5.00 for out-of-state vehicles and $2.00 for vehicles with Wyoming plates.

AYRES NATURAL BRIDGE

One of the prettiest spots near the emigrant route, **Ayres Natural Bridge** actually sits about a mile south of the Oregon Trail. But it's no wonder travelers went out of their way to see it. The site was donated to Converse County, Wyoming, by Andrew Clement Ayres in May 1920, and the county has preserved it as a pleasant park. (Some maps and guidebooks refer to the site as Ayers Natural Bridge; Wyoming Highway department signs on I–25, shying from the spelling dispute, simply call it "Natural Bridge.")

LaPrele Creek is responsible for nature's handiwork at Ayres Natural Bridge. Over time, the creek wore its way through a sandstone monolith, carving a passageway and creating one of Wyoming's earliest tourist attractions. Ayres remains the only natural bridge with a stream running under it in the

Visitors are dwarfed by the Ayres Natural Bridge west of Douglas, Wyoming.

United States, and red rock formations and leafy shade trees add to the park's overall beauty.

Activities at the park include picnicking, fishing, and hiking. Campers are welcome, too, though they must seek written permission from the caretaker, and there's a three-day limit. The park is open for day use from 8:00 A.M. to 8:00 P.M. April 1 through October 31, and admission is free. To get there, take the Natural Bridge exit off of I-25 11 miles west of Douglas, then follow the signs 5 miles south to the park. The access road's last stretch may be too winding and steep for vehicles towing trailers. Call (307) 358–3532 for more information.

Douglas, Wyoming, was founded in 1886 as a supply post for cattlemen and a rail distribution point. Today, it serves as home to 5,100 people and as world capital of the jackalope, a uniquely Western mix of jackrabbit, prong-horn antelope, and frontier fable. Specimens are available on many postcard racks and bars in Wyoming, and skeptics can see a 10-foot replica at Third and Center Streets in Douglas. The Converse County seat is also home to the Wyoming State Fair, held every third week in August since 1905, and to the Wyoming Pioneer Museum, located at the state fairgrounds.

In addition to these in-town activities, Douglas is at the hub of a wide range of outdoor attractions. Medicine Bow National Forest begins south of town and sprawls out across 1,665,755 acres in southeast Wyoming. The Douglas District includes Laramie Peak and the rest of the rugged Laramie Mountains. To the north, Thunder Basin National Grassland was turned into a dust bowl by homesteaders who used farming techniques more suited to wet climates. Today, the reclaimed 1.8 million-acre grassland is used primarily for grazing and energy resources development.

Even farther north is Devil's Tower National Monument, which is definitely worth a visit for those with an extra day. The stump-shaped rock monolith rises 867 feet from the ground and was proclaimed the first U.S. national monument in 1906 by President Theodore Roosevelt. Campers and climbers enjoy the grounds, and the nearby Belle Fourche River offers good fishing, swimming, and tubing opportunities. A prairie dog town rounds out the attractions at this fascinating site. Devil's Tower is 28 miles northwest of Sundance via WY 24, about 190 miles from Douglas.

After leaving Ayres Natural Bridge and returning to I-25, it's less than an hour's drive to Casper, one of Wyoming's largest cities and a major center of Oregon Trail interpretation.

CASPER

For more than 400 miles—past Chimney Rock, Scotts Bluff, and Fort Laramie—the emigrants had traveled within sight of the Platte River. Now, they were about to leave it behind for the final dusty approach to South Pass,

Indian Sites in Northeast Wyoming

The opening of the Oregon Trail had a profound effect on Euro-American history, but it had an equally large impact on the lives of the North American Indians. For centuries, tribes had lived basically simple lives close to the land of the plains and mountains of the West. When the whites' emigration began, relations between the cultures were mostly cordial. But increased traffic on the paths the Indians pioneered eventually led to misunderstandings, conflict, and violence.

Northeast Wyoming has a high concentration of sites that trace the clash between the Indians and whites. One of the earliest events—and one tied directly to the migration—was the Grattan Massacre, which took place near present-day Lingle. In August 1854, a Mormon wagon train traveling along the route to Oregon camped 10 miles below Fort Laramie. After a stray cow belonging to the Mormons was killed by an Indian, a group of twenty-nine soldiers led by Second Lieutenant John Grattan was dispatched to the Indian camp to arrest the guilty man. The ensuing fight resulted in the deaths of Grattan and half his men, as well as an Indian chief. But even more crucially, the fight marked the start of years of intermittent hostilities along the trail. A monument to the incident stands 3 miles west of Lingle on WY 157. The U.S. soldiers who died were first buried on the battlefield then later removed to Fort McPherson National Cemetery back in Nebraska.

Fort Fetterman, 11 miles northwest of Douglas on WY 93, was located near the intersection of the Oregon and Bozeman Trails. The Indians hated the "Bloody" Bozeman Trail, for it cut across their hunting grounds to the goldfields of Montana. The fort was established in 1867 and rapidly became a major supply post during U.S. military campaigns against the Indians. It is now a state-run historic site where the restored officers' quarters and ordnance building may be seen. A museum displays weapons, clothing, and artifacts from the period.

Some of the most famous events of the 1860s occurred near Fort Phil Kearny, which is about 145 miles north of Casper (take exit 44 off of I–90 north of Buffalo, Wyoming). Battles involving such famous Indians as Red Cloud and Crazy Horse were fought nearby, and exhibits at the fort museum help explain the events, which included the Fetterman Massacre of William Fetterman and his eighty-two men in 1866 and the Wagon Box Fight, in which soldiers shielded by wagon boxes and backed by new Springfield breech-loaded rifles survived a Sioux assault in 1867. The actual sites of these battles are within 3 miles of Fort Phil Kearny.

Those interested in the West's military history might want to keep driving north on I–90 into Montana and the site of the Battle of the Little Bighorn. Here, Lieutenant Colonel George A. Custer and the 210 men of the Seventh Cavalry Regiment made their last stand against the Sioux and Northern Cheyenne in 1876. The main entrance is via exit 510 on I–90, about 70 miles north of Sheridan, Wyoming. Tours are available. For more information on these sites, call Fort Fetterman at (307) 358–2864, Fort Kearny at (307) 684–7629, or the Little Bighorn Battlefield National Monument at (406) 638–2621. ◢

where they'd enter the Oregon Territory.

Many emigrants crossed the North Platte at the site of present-day Casper and took the northern route through Emigrant Gap and past Poison Spring, where pristine ruts still exist. Others waited a few more miles and made the ford upstream at Bessemer Bend. In either case, the North Platte crossing marked the beginning of some miserable travel, with good water and good grazing in very short supply. This was a truly pivotal point along the trail, one that is thoroughly interpreted at the new National Historic Trails Interpretive Center and Fort Caspar, as well as through the outdoor activities offered by a local company, Historic Trails West.

The **National Historic Trails Interpretive Center** is set to open in late 2001 or early 2002. Situated on a bluff overlooking Casper (take exit 189 off of I–25), the center has the ideal vantage point to survey an area where many major historic routes—the Oregon, California, Mormon, Pony Express, Bozeman, and Bridger Trails—converged. Inside, visitors move through exhibits that tell of the Native Americans, who have lived in the Casper area for 10,000 years, and of the myriad forces that compelled the United States to look westward. The Oregon Trail section includes a simulated crossing of the North Platte River, while the Mormon Trail exhibit explains how the Latter-day Saints made advances in trail travel (with a primitive odometer, for example) while enduring tremendous hardship. The California Trail area examines how the trek changed with the increased traffic of the gold rush years, while the Pony Express section gives visitors a chance to read letters carried by the lightning mail service.

The center includes a gift shop and Wyoming travel information desk. Hours and admission prices were not set at presstime, but the center will likely be open daily April through October, with somewhat reduced hours the rest of the year. For updated information, call (307) 261–7600.

From the center, proceed to the modern-day reconstruction of **Fort Caspar.** Until 1847, pioneers crossing the North Platte had to either improvise a ferry or hope for low water at the usual ford, 4 miles northeast of Fort Caspar. In 1847, Mormon leader Brigham Young established a ferry across the river and charged $4.00 to $5.00 per wagon. When he founded the ferry, Young was on his way to establish the Mormon community near the Great Salt Lake. He left nine men behind to operate the ferry, which helped raise money for the Mormon's new stronghold. The ferry stayed in operation through 1851.

Sometimes emigrants balked at either the fee or the time spent waiting to use the Mormon Ferry and tried to make their own crossing, even in high water. Emigrant James A. Pritchard wrote of one such instance in 1849, when his wagon train arrived on a Sunday and found 175 wagons already waiting to use the ferry: "We however joined another company or two and constructed a raft to cross our wagons on. After several efforts we succeeded in crossing two

Fort Caspar, Wyoming.

wagons, but we found the current so strong and the raft so heavy and unwieldy that we abandoned the project and awaited our turn which came in on Wednesday morning."

In 1852, John Richard—or Reshaw, as he was better known—built a wooden toll bridge over the North Platte at what is now Evansville, Wyoming, 3 miles from Casper. Reshaw's bridge served the emigration off and on until 1865, and some historians say it put the Mormon Ferry out of business. In later years, however, Reshaw had competition from a 1,000-foot log bridge built in 1858 at the site of the Mormon Ferry by Louis Guinard.

Guinard charged a toll of $1.00 to $6.00, depending on river conditions. His bridge was used until 1867, when it was burned by Indians after the abandonment of Fort Caspar. Guinard also established a trading post at the site, and it became known as Platte Bridge Station. Later, the site was renamed in honor of Lieutenant Caspar Collins, who was killed while protecting a supply train from Indian attack in 1865. (An early recorder's spelling error accounts for the discrepancy between the name of the fort and the city that followed.)

As a military post, Fort Caspar played a key role in protecting the emigration as it moved up the Sweetwater Valley. It also helped preserve communications during the era by protecting a Pacific Telegraph office built at the south end of Guinard's bridge.

Start a visit to Fort Caspar with a stop in its museum, which explains the history of the area and other Wyoming lore. Visitors can also pick up brochures for a self-guided tour of the reconstructed fort, which includes a sutler's store (where soldiers could purchase provisions), blacksmith's shop, officers' quarters, and several other buildings. Another self-guided trail combines nature and history, making its way past the piled earth and rock on which Guinard's bridge rested, the Oregon Trail itself, and "The Sand Bar," an infamous district well known in Casper's early days for its gambling and prostitution. The area was cleaned up in the 1940s, but a small white house—once a bordello—was saved as evidence of the former red-light district.

Fort Caspar is the site of several special events, including a mountain man rendezvous, a Civil War encampment every odd-numbered year, a lecture series, and Christmas candlelight tours. The complex also includes Centennial Park, where kids can have a ball on the playground. It's all located off Wyoming Boulevard in the city's west end.

The fort is open from 8:30 A.M. to 6:30 P.M. Monday through Saturday and noon to 6:30 P.M. on Sunday during the summer only. The museum is open year-round, from 8:00 A.M. to 7:00 P.M. Monday through Saturday and noon to 7:00 P.M. on Sunday in the summertime, and from 8:00 A.M. to 5:00 P.M. weekdays and 1:00 to 4:00 P.M. on Sunday the rest of the year. Admission is free. For more information, call (307) 235–8462.

Fort Caspar is the jumping-off spot for many trips led by **Historic Trails West,** one of very few companies along the Oregon Trail dedicated to giving modern travelers a firsthand taste of what pioneer travel was really like. Historic Trails West is operated by Morris Carter, who—with his four daughters—traveled the entire length of the Oregon Trail during its sesquicentennial year in 1993. The family also traveled the California Trail in 1999 in an official celebration of that route's 150th anniversary. Today's trips are led by such people as Carter himself or Bruce Berst, a Casper high school history teacher who is also an avid student of the historic trails and Civil War eras.

On most trips, people have the option of riding in an authentic reproduction covered wagon, going on horseback, or walking alongside the wagons as the pioneers did. People with little time to spare can opt for a four-hour jaunt including a tour of Fort Caspar and a meal at a riverside teepee village at a cost (in 2000) of $45 per person, $35 for children ten years or under, or $55 for horseback riders. Even these short excursions include time along the actual Oregon Trail, a white-knuckle ride down Roughlock Hill (documented in emigrant journals), and plenty of historical interpretation.

Plenty of longer adventures also are available. The overnight trip includes accommodations in the teepee village and a chance to help prepare meals and care for the horses. A two-day trip features a re-creation of the Red Butte Battle, with participants joining either the Indian band or cavalry. Three- and

Bruce Berst and Morris Carter Sr. hitch the team for a Historic Trails West trip.

five-day trips begin on the Sweetwater River and include stops at all the major Wyoming trail sites including Independence Rock, Devil's Gate, Split Rock, and the crossing of the Continental Divide at South Pass. You'll probably see plenty of antelope. Nights are spent in teepees, and prices include all meals. In 2000, the three-day wagon train cost $550 per adult or $395 for children ten and under, The five-day excursions cost $895 for adults and $695 per child. (Horseback riders are charged $650 for three days, $995 for five days.)

Trips are available May through October. (The longer treks take place mostly in the summer months.) Bus tours, scout troops, and other groups are welcome. For more information, call (307) 266–4868 or (800) 327–4052 outside Wyoming, or see the Web site at www.historictrailswest.com.

From Fort Caspar, take a right on Wyoming Boulevard and proceed south to CY Avenue, which turns into WY 220, the main route to Bessemer Bend and Independence Rock.

BESSEMER BEND AND THE RED BUTTES

Not everyone had the time or money to use the ferry or toll bridge at present-day Casper. Many parties continued along the Platte to **Bessemer Bend,** the last place they could cross and, after 1848, the site of an early U.S. Mail station. Today, Bessemer Bend is marked with a Bureau of Land Management (BLM)

Bruce Berst drives the team for Historic Trails West out of Casper, Wyoming.

Urban Wyoming

With not quite a half-million residents—fewer than five per square mile—Wyoming ranks dead last among the fifty states in population. But even Wyoming has its pockets of city life.

Although emigrant trail commerce and cattle ranching were Casper's earliest industries, the town really took off in 1889 when the first oil well was tapped. From that modest beginning, Casper grew into the hub of the Rocky Mountain oil-and-gas industry. The boom created prosperity, and scandal too: In 1927, U.S. Secretary of the Interior Albert Fall went to prison for secretly leasing the nearby Teapot Dome oil field to the Mammoth Crude Company without seeking bids from other companies.

In Wyoming's early days, Casper and Cheyenne vied to be the state's capital. The rivalry continues today as the two towns see-saw in their bids to be Wyoming's largest city. (Each town's population fluctuates between 45,000 and 50,000.)

Casper seems to have the edge culturally. The Nicolaysen Art Museum at 400 East Collins Street is housed in a refurbished warehouse and includes permanent and traveling exhibitions of major regional and national artists. The Discovery Center, a children's museum, is on the same site. The Casper Municipal Band plays each Thursday evening in Washington Park on McKinley Street, and several other groups showcase local dramatic, musical, and artistic talent. Rockhounds may want to visit the Tate Geological Museum, open weekdays on the Casper College campus. The Werner Wildlife Museum at 405 East Fifteenth Street is another popular attraction.

Casper's biggest annual event is the Central Wyoming Fair and Rodeo, held the last week of July. Recreational opportunities include the Casper Recreation Center at 1801 East Fourth Street and the Casper Family YMCA at 315 East Fifteenth. Both offer daily passes. Visitors can also take advantage of four city pools or the Casper Community Golf Course, at 2120 Allendale Boulevard. Casper Mountain and Edness K. Wilkins State Park, both south of town, cater to outdoor fun and adventure. For shopping, try downtown or the Eastridge Mall, located at East Second and Wyoming Boulevard off of I–25.

Cheyenne's claim to fame is Frontier Days. The main attraction is the world's oldest and largest rodeo, also known as the "Daddy of 'em All," but free pancake breakfasts (with the batter mixed by cement truck) and the overall party-hearty atmosphere keep everyone happy, no matter what their interests. Be forewarned that Cheyenne motel prices double (and even then, rooms can be hard to find) during Frontier Days, so plan accordingly. If you miss the rodeo, check out the Cheyenne Frontier Days Old West Museum at Eighth and Carey Streets, open all year.

Tours are available at the Wyoming state capitol, open to visitors from 8:00 A.M. to 4:30 P.M. weekdays. The Cheyenne Club at 1617 Capitol Avenue features live country music entertainment, and the Old Atlas Theater at 211 West Sixteenth Street offers vaudeville-style melodramas each summer. Frontier Mall, with seventy-five stores on Dell Range Boulevard, is Cheyenne's largest shopping center, and the Sierra Trading Post outlet store east of town has great deals on outdoor clothing and gear.

Although only about half the size of Cheyenne, Laramie is home to the state's only four-year institution of higher learning, and thus it's Wyoming's intellectual and cultural capital. The University of Wyoming holds a Western music festival each June, along with other arts activities year-round. But this is still Wyoming, and outdoor activities reign supreme. Popular spots include Curt Gowdy State Park (named for the sportscaster, a native Wyomingite) and Vedauwoo, both southeast of Laramie via I–80. Vedauwoo is one of North America's finest rock climbing sites. In the summer, consider a scenic drive over the 10,847-foot Snowy Range Pass Highway between Rawlins and Laramie. The Wyoming Territorial Prison and Old West Park, supposedly the only place where outlaw Butch Cassidy was ever jailed, is full of interesting frontier-era exhibits and living-history characters.

For more information, contact the chambers of commerce in Casper (800–852–1889, www.casperwyoming.org), Cheyenne (800–426–5009, www.cheyenne.org), or Laramie (800–445–5303, www.laramie-tourism.org. ▲

interpretive shelter and by nature itself—the Red Buttes that served as a landmark to Indians, fur traders, and emigrants may still be seen south of the river.

Bessemer Bend was a popular campsite, used as early as 1812 by Robert Stuart and the Astorians, who were returning to St. Louis from the Pacific. From here, the route west to the Sweetwater River involved three days of rough, dry country and poisonous alkali water. John Fremont, passing through in 1842, commented on "innumerable quantities of grasshoppers," which had destroyed the grass. Today, Bessemer Bend is a popular put-in for floating downriver to Casper, a 7-mile trip. Picnic tables are available.

To get to Bessemer Bend, take WY 220 6 miles south of Casper. Turn right on the Bessemer Bend Road and continue 3 miles.

From here, Oregon Trail explorers have two choices. Stay on WY 220, or follow the pioneers' route more closely by taking a 40-mile trip along back roads that meet WY 220 just north of Independence Rock. The dirt road alternative includes such trail landmarks as Emigrant Gap, Avenue of Rock, Willow Spring, and Poison Spring, but the way is not well marked. For exact directions and road conditions, inquire locally at Fort Caspar (307–235–8462), the Casper Chamber of Commerce (307–234–5311), or the Casper BLM district office (307–261–7600).

Travelers who stay on WY 220 will glimpse several sweeping vistas of Alcova and Pathfinder Reservoirs. Boating, fishing, swimming, and camping are all enjoyed along the shores of these great lakes. The BLM maintains a scenic byway through the Seminoe Mountains, the jagged peaks that rise up southwest of Casper. The northern access is at Alcova, and the scenic byway is described in detail in the *Scenic Driving Back Country Byways* guide from The Globe Pequot Press.

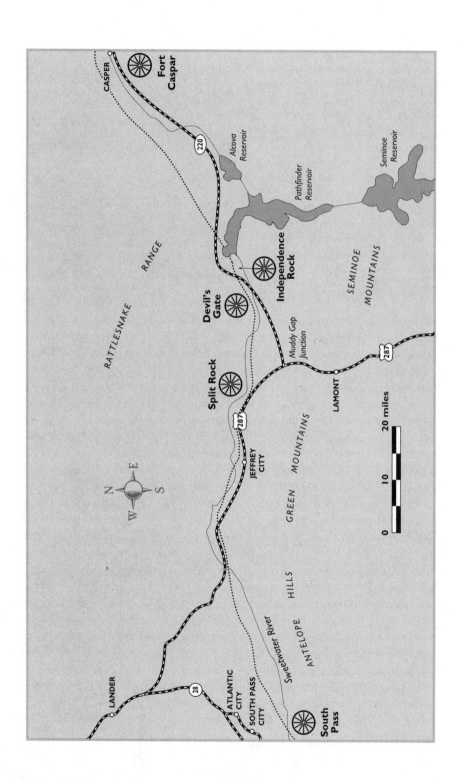

WYOMING RANCH STAYS

To many people, a Wyoming vacation means a ranch stay. If you have some extra time (many ranches require a minimum stay of a few nights to a week), you might want to treat yourself to this experience, too.

Working ranches near the Oregon Trail include Cheyenne River Ranch, 50 miles north of Dubois (307–358–2380); Grant Ranch, near the US 26/I–25 junction (307–322–2923); Deer Forks Ranch, 24 miles south of Douglas (307–358–2033); and Deer Creek Ranch, 33 miles southeast of Shoshoni (307–457–2451). For more information on these ranches and others, see the Web site at www.wyomingbnb-

ranchrec.com. Or you can get a copy of their print directory by calling WHOA-B&Bs, Inns, and Ranches of Wyoming at (307) 237–3526, or by writing to P.O. Box 40048, Casper, WY 82604.

City Slickers of Wyoming near Evanston is more of a guest ranch than a working cattle facility, though visitors still can get out on a cattle drive if they like. The company also specializes in horseback trips to historic trails sites, along with fishing, roping, country dance lessons, dutch-oven dinners, and more. Call (307) 789–3378 or see the Web site at www.cityslickersofwyoming.com for more information. ▲

Check the gas gauge at Alcova before continuing west on WY 220. It's 43 miles to the next filling station at Muddy Gap Junction.

INDEPENDENCE ROCK

One of the most famous sights along the Oregon Trail, **Independence Rock** is located 50 miles southwest of Casper, rising like a turtle or whale above the desert. During pioneer days, Independence Rock was used as a landmark, lookout, campsite, trail register, and bulletin board. Today, it serves as backdrop for a conveniently located Wyoming state rest area and interpretive site along WY 220.

To fully appreciate Independence Rock, visitors should climb to the top. It only takes about twenty minutes up and back, although you might want to pack a snack and spend time enjoying the expansive views and emigrant signatures at the top. In 1860, Sir Richard Burton calculated that 40,000 to 50,000 autographs had been placed on the rock in previous decades. Most either chiseled their names or wrote them with a mixture of pine tar, gunpowder, and hog fat. Although most signatures have worn away, some are still visible, both at the top and within sheltered areas elsewhere on the rock, particularly on the south side. While on top, look for the Sweetwater River—which would guide the emigrants to South Pass—and for Devil's Gate, both to the west.

Howard Stansbury, who passed by on July 31, 1849, noted the rock "was covered with the names of passing emigrants, some of whom seemed determined, judging from the size of their inscriptions, that they would go down in posterity in all their fair proportions." Some trail entrepreneurs made money chiseling or writing autographs for their illiterate companions, charging up to $5.00 depending on the signature's location.

John Fremont, seeing all the names in 1842, thought the rock was actually a large gravestone. According to the government Writers Project of 1939, Fremont decided to honor the dead by placing a large cross on the rock. Later, some emigrants hostile to Roman Catholicism dynamited the section where Fremont had left the cross, which they looked upon as a symbol of the Catholic "sect."

Most stories on the naming of Independence Rock credit the fur trappers who traveled through the area before the Oregon-bound emigrants. One tale holds that a group of traders celebrated the Fourth of July at the rock in 1824. Another version maintains that William Sublette, leader of the first wagon train to the Continental Divide, spent July 4, 1830, at the rock and so named it in honor of the nation's birthday. However it was named, travelers by the time of the Oregon emigration looked forward to Independence Rock as a

Many emigrants celebrated at Independence Rock because they were almost halfway to Oregon.

Expansive views and emigrant signatures are rewards for scrambling to the top of Independence Rock. Photo courtesy of the Wyoming Division of Tourism.

place to celebrate, whether or not they arrived on the Fourth of July. By now, they'd moved 814 miles from Independence, Missouri. They were almost halfway to Oregon.

Many emigrants mentioned Independence Rock in their journals. Robert Canfield visited on the Fourth of July, 1847, and noted that his party fired a cannon from atop the rock and planted a flag there. E. W. Conyers, describing a Fourth of July celebration in 1852, had this to say: "No person left the table hungry. After our feast, patriotic songs were indulged in, winding up with three cheers for Uncle Sam and three for Old Glory . . . a Fourth of July on the plains never to be forgotten."

A few miles past Independence Rock, the travelers marveled at **Devil's Gate,** a nasty-looking chasm carved through solid granite by the Sweetwater River. Wagons couldn't go through the gap and passed to the south, but some emigrants hiked over to view it up close. According to Arapaho-Shoshone legend, a powerful evil spirit in the form of a big beast with tusks once wandered the Sweetwater Valley, preventing Indians from hunting or camping. A prophet told the tribes that the Great Spirit wanted them to destroy the beast, so they launched an attack from nearby mountain passes and ravines, shooting countless arrows into the animal. The enraged creature, with a mighty upward thrust of its tusks, ripped a gap in the mountains, disappeared through the opening, and was never seen again.

Devil's Gate, once situated on the privately owned Sun Ranch, was long inaccessible to the public. But the Church of Jesus Christ of Latter-day Saints acquired the land and turned it into the **Mormon Handcart Visitor Center.** This area is a bittersweet one for the Mormons because near here, at Martin's Cove, an exhausted band of Mormon handcart emigrants sought shelter from an early winter storm in 1856. Dozens of people died in the blizzard before rescue parties from Utah reached them.

Take time to look through the center's interpretive exhibits, which include a moving video telling the Mormon Trail story from the perspective of a thirteen-year-old boy whose family made the trip. An adjacent building holds the Peoples of the Sweetwater Museum, recounting the lives of Native Americans and of the Sun family, who settled and ranched here starting in 1866. Next, make the 1-mile round-trip hike to Devil's Gate. It's well worth the time, although you'll definitely want insect repellent. People especially interested in the Mormon Trail can even borrow a reproduction handcart and make the trek to Martin's Cove. The Mormon Handcart Visitor Center is open daily from 8:00 A.M. to 7:00 P.M. Admission is free, and picnic tables are available. For more information, call (307) 328-2953.

Another turnout area west of Devil's Gate offers opportunities to see pronghorn, the antelope-like animals that can run up to 70 miles per hour. According to a display at the site, the pronghorn population once dwindled down

This view of the Sweetwater River gives one a sense of how the terrain became more rugged the farther west the emigrants traveled. Photo courtesy of the Wyoming Division of Tourism.

SIDE TRIP: YELLOWSTONE AND GRAND TETON NATIONAL PARKS

Wyoming is blessed with Grand Teton and Yellowstone National Parks, two of America's most spectacular natural areas. Grand Teton is a 132-mile drive northwest of Lander, and Yellowstone is another 60 miles north. A detour through these parks may well be in order, or better yet, plan another vacation to savor the magic that is northwest Wyoming.

Few people forget their first sight of the Tetons, which are among the youngest mountains in North America. These soaring, craggy peaks provide the setting for some of the greatest hiking in the world. The Cascade Canyon Trail is among the most popular treks, and the hikes to Hermitage Point or on the Paintbrush Trail often reward visitors with wildlife views. Mountain climbing instruction and guides are available.

It's difficult to pull your gaze away from the mountains, but the lakes and Snake River are lovely, too. Activities include scenic boat trips, boat rentals, sailboarding on Jackson and Jenny Lakes, and floats down the Snake. Horseback riding, fishing, and camping offer still more pleasures.

Yellowstone was the world's first national park, so declared by President Ulysses S. Grant in 1872. Known for its geysers, waterfalls, and wildlife (not to mention the 1988 fires that burned more than a third of the park), Yellowstone is among the most frequently visited national parks, so it can be crowded. Still, Yellowstone is a big place, with more than a thousand miles of trails. Solitude is available for those who seek it out. Yellowstone is mostly in Wyoming, although Idaho and Montana share narrow strips of the park's northwest corner.

Yellowstone boasts so many spectacular sights that it's hard to know where to begin. Artist Point and Inspiration Point offer vistas of the Grand Canyon of the Yellowstone River and its famous falls. Old Faithful is but one example of the park's intense thermal activity, all triggered by an immense volcanic eruption 600,000 years ago. Norris Geyser Basin and the Fountain Paint Pots area offer the park's most concentrated displays of these steaming, bubbling natural features.

Sight-seeing is definitely the main attraction at Yellowstone. But other opportunities available include fishing (a permit is required), backcountry camping and hiking, and canoeing (especially on Shoshone Lake). Power boaters are permitted on Yellowstone and Lewis Lakes. One $20 vehicle permit is good for entrance at both Grand Teton and Yellowstone National Parks for up to seven days. Both parks also honor the $50 annual permits to all U.S. national parks, the $10 lifetime Golden Age Passports for U.S. citizens over sixty-two, and the free lifetime Golden Access Passports available to U.S. citizens with physical impairments.

The town of Jackson sits south of Grand Teton National Park. Like other mountain resort towns, Jackson has gone through a lot of changes in recent decades. It no longer qualifies as a "typical" Western town, but it certainly is a fun place to visit. Jackson crackles with energy, from its creative restaurants and lively nightlife (don't miss the Million Dollar Cowboy Bar) to its wide recreational menu and active arts scene.

Another northwest Wyoming town, Cody, is famous for the Buffalo Bill Historical Center, considered by many to be the best overall Western museum in the United States. The four-part complex includes the Buffalo Bill Museum, which documents Colonel William Cody's colorful life; the Whitney Gallery of Western Art, featuring original works by such famous names as Russell and Remington; the Plains Indian Museum, with extensive displays on the life and times of the region's great tribes; and the Cody Firearms Museum. Cody is 80 miles east of the Fishing Bridge junction at Yellowstone National Park.

For more information, contact Grand Teton National Park at (307) 739–3600, Yellowstone National Park at (307) 344–7381, the Jackson Hole Area Chamber of Commerce at (307) 733–3316, or the Cody Country Chamber at (800) 393–2639.

to 5,000 animals. But the state prohibited hunting of the species between 1908 and 1915, and the pronghorn rapidly recovered. Today, there are about a half-million pronghorn, and two-thirds of the world's pronghorn population lives within a 300-mile radius of Casper.

Muddy Gap Junction marks the end of WY 220. From here, US 287 leads south to Rawlins and north to Lander (and on to Yellowstone and Grand Teton National Parks). Turn right and head north.

Eleven-and-a-half miles from the junction, the Bureau of Land Management has another interpretive site, this one telling about **Split Rock,** the notch landmark that has been visible since Devil's Gate. Another turnout 2 miles west offers another view of the split and of the "Old Castle" or "Castle Rock," a smaller landmark south of the trail and highway.

The **Ice Spring Slough,** located 9.5 miles west of Jeffrey City, amazed and delighted the emigrants. Here, travelers could dig down a couple feet and discover ice, even in the searing summer heat. Peat-like turf once covered this marsh, insulating the frozen water beneath the surface. Today, the slough is nearly dry and little ice forms in the winter, but the area is still moist enough to produce occasional beautiful displays of wildflowers. The site is marked by a turnout and sign.

Jeffrey City, a once-booming uranium town that is now only slightly bigger than Muddy Gap Junction, offers another oasis on beautiful but remote US 287. Be cautious when driving this route in late summer—the setting sun glares against the windshield, and deer and pronghorn play on the roadside. Sweetwater Station, a rest area at the intersection of US 287 and WY 135, has an excellent Oregon Trail map and display from the Fremont County Historical Society, along with some play equipment for children and shaded picnic tables.

From here, the trail is about 2 miles south, paralleling the highway. Most travelers will want to continue northwest to the intersection with WY 28, the major route to South Pass. But those with time and inclination can drive the Hudson–Atlantic City Road, which follows the trail corridor more closely. The maintained dirt road is open from June through October. It turns south from US 287 about 6 miles west of Sweetwater Station and leads to the South Pass–Atlantic City historic mining district (which also is accessible via WY 28). It takes ninety minutes to two hours to drive the 31-mile route. Passenger cars can make it, but check the skies first; two-wheel-drive vehicles are better off sticking to the highway in wet weather. The Lander office of the BLM at (307) 332–8400 is a good source of information on this and other back roads in the South Pass area.

Lander makes a fine spot to spend the night before continuing on to South Pass and Fort Bridger. A town of about 8,000 people, Lander lives for the outdoors. Home of the National Outdoor Leadership School, it's a major gateway to Grand Teton and Yellowstone National Parks, the Wind River Range, and vast tracts of national forest. Sinks Canyon State Park, located 9 miles southwest of town, features the beautiful Popo Agie River (pronounced Po-PO-zsha), a couple of great nature trails, and one of the most pleasant state park campgrounds you'll find anywhere. The park was named for the way the Popo Agie suddenly disappears into a large cavern before reappearing about a half-mile down the river canyon. If you're traveling with children, be sure to let them feed the big trout at "The Rise," where the river resurfaces. Vending machines dispense trout chow for 25 cents. Visit the Lander Chamber of Commerce at 160 North First Street, or call (800) 433–0662 or (307) 332–3892 for more information on activities and sights in the area.

The Wind River Indian Reservation, home to the Shoshone and Arapahoe tribes, is north of Lander. Special events on the reservation include a Labor Day powwow at Fort Washakie, rodeos throughout the summer, and three days of sun dances in July. A cemetery near Fort Washakie is said to be the resting place of Sacagawea, the Shoshone woman who accompanied Lewis and Clark. This is a point of controversy; although Wind River–area residents say Sacagawea died an old woman among them, most historians believe she probably died just a few years after the expedition ended, at Fort Manuel on what is now the South Dakota–North Dakota border. Whatever the truth, the gravesite here is a moving tribute to one of America's great heroines.

SOUTH PASS

As mountain passes go, **South Pass** wasn't much to look at in the nineteenth century, and it still isn't today. Many emigrants figured they'd be crossing through "a narrow defile in the Rocky Mountains walled in by perpendicular rocks hundreds of feet high," as Lorenzo Sawyer wrote in 1850. "The fact is they are in the South Pass all the way up the Sweetwater."

Because South Pass hardly looks like a mountain pass, emigrants who crossed the Continental Divide here scarcely knew they'd done so until they saw water flowing the "wrong" way on the other side. But the broad rise, 29 miles wide, was the key to the whole Oregon Trail. It was the only place that allowed an easy passage through the Rocky Mountains, thus enabling wagons to roll over the divide with a minimum of difficulty. Aside from that, South Pass marked the emigrants' arrival in what was then Oregon Territory. Although travelers were little more than halfway to their destination, the pass was an important psychological benchmark.

South Pass was known and used by Indians for a long time before white men came along. Robert Stuart led his Astorians through the area in 1812 as the party returned from the Pacific coast. A party of mountain men including Jim Bridger and Jed Smith rediscovered the way in 1824. A wagon train led by Captain Benjamin Bonneville rolled through in 1832. Just over a decade later, the great emigration was on, with about 1,000 people traversing the pass in 1843.

Emigrants rarely stopped at the pass, although many made note of it in their journals. Kit Carson guided John Fremont's party through in 1842, and Fremont wrote: "The ascent had been so gradual that, with all the intimate knowledge possessed by Carson, who had made this country his home for 17 years, we were obliged to watch very closely to find the place at which we had reached the culminating point."

Some writers grasped the full impact of the crossing. One emigrant woman, writing poetically of her party's last crossing of the Sweetwater River, noted they "forever took leave of the waters running toward the home of our childhood and youth." Another diarist, Theodore Talbot, said only: "Today we set foot in Oregon Territory . . . 'The land of promise' as yet only promises an increased supply of wormwood and sand."

Although it is barely interpreted, South Pass is worth a visit. And while an exhibit along WY 28 provides a good view of the pass, it is easy enough to drive to the real thing and see it up close. The access road is 42 miles south of Lander. (A turnoff 26 miles south of Lander is the start of a loop road leading to Atlantic City and South Pass City, two old mining towns worth a visit while en route to South Pass itself. [See sidebar, page 114.] This loop road leads back to WY 28 north of the South Pass turnoff.)

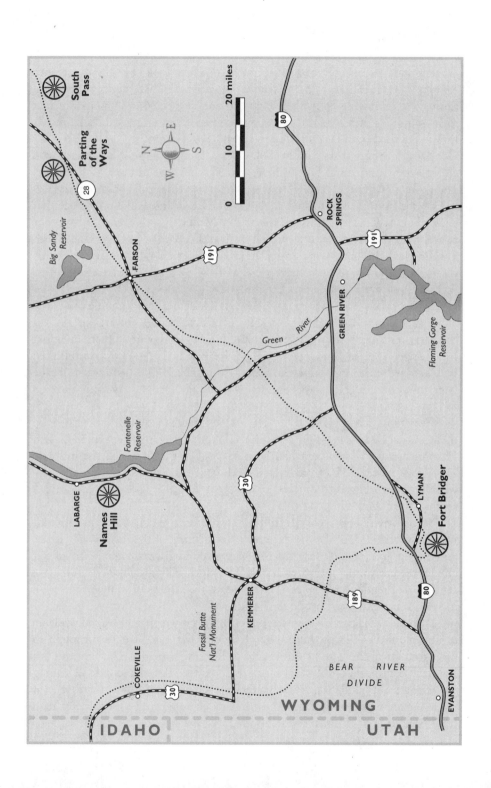

Stone monuments mark the summit of South Pass.

Just before the turnoff, the highway crosses the Sweetwater River a final time and climbs. At the crest, 0.7 mile past the bridge, watch for a sign for the Bridger Wilderness (on your right when heading south). Turn left instead, onto Oregon Buttes Road. Drive about 2.75 miles to an old railroad bed. Drive another 0.4 mile to a Y intersection, bear right, then immediately right again. In another 0.2 mile, bear right yet again. South Pass is just ahead, past the cattleguard 0.6 mile away. Park by the cattleguard and stroll into history.

The pass is marked only by two small monuments. The one reading OLD OREGON TRAIL 1843–57 was placed on the Continental Divide by Ezra Meeker, the pioneer who went west in 1852 and later returned to mark the route. The other stone honors Narcissa Whitman and Eliza Spalding, the first white women to cross the pass.

Near the pass, take time to look at the landscape, which has changed little since pioneer times. Here, the travelers had a natural corridor to follow, flanked on the north by the Wind River Range, its towering peaks cloaked in snow even in summer, and to the south by the Oregon Buttes and Antelope Hills.

From the pass, return to WY 28. The roadside exhibit 5 miles south offers another perspective on the South Pass area. It also points out **Pacific Springs,** where the emigrants often camped after crossing the divide. The springs are now on private land.

HISTORY ON THE CONTINENTAL DIVIDE

After Oregon Trail travel tapered off with the coming of the transcontinental railroad, the South Pass region was the scene of much mining activity. South Pass City was built north of the Oregon Trail in 1867 after the Carissa Mine struck a rich vein of gold. The town's population boomed to 2,000 within a year, and more than thirty mines started working the hillsides. The bust hit in 1872, and most folks moved away.

South Pass City is now a state historic site with twenty-four structures intact (out of about 300 that once existed). Summer activities include living-history displays and one of Wyoming's oldest and largest Fourth of July celebrations. Visitors can buy gold-panning equipment and try their luck in nearby Willow Creek, tour the remaining buildings, or enjoy a picnic lunch on the pleasant grounds. Admission is $2.00 for non-residents and $1.00 for Wyoming residents; children and teens get in free. Buildings are open from 9:00 A.M. to 6:00 P.M. daily May 15 through October 15, and the grounds are open year-round. It's a fascinating place, so allow at least an hour. For more information, call (307) 332–3684.

A museum in the visitor center tells the town's history, including its substantial role in the women's rights movement: In 1869, South Pass City's representative in the Wyoming territorial legislature, William Bright, introduced a bill giving women the right to vote, to run for office, and to hold property. It passed, making Wyoming the first state or territory to extend these rights to women and leading to its nickname, "the Equality State." Two months later, Esther Morris was appointed South Pass City's first justice of the peace and the nation's first female judge.

If you're interested in vintage clothing, check out the South Pass Trading Company, just outside the state historic site in the old Masonic lodge. It's open during the summer months and stocks a variety of authentic reproduction clothing and accessories from the 1860s through the 1940s, as well as Wyoming souvenirs and snacks.

Atlantic City, another old gold camp, is just northeast of South Pass City. The town was so named because it was located east of the Continental Divide. It too has escaped becoming a complete ghost town, with several small businesses catering to the tourist trade, including several places to eat and stay overnight. Campers will find two Bureau of Land Management campgrounds near Atlantic City.

Make sure to have a jacket or sweater handy when visiting South Pass City or Atlantic City. Elevations are near 8,000 feet, and the area gets some of Wyoming's harshest weather year-round. ♠

Another 5 miles down WY 28, a group of historical markers tell about the **"Parting of the Ways,"** the first of many major divisions in the trail where emigrants branched off to their various destinations. The actual jumping-off onto the Sublette Cutoff was 8 miles west of this site; another turnout 8 miles northwest of Farson on US 191 marks the route as it entered the Little Colorado Desert.

The Sublette Cutoff was opened in 1844 by a California-bound wagon train, but it didn't become popular until the gold rush of 1849. It originally was known as the Greenwood Cutoff (for one of the pioneering wagon train's guides, eighty-one-year-old Caleb Greenwood), but an 1849 guidebook error forever changed its name. Although the Sublette Cutoff saved the travelers 85 miles and five or six days of travel, it was tough going, with dry stretches and mountainous terrain.

Farson, at the junction of WY 28 and US 191, is a good pit stop for today's traveler. Gas, food, and lodging are available, not to mention what may be the biggest ice-cream cones in Wyoming at the Farson Merc. Present-day Farson also is where the main Oregon Trail crossed the Big Sandy River before following its north bank to the Green River. Here, Jim Bridger and Brigham Young met for the first time in 1847. Bridger gave Young a description of the Salt Lake Valley, which the mountain man was credited with discovering in 1824. In return, Young gave Bridger a free pass for the the Platte River ferry at Casper. A plaque by the Big Sandy bridge commemorates the encounter.

From Farson, stay closest to the trail by driving WY 28 to WY 372, which accesses the Seedskadee National Wildlife Refuge, famous for its wide variety of birds. WY 372 runs southeast to I–80 and northwest to US 189. Head north on US 189 to see Names Hill, where many emigrants on the Sublette Cutoff carved their names on a cliff. One of the signatures is supposed to be that of Jim Bridger, though that's doubtful since the famous mountain man could neither read nor write and typically made an "X" mark to sign his name. From here, you can bypass Fort Bridger and go on to Kemmerer via US 189 south, or go to Fort Bridger via US 189 south and WY 412.

Or bypass Names Hill and travel south from Farson on US 191 to I–80 and the Rock Springs–Green River area, the biggest metropolitan region in western Wyoming with a population of about 35,000. Rock Springs started out in 1862 as a stop on the Overland Stage route, and it remains an important transportation center. To the north, the Red Desert region stretches more than 100 miles and serves as home to one of the nation's largest wild horse populations. The Bureau of Land Management controls the herd's size by rounding up some of the animals and offering them for adoption.

Visitors aren't allowed to watch the wild horse roundups, but they are welcome at the Red Desert Roundup, a major rodeo held each July. Arts-minded travelers may want to stop at the Rock Springs Community Fine Arts Center, located in the public library at 400 "C" Street. This collection includes hundreds of works by Wyoming and other Western artists. The local Recreation Center at Reagan Avenue and Sweetwater Drive has year-round sports facilities open to the public.

Rock Springs and Green River are known for their nearby deposits of trona, used to make soda ash, which in turn is used to produce glass, detergents, and baking soda. Two-thirds of the world's soda ash comes from southwest Wyoming. Green River is the seat of Sweetwater County and home of the local historical museum at 80 West Flaming Gorge Way. Its exhibits include a large collection of historical photographs from the region.

Both towns abound in visitor services and serve as gateways to Flaming Gorge National Recreation Area. For more information, contact the Rock Springs Chamber of Commerce at (307) 362–3771 or the Green River Chamber of Commerce at (307) 875–5711. From Green River, it's about an hour's drive west on I–80 to Fort Bridger.

The Shoshone National Forest west of WY 28 is another favorite recreational area, particularly for Wyomingites who want to avoid the crowds that often congregate at their state's national parks. Fiddler's Lake and Louis Lake are among the popular spots in this scenic area. For information, call the forest headquarters at (307) 527–6921 or stop by the turnout on the west side of the highway about 30 miles south of Lander.

FORT BRIDGER

By the early 1840s, the fur trading days of the American West were coming to a close, and Jim Bridger needed something new to occupy his time. He decided to build a fort to capitalize on the coming westward migration, a place where emigrants could buy supplies, fix their wagons, and rest before resuming their trips. His first post was situated almost a mile north of the present-day town of Fort Bridger; a second fort, erected in 1844, was on the ground now occupied by **Fort Bridger State Historic Site.**

By most accounts, Fort Bridger wasn't a pretty place. In *The Oregon Trail Revisited,* Gregory Franzwa described the post as "a raunchy adobe emplacement surrounded by a stockade—always a disappointment to trail-weary emigrants." But, as Franzwa noted, what the fort lacked in aesthetic appeal it made up for by its surroundings. Emigrant diarists wrote of abundant clear, sweet water and good grass for their livestock. They also couldn't help but notice the beautiful Uinta Mountains to the south, nor the high, wide blue skies that prevailed then and now over Wyoming.

Despite their new roles as shopkeepers, Bridger and his partner Louis Vasquez were still mountain men at heart, and some visitors to the fort reported the proprietors were nowhere to be found. When they did stick around,

The officers' quarters at Fort Bridger State Historic Site offer a unique glimpse of the past. Photo courtesy of the Wyoming Division of Tourism.

FLAMING GORGE, DINOSAUR, AND FOSSIL BUTTE NATIONAL MONUMENTS

A detour off I–80 leads to Flaming Gorge National Monument, a spectacular area of bright red canyons, towering green ponderosa pines, and abundant recreational opportunities. The most scenic route through the area is US 191, which heads south between Rock Springs and Green River.

Fishing and boating are the most popular activities at Flaming Gorge, which was named by Major John Wesley Powell during his explorations of the area in 1869. Numerous boat and tackle rental shops dot the area near the Wyoming-Utah border. The Flaming Gorge Dam Visitor Center at Dutch John offers tours, self-guiding maps, and coloring books for the kids. The Red Canyon Visitor Center on UT 44 boasts a spectacular quarter-mile-high vista above the lake and canyon. Primitive camping is available here, too. For more information, call (801) 889–3713.

Dinosaur fans young and old will enjoy a side trip to Dinosaur National Monument, about 12 miles south of I–80 at Jensen, Utah. (Take UT 149 from Jensen to the site.) Fossilized bones from *brontosaurus* and other prehistoric creatures were found here in one of the largest concentrations anywhere in the world. A visitor center displays many bones and related exhibits. Admission to the monument is $10 per vehicle, good for seven days. Call (435) 789–2115 for more information.

Prehistoric life is also the focus at Fossil Butte National Monument, 15 miles west of Kemmerer, Wyoming. During the Eocene Age 50 million years ago, this area was covered with a freshwater lake. As the lake dried up, it left behind a wealth of beautifully fossilized fish and other aquatic creatures. The area is a geological wonderland, with its buff-colored Green River formation layers mingling with the red, pink, and purple Wasatch formation.

The monument's visitor center exhibits a variety of fossils and an artist's rendition of what the area might have looked like during prehistoric times. A 2.5-mile trail leads to the area where the fossils were quarried. The visitor center is open daily from 8:00 A.M. to 7:00 P.M. June through August, with regular interpretive programs, and from 8:00 A.M. to 4:30 P.M. the rest of the year. Grounds are open year-round. Admission is free. For more information, call (307) 877–4455. ◆

however, Bridger and Vasquez received good notices from their patrons. James Reed, who stopped by in July 1846, called them "two very excellent and accommodating gentlemen . . . they can be relied on for doing business honorably and fairly."

Some other deals that went down here were shadier; Fort Bridger was to be the rendezvous site for Lansford Hastings and the Donner Party, which he had promised to lead on his new shortcut to California. When George Donner and his party arrived, Hastings had already moved on. The party used the Hastings route anyway, following his tracks. Within days, however, the Donner Party had lost the way. Three months later, they found themselves trapped by an early blizzard in the Sierra Nevada of California.

Fort Bridger also played a pivotal role for members of the Church of Jesus Christ of Latter-day Saints, or Mormons, who were headed for religious freedom in what would become Utah. This, in fact, was the point where the Mormon Trail—which had paralleled the Oregon Trail since Fort Kearny—left the track bound for Oregon and California and struck off southwest toward the Great Salt Lake. About 70,000 Mormons followed the trail from Nauvoo, Illinois, to Salt Lake City between 1847 and 1869, many of them using handcarts instead of covered wagons. From their base in Salt Lake City, the Mormons went on to settle more than 300 communities in the West.

The Mormons ended up buying Fort Bridger in 1855, but the occupation was destined to be short-lived, lasting only two years. Tensions mounted between the Mormons and the federal government, and President Buchanan sent troops to the area in 1857. Rather than fight, the Mormons burned Fort Bridger and their nearby Fort Supply and retreated to Salt Lake City.

From 1858 on, Fort Bridger became a military site and remained so until its final abandonment in 1890. Soldiers rebuilt the fort, and it is these army-era buildings that are the site's main attractions today. Visitors can easily walk the grounds and tour several buildings and the fort museum in about an hour. The museum features good displays on all aspects of the fort's history, from the Oregon Trail to the military to its use by Indians.

One of the most fascinating characters in Fort Bridger history was William A. Carter, who started as a sutler at the trading post and went on to become a judge, living here until his death in 1881. Carter's clan enjoyed comforts known by few other frontier families, including one of the region's largest libraries. Today's Fort Bridger is especially well suited for people with disabilities, with its flat walkways and Braille signs provided by the Lions Club from the nearby town of Lyman.

Modern-day Fort Bridger also includes a replica of the Bridger-Vasquez trading post, open May through September. Tucked back in the site's northwest corner, the post stocks fur trade and emigrant-era goods such as skins, pelts, beads, and hats. Fort Bridger hosts a mountain man rendezvous each Labor Day weekend, with associated events including a demolition derby and other entertainment.

Fort Bridger State Historic Site is located near exit 34 off I–80. It's open daily from 9:00 A.M. to 4:30 P.M. May through September. The fort also is open weekends in March, April, October, and November. It's closed December through mid-March. For more information, call (307) 782–3842.

Visitor services are available in the town of Fort Bridger and nearby communities including Lyman and Mountain View. From Fort Bridger, the Oregon Trail turned north toward present-day Idaho. Modern travelers can backtrack on I–80 to WY 412, follow it north to its junction with US 189, then drive north to Kemmerer, home of the first J.C. Penney store and a fine little museum (the Fossil Country Frontier Museum at 400 Pine Avenue). Evanston, 28 miles west of Fort Bridger, is another possible overnight stop; from Evanston, backtrack 13 miles east to US 189 and drive north to Kemmerer. From Kemmerer, take US 30 55 miles west then north into Idaho.

Lodgings, campgrounds and restaurants listed below are a representative sampling of what is available. Listing in these pages does not imply endorsement, nor is this a complete listing of all reputable businesses. For more complete listings, contact the visitor information bureau or chamber of commerce in each town. Room rates were accurate as of summer 2000, but are subject to change.

LODGING

TORRINGTON, WYOMING
Holiday Inn Express, (307) 532–7600, 1700 East Valley Road, $76.
Maverick Motel, (307) 532–4064, US 26 and US 85, $34.
Oregon Trail Motel, (307) 532–2101, US 26 East, $22–$32.

FORT LARAMIE, WYOMING
Fort Laramie Motel, (307) 837–3063, 211 Laramie Avenue, $30.

GUERNSEY, WYOMING
Annette's Whitehouse Bed & Breakfast, (307) 836–2148, 239 South Dakota Street.
Bunkhouse Motel, (307) 836–2356, US 26, $49.
Sage Brush Motel, (307) 836–2331, $35.

GLENDO, WYOMING
Howard's Motel, (307) 735–4252, I-25 exit 111, $30.

DOUGLAS, WYOMING
Best Western Douglas Inn, (307) 358–9790, 1450 Riverbend Drive, $80–$90.
Chieftain Motel, (307) 358–2673, 815 East Richards Street, $36.
First Interstate Inn, (307) 358–2833, 2349 East Richards Street, $50.
Plains Motel, (307) 358–4484, 628 East Richards Street, $32.

GLENROCK, WYOMING
All-American Inn, (307) 436–2772, 500 West Aspen, $33.
Hotel Higgins, (307) 436–9212, 416 West Birch Street, $45–$60.

CASPER, WYOMING

Best Western Casper, (307) 234–3541, 2325 East Yellowstone Highway, $60–$85.
EconoLodge, (307) 266–2400, 821 North Poplar Street, $50–$65.
Parkway Plaza Hotel, (307) 235–1777, 123 West "E" Street, $55.
Sage & Sand Motel, (307) 237–2088, 901 West Yellowstone Highway, $30.
Shilo Inn, (307) 237–1335, I–25 at Curtis Street (Evansville), $55–$100.
Super 8 Motel, (307) 266–3480, 3838 CY Avenue, $65–$70.
Westridge Motel, 307) 234–8911, 955 CY Avenue, $40–$50.

LANDER, WYOMING

Blue Spruce Inn B&B, (307) 332–8253, 677 South Third Street, $80.
Downtown Motel, (307) 332–3171, 569 Main Street.
Holiday Lodge National 9, (307) 332–2511, 210 McFarlane Drive, $45–$50.
Maverick Motel, (307) 332–2300, 808 Main Street, $45.
Pronghorn Lodge, (307) 332–3940, 150 East Main Street, $60–$75.

ATLANTIC CITY, WYOMING

Atlantic City Mercantile, (307) 332–5143, $55.
Miner's Delight Bed & Breakfast, (307) 332–0248, $60–$75.

FARSON, WYOMING

Sitzman's Motel, (307) 273–9246, 4066 US 191, $35.

ROCK SPRINGS, WYOMING

Cody Motel, (307) 362–6675, 75 North Center Street, $32.
Comfort Inn, (307) 382–9490, 1670 Sunset Drive, $60–$70.
Holiday Inn, (307) 382–9200, 1675 Sunset Drive, $68–$80.
Inn at Rock Springs, (307) 362–9600, I–80 exit 102, $48–$80.
Motel 6, (307) 362–1850, 2615 Commercial Way, $46.

GREEN RIVER, WYOMING

Coachman Inn Motel, (307) 875–3681, 470 East Flaming Gorge Way, $40–$48.
Oak Tree Inn, (307) 875–3500, I–80 exit 89, $55–$60.
Super 8 Motel, (307) 875–9330, 208 West Flaming Gorge Way, $50–$57.
Western Motel, (307) 875–2840, 890 West Flaming Gorge Way, $45–48.

LITTLE AMERICA, WYOMING

Little America Hotel, (307) 875–2400, I–80 exit 68, $70–$90.

LYMAN, WYOMING

Valley West Motel, (307) 787–3700, 106 East Clark Street, $35–$45.

FORT BRIDGER, WYOMING

Wagon Wheel Motel, (307) 782–6361, located across from Fort Bridger State Historic Site, $40–$50.

EVANSTON, WYOMING

Best Western Dunmar Inn, (307) 789–3770, 1601 Harrison Drive, $75–$105.

Motel 6, (307) 789–0791, 261 Bear River Drive, $41–$46.

Pine Gables B&B Inn, (307) 789–2069, 1049 Center Street, $55–$90.

Weston Plaza, (307) 789–0783, 1983 Harrison Drive, $70.

KEMMERER, WYOMING

Antler Motel, (307) 877–4461, 419 Coral Street, $36.

Energy Inn, (307) 877–6901, junction of US 30 and US 189 (Diamondville), $48.

Fairview Inn, (307) 877–3938, US 30 and US 89, $40.

Fossil Butte Motel, (307) 877–3996, 1424 Central Avenue, $35.

COKEVILLE, WYOMING

Valley Hi Motel, (307) 279–3251, 10716 US 30, $42.

CAMPING

TORRINGTON, WYOMING

Kountry Kids, east of town on US 26.

Pioneer Municipal Park, West Fifteenth Avenue and "E" Street. Free.

Traveler's Trailer Court & Campground, (307) 532–5517, 745 South Main Street.

LINGLE, WYOMING

Pony Soldier RV Park, (307) 837–3078.

FORT LARAMIE, WYOMING

Chuckwagon RV Park, (307) 837–2304.

Fort Laramie Municipal Park, (307) 837–2711, on Fort Laramie Avenue. Free.

GUERNSEY, WYOMING

Guernsey State Park, (307) 836–2334, 3 miles north of Guernsey.

Larson's Park, by Register Cliff.

GLENDO, WYOMING

Collins Corral, south of town on WY 319.

Glendo Marina, (307) 735–4216, 383 Glendo Park Road.

Glendo State Park, (307) 735–4433, 4 miles east of Glendo.

DOUGLAS, WYOMING

Ayres Natural Bridge, (307) 358–3532, I–25 exit 151.

Jackalope KOA, (307) 358–2164, I–25 exit 140 or 146.

Lonetree Village RV Park, (307) 358–6669, I–25 exit 140

Several USDA Forest Service campgrounds are located in the Medicine Bow National Forest south of Douglas. Call (307) 358–4690 for information.

GLENROCK, WYOMING

Deer Creek RV Park, (307) 436–8121, 302 Millar Lane.

CASPER, WYOMING

Casper KOA, (800) 423–5155, 2800 East Yellowstone Highway.

Casper Mountain Park, (307) 234–6821, 6 miles south on Casper Mountain Road.

Fort Caspar Campground, (307) 234–3260, west of Fort Caspar on Thirteenth Street.

ALCOVA, WYOMING

Alcova Lake Campground, (307) 234–6821, 30 miles southwest of Casper on WY 220.

Pathfinder Lake Campground, (307) 234–6821, 7 miles south of WY 220 on Pathfinder Road.

JEFFREY CITY, WYOMING

Cottonwood Campground, (307) 332–7822, 6 miles east on US 287, then 8 miles south on Green Mountain BLM Road. Primitive sites.

LANDER, WYOMING

Ray Lake Campground, (307) 332–9333, 9 miles northwest on US 287.

Rocky Acres Camper and Trailer Park, (307) 332–6953, 4 miles northwest on US 287.

Sinks Canyon State Park, (307) 332–6333, 6 miles southwest on WY 131.

Several Forest Service campgrounds are located in the Shoshone National Forest southwest of Lander. Check the roadside display on WY 28 or call (307) 332–5460 for information.

ATLANTIC CITY, WYOMING

Atlantic City BLM campgrounds, (307) 332–7822, 28 miles south of Lander; follow signs from WY 28. Primitive sites.

FARSON, WYOMING

Big Sandy State Recreation Area, (307) 332–3684, 8 miles north on US 191, then 2 miles east on county road. Primitive sites.

ROCK SPRINGS, WYOMING

Rock Springs KOA, (307) 362–3063, 86 Foothill Boulevard. Kamping Kabins.

GREEN RIVER, WYOMING
Tex's Travel Camp, (307) 875–2630, between I–80 exits 85 and 89.

LYMAN, WYOMING
Lyman/Fort Bridger KOA, (307) 786–2188, I–80 exit 413.

EVANSTON, WYOMING
Phillips RV & Trailer Park, (307) 789–3805, 225 Bear River Drive.

KEMMERER, WYOMING
Foothills RV Park, (307) 877–6634, US 189 North.
Riverside RV Park, (307) 877–3416, 216 Spinel Street.

RESTAURANTS

TORRINGTON, WYOMING
Granny's Café, (307) 532–5856, 530 West Valley Road.
State Line Oasis, 307–532–4990, US 26 East.
Vi's Diner, (307) 532–2740, 1500 East Valley Road.

LINGLE, WYOMING
Lira's Restaurant, (307) 837–2826.

FORT LARAMIE, WYOMING
Garhart's Pioneer Inn, (307) 837–3065, US 26.
The Outfitters, (307) 837–2570, 302 Pioneer Court.

GUERNSEY, WYOMING
Lunch Box, (307) 836–3188, 262 East Whalen.
S&S Café, (307) 836–2301, US 26.
Trail Inn, (307) 836–2573, 37 North Wyoming.

GLENDO, WYOMING
Flying Dutchman Bar & Steakhouse, (307) 735–4279, 115 South Yellowstone Avenue.

DOUGLAS, WYOMING
Big Wheel Truck Stop, (307) 358–4446, east of Douglas off of I–25. Open twenty-four hours.
Chutes Wyoming Eatery, (307) 358–9790, in Best Western Douglas Inn, 1450 Riverbend Drive.
Country Inn, (307) 358–3575, 2341 East Richards. Family dining.

GLENROCK, WYOMING

The Paisley Shawl, (307) 436–9212, in Hotel Higgins, 416 West Birch Street. Prime rib and steaks, Victorian atmosphere.

CASPER, WYOMING

Botticelli Ristorante Italiano, (307) 266–2700, 129 West Second Street. Upscale Italian.

El Jarro Family Restaurant, (307) 577–0538, 500 West "F" Street. Homemade Mexican food.

Garden Creek Café, (307) 265–9018, 251 South Center. Breakfast and lunch daily; sushi weekend evenings.

Goose Egg Inn, (307) 473–8838, 5 miles southwest on WY 220. Prime rib. Established in 1936.

Granny's Diner, (307) 234–4204, 1705 East Second Street. 1950s-style atmosphere.

Karen & Jim's Restaurant, (307) 473–2309, 915 CY Avenue. Gyros and more.

South Sea Chinese Restaurant, (307) 237–4777, 2025 East Second Street. Chinese and American cuisine.

ALCOVA, WYOMING

Alcova Lakeside Marina, (307) 472–6666, 24025 Lakeshore Drive. Restaurant, lounge, and grocery store.

JEFFREY CITY, WYOMING

High Plains Bar & Cafe, (307) 544–2361, 2311 WY 789.

LANDER, WYOMING

The Hitching Rack, (307) 332–4322, 785 East Main Street. Steaks and seafood.

J.B.'s Sausage and Smokehouse, (307) 332–2065, 628 Main Street. Deli sandwiches.

Judd's Grub, (307) 332–9680, 634 Main Street. Drive-in style fast food.

Sweetwater Grille, (307) 332–7388, 148 Main Street. Brew pub, wide menu, families welcome.

ATLANTIC CITY, WYOMING

Atlantic City Mercantile, (307) 332–5143. Specializing in "Aspen barbecue rib-eye steak."

Miner's Delight, (307) 332–0248. Dinner served Friday and Saturday nights by reservation.

FARSON, WYOMING

Mitch's Café, (307) 273–9606, 4066 US 191.

Oregon Trail Cafe, (307) 273–9631, 4052 US 191. Local gathering spot.

ROCK SPRINGS, WYOMING

Bitter Creek Brewing, (307) 362–4782, 604 Broadway. Microbrewery with family dining.

Outlaw Inn Restaurant, (307) 362–6623, in the Best Western, 1630 Elk Street. Western and gourmet dining.

Santa Fe Trail, (307) 362–5427, 1635 Elk Street. Mexican and American food.

Ted's Supper Club, (307) 362–7323, 3 miles west on I–80. Steak, seafood, chicken.

GREEN RIVER, WYOMING

China Buffet, (307) 875–6888, 160 Uinta Drive.

Don Pedro Mexican Family Restaurant, (307) 875–7324, 520 Wilkes Drive.

Embers Family Restaurant, (307) 875–9983, 95 East Railroad. Charbroiled steaks.

Red Feather Inn, (307) 875–6625, 211 East Flaming Gorge Way. Lunch, dinner, lounge.

Trudel's Restaurant, (307) 875–8040, 3 East Flaming Gorge Way.

LITTLE AMERICA, WYOMING

Little America Restaurant, (307) 872–2656, I–80 exit 68. Open twenty-four hours.

LYMAN, WYOMING

Longhorn Resataurant, (307) 787–6366, 302 East Clark Street.

MOUNTAIN VIEW, WYOMING

Mountain View Drive-In, (307) 782–6952, 551 North WY 414.

FORT BRIDGER, WYOMING

Wagon Wheel Cafe, (307) 782–3585, located across from Fort Bridger State Historic Site.

EVANSTON, WYOMING

Dunmar's Legal Tender, (307) 789–3770, in the Best Western, 1601 Harrison Drive.

Last Outpost, (307) 789–3322, 203 Bear River Drive. Ranch-raised buffalo steaks, chuck wagon fare.

Main Street Deli, (307) 789–1599, 1025 Main. Specialty sandwiches, soups, doughnuts.

Michael's Bar & Grill, (307) 789–1088, 1011 Front Street. Fine dining, lunch and dinner.

KEMMERER, WYOMING

Lake Viva Naughton Marina Restaurant, (307) 877–9669, 15 miles north on WY 233.

Luigi's, (307) 877–6221, 819 Susie Avenue (Diamondville). Steaks, seafood, Italian specialties.

New Little Mexico, (307) 877–1166, 801 South Main.

Polar King, (307) 877–9448, US 189. Breakfast anytime.

CHAPTER FIVE

TOUGH GOING: IDAHO

"Traveled 15 miles today over the most torturous road I ever could have imagined. Nothing but rock after rock . . . nothing but sage."
—Emigrant Esther McMillan Hanna, 1852

CLOVER CREEK AND SODA SPRINGS

*T*he pioneers had a curious saying to describe a key passage of their progress west. As parties started out, spirits were usually high. Eventually, however, the travelers would "see the elephant." This meant they had finally come face to face with the bitter realities of their journey—the untimely deaths, lost possessions, crazy weather, and tortuous terrain. And by the time they passed through Idaho, the emigrants had "seen the elephant" many times over. Retrace their route by driving along US 30, which closely parallels the trail.

Soon after entering present-day Idaho, the wagon trains had to ford the **Thomas Fork,** where steep, muddy inclines in and out of the stream made crossing most difficult. In 1850, emigrants built two bridges on the site, but a toll collector soon started charging for the bridges' use. The fee, $1.00 per wagon, was more than many could afford by this point.

Just a few miles farther west, the emigrants came to a high ridge that became known as **"the Big Hill"** east of what is now Montpelier. Many pioneers thought this was the steepest, longest hill they'd yet seen. "The ascent is very long and tedious, but the descent is still more abrupt and difficult," Theodore Talbot wrote in 1843. "It is about one mile to the plain, and generally very steep and stony, but all reached the plain safely and were truly thankful that they had safely passed one of the most difficult mountains on the road," Joel Palmer wrote in 1845. Many wagons were let down by ropes tied to trees that are now long gone.

Once they descended the hill, the emigrants looked forward to a few days' rest along Clover Creek. An interpretive facility on that very site, the **National Oregon/California Trail Center,** isn't as comprehensive as its name suggests, but it does have live actors on hand to lead you through an interesting glimpse of life on the trail. After buying your admission ticket, you're guided through a

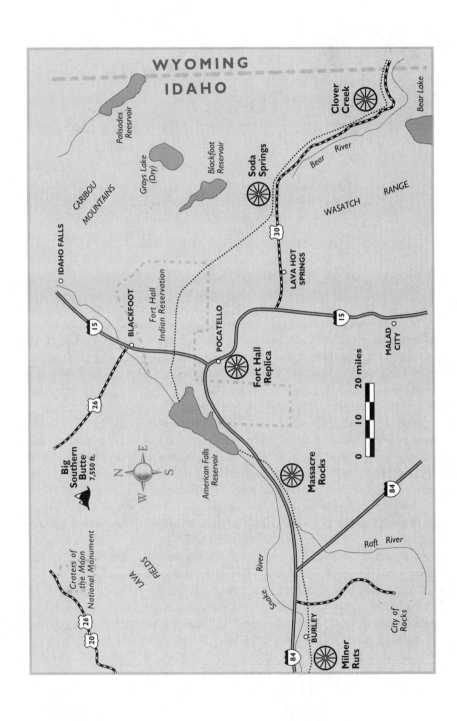

street scene reminiscent of nineteenth-century Independence, Missouri, where you learn how to gear up for your trip. Then, after a short simulated wagon ride, you arrive at the Clover Creek encampment, where you're welcomed by pioneers who'll regale you with some amazing true trail tales. Visitors become part of the dramatic experience, which includes beautiful sets and realistic lighting. The center also includes a set of trail paintings by Idaho artist Gary Stone, as well as the Rails to Trails Museum, a repository of local history.

The center is open from 10:00 A.M. to 5:00 P.M. Memorial Day through Labor Day, with tours every half-hour. It's at 322 North Fourth Street, near the junction of US 89 and US 30. Admission is $5.50 for adults and teens, $3.50 for children ages five to twelve (kids ages four and under are free), and $5.00 for seniors. Ask about family discounts. For more information, call (208) 847–3800 or see the Web site at www.oregontrailcenter.org. Montpelier-area trail buffs also put on an Oregon Trail Rendezvous Pageant most years in late July.

Once in the Bear River Valley, travelers found a trading post established in 1848 by Thomas L. "Peg Leg" Smith, a mountain man from Utah who had to amputate his own leg twenty years before. In 1849, gold-seekers rushing to California passed here by the thousands, and Smith reportedly made $100 a day. No traces of the post remain.

But unquestionably, **Soda Springs** was the major attraction in the Bear River country. Here, the emigrants marveled at springs, geysers, and a landscape marked by cones and craters formed by mineral deposits. "These soda springs are well worth a notice, possessing all the properties of pure soda water," emigrant Samuel Hancock wrote in 1845. William J. Scott, who passed through the area a year later, said he drank a whole gallon of the stuff. The most popular site may have been the one known as Beer Spring. Rufus B. Sage, who visited in 1842, had this to say: "The draught will prove delicious and somewhat stimulating, but, if repeated too freely, it is said to produce a kind of giddiness like intoxication."

There once were more than 100 such springs in the area. Most have disappeared, but one, Hooper Spring, has been preserved at a city park north of the town of Soda Springs. To get there, turn north from US 30 onto Third Street East. Drive 1.5 miles north, then turn left and proceed to the park. The spring is located under a shady pavilion, and a plaque encourages visitors to "drink deeply of nature's best beverage." Visitors really can drink the water, which is full of such yummy ingredients as silica, iron, calcium, magnesium, and bicarbonate radicle.

Another spring regularly gave off a sound like that of a steamboat. It is now drowned beneath the reservoir, but it hasn't disappeared entirely. The best way to see it is to play nine holes at the Oregon Trail Country Club. Look south to the reservoir from either the No. 1 green or the No. 8 tee. On a calm day, watch for a slight disturbance on the water's surface. That is Steamboat

The geyser at Soda Springs is still an attraction to visitors.

Spring, still percolating and puffing away. The golf course also boasts a fine Oregon Trail swale that emerges from the lake, cuts across the No. 9 fairway, and skirts the No. 1 green before traversing the No. 8 fairway. This most unusual hazard, sometimes cursed by local golfers, has even made the pages of *National Geographic.*

The local cemetery was built around the Wagonbox Grave, which commemorates the deaths of eight members of an emigrant family who were allegedly killed by Indians in 1861. Nearby, the world's only captive geyser erupts for about five minutes every hour on the hour unless the wind is blowing in a westerly direction. The geyser, discovered in 1937 while officials were trying to find a hot-water source for the local swimming pool, is now capped and controlled by a timer. A small park across the street from the geyser offers a place to picnic or relax on the front-porch-style swings until the show begins.

West of Soda Springs, at a landmark called Sheep Rock or Soda Point, some emigrants left the main trail and struck west for California on a route that came to be known as Hudspeth's Cutoff. Originally used by Indians, the route became popular in 1849 even though it saved only two days' travel and 25 miles. The main trail set off on a northwesterly course before emerging north of present-day Pocatello at Fort Hall. No good roads parallel the trail through this mountainous region, but the modern route is absolutely delightful. Follow US 30 west to I–15. From the junction, it's just 20 miles to Pocatello and a fine Fort Hall replica.

FORT HALL

Established in 1834 as a fur trading post, **Fort Hall** later became an important resting stop for the emigrants. The post was originally situated 14 miles north of Pocatello near what is now the shore of American Falls Reservoir, but the Bannock County centennial committee built a replica in Pocatello's Ross Park in 1963. To get there, follow the signs from exit 67—the first Pocatello exit coming from the south—off of I–15.

Actually, Fort Hall was the result of a grudge. Massachusetts native Nathaniel Wyeth originally wanted to start a trading post at the mouth of the Columbia River, but en route, he was convinced by fur traders Milton Sublette

BEAR LAKE AND LAVA HOT SPRINGS

Much of southern Idaho is a high, dry desert. But the state's southeast corner is blessed with abundant water-based recreation, especially at Bear Lake and Lava Hot Springs.

Bear Lake lies 18 miles south of Montpelier on US 89. Not only is the water unbelievably blue; it also is home to several species of fish found nowhere else in the world, including the Bonneville Cisco. Fishing, camping, and boating are popular here. A national wildlife refuge on the lake's north end is home to deer, moose, and numerous waterfowl species. For more information, contact the Bear Lake Convention and Visitors Bureau at (800) 448-2327.

Lava Hot Springs was once a winter campground for the Bannock and Shoshone Indian tribes. White men discovered the site in 1812, and it became known as "Dempsey's Bath Tub." The springs lost their importance as an Indian camp after 1868, when tribal members were ordered to the Fort Hall Reservation. But Lava Hot Springs remains a popular gathering spot and is a growing retirement area.

A sea of green grass surrounds a huge, award-winning pool complex operated by the state of Idaho. Across town, another set of smaller pools maintain 110°F year-round. Several local hotels have their own private hot-water baths for guests, too. As if all this water isn't enough, the Portneuf River running through town provides plenty of trout-fishing and tubing action.

Special events include a mountain man rendezvous and "Pioneer Days" celebration in mid-July. Autumn is another great time to visit, when the surrounding hillsides come alive with some of Idaho's most colorful fall foliage. For more information, call the Lava Hot Springs Foundation at (208) 776-5221 or see the Web site at www.lavahotsprings.com. ▲

and Thomas Fitzpatrick to bring them $3,000 worth of goods they could sell at their Green River rendezvous the following year. When Wyeth and his men returned the next spring, the Rocky Mountain Fur Company had dissolved and Wyeth was stuck with his wares. "Gentlemen," he reportedly told the traders, "I will yet roll a stone into your garden that you will never be able to get out." Wyeth built Fort Hall that summer, placing it on land he'd seen on earlier trips and naming it in honor of Henry Hall, the senior partner in the Boston firm that had financed his venture.

Like Jim Bridger, Wyeth became something of an absentee landlord. He was still interested in building a fort farther west, and he soon set off to pursue that idea. Eventually, however, he gave up and headed back east to pursue a career as an inventor. He sold Fort Hall to the Hudson's Bay Company (HBC) in 1837 at a reported loss of $30,000. HBC set about improving the fort by encasing the log structure in adobe brick.

Despite the facelift, the reality of Fort Hall never quite matched up to the emigrants' expectations. One display in the replica museum notes that travelers often "wrote about seeing the whitewashed walls of the stockade glisten like a beacon in the distance. They also spoke of being disappointed by the roughness of the structure once they arrived." It's difficult to imagine the pioneers

Fort Hall offers exhibits and replicas representing the fort's history and its influence on travelers along the Oregon Trail.

being let down by any fort when, after all, they had been on the road for many weeks with few signs of "civilization." Still, many of the pioneers were, after all, former urbanites whose notions of cities didn't quite gibe with the rough-and-ready settlements that passed for town life in the West.

After the British-based HBC bought the fort, emigrants were often convinced to abandon their plans to move to Oregon and head instead for California. In doing this, Hudson's Bay employees hoped to stem the tide of Americans flowing into the Northwest and preserve the region for their own country. Early parties that insisted on going to Oregon were talked into trading their wagons for pack trains since, the Hudson's Bay staff said, wagons couldn't stand the rugged terrain past this point.

But Marcus and Narcissa Whitman had already proved this conventional "wisdom" false. The missionary couple arrived here with their wagon in 1836. It was falling apart, but rather than switch to pack animals, Marcus Whitman converted the wagon to a cart and took it all the way to Fort Boise, nearly 300 miles away. Seven years later, Whitman passed this way again, leading the first great emigration to Oregon, a thousand people strong.

Exhibits at the Fort Hall replica include a blacksmith's shop, which lauds the blacksmith as an all-around craftsman, and a display on Indian lifestyles. Ask a staff member to run the videotape on Fort Hall's history.

The Fort Hall replica is open from 10:00 A.M. to 2:00 P.M. Tuesday through Saturday during April and May, daily from 10:00 A.M. to 6:00 P.M. Memorial Day through Labor Day, and daily from 10:00 A.M. to 2:00 P.M. the day after Labor Day through the end of September. Admission is $2.50 for adults, $1.75 for youth ages twelve to eighteen and seniors ages sixty and up, and $1.00 for children ages six through twelve.

Ross Park also includes the Bannock County Historical Museum, a pool, a rose garden, picnic areas, a playground, and a fenced field in which deer, antelope, elk, and bison roam. For more information, call (208) 234–1795. See also the following information on touring the original fort site at Fort Hall Bottoms.

After touring Fort Hall, spend a little time in Pocatello, Idaho's second-largest city with about 52,000 people. Long known as a railroad town and seat of higher learning (as home of Idaho State University), Pocatello also has an abundance of interesting historical buildings, including the Standrod House at 648 North Garfield, usually considered the finest example of Victorian architecture in Idaho. A self-guiding architectural tour brochure is available at the Fort Hall replica. The Idaho Museum of Natural History on the ISU campus is another local favorite.

Pocatello offers a streetcar route that takes passengers to such places as Ross Park, the ISU campus, downtown, a golf course, and the town's two major malls. Fare is 60 cents, and the entire trip around town takes about an hour. For those looking for bed or board, Pocatello and its main suburb to the north, Chubbuck, offer wide selections of motels and restaurants. More information on area attractions can be found by calling (208) 233–7333 or visiting the Web site at www.pocatelloidaho.com.

The Fort Hall Indian Reservation north and west of Pocatello is home to more than 3,300 members of the Shoshone and Bannock tribes. The tribal government is headquartered at the town of Fort Hall, 8 miles north of the junction of I–15 and I–86 near Pocatello. The Shoshone-Bannock Indian Festival and All-Indian Rodeos are held the second week of each August, and the tribe also operates a museum at exit 80 off I–15. The **Original Fort Hall** site is generally inaccessible to the public since it's on reservation land, but tours of it and other area Oregon Trail landmarks are available through local historian Robert Perry Sr. For more information including times and prices, call him at (208) 238–0097, or write Oregon Trail Tours, Route 6 Box 666, Pocatello, ID 83202. Perry's tours are a great opportunity to experience some seldom-seen trail sites and hear the Native American viewpoint. The city of Blackfoot, 10 miles north of Fort Hall on I–15, is home to the Eastern Idaho State Fair, usually held in early September.

From Pocatello or points north, take I–15 to I–86 and continue west to Massacre Rocks State Park, 12 miles west of American Falls.

MASSACRE ROCKS

Most emigrant wagon trains that traversed southern Idaho encountered no trouble from the Indians. There were, however, occasional skirmishes. One such incident took place in August 1862, when ten emigrants and an unknown number of Indians were killed in two days of fighting. The battles painted this area with its unfairly harsh and gory name, **Massacre Rocks.**

During the trail era, the area was known as "Gate of Death" or "Devil's Gate," which referred to a narrow break in the rocks through which the wagon trains passed. (The natural gap disappeared in 1958 when rocks were blasted to construct I–86.) Neither name is associated with the 1862 battles. In fact, those skirmishes took place east of the present-day state park. Local folks say it wasn't until the 1920s that the site became known as Massacre Rocks, but the name now seems stuck for good.

Happily, there is more to Massacre Rocks than historical hype. This state park has made the very most of its 900 acres, bounded on one side by the Snake River and on the other by I–86. About 7 miles of hiking trails offer the visitor close-up looks at everything from Oregon Trail remnants to more than 200 species of birds (including whistling swans, pelicans, blue herons, plus bald eagles in the winter); numerous desert plants (especially sagebrush, Utah juniper, and rabbit brush); and geological features.

Two trails in the area lead to a section of Oregon Trail ruts. There's a gate at the fishing access parking lot; ask park staff for a key or have them unlock the gate so you can drive 1.5 miles to the trailhead, from which the ruts are 0.8 mile one-way. (Or you could park at the gate and walk the 2.3 miles.) The ruts may also be reached via the westbound rest area just past exit 33 (Neeley Area) off of I-86. A trailhead at the rest area's west side leads to the Oregon Trail display for about a 1.5-mile round-trip hike. The rest area access may be more convenient for people who don't have much time to spend.

Massacre Rocks State Park has a small visitor center. Exhibits include the diary of Jane A. Gould, who traveled from Iowa to California in 1862 along the Oregon Trail and was in the area at the time of the skirmishes. Other facilities at the park include a campground with fully equipped rest rooms, picnic areas, fishing access sites, and boat ramps. Camping is available year-round, and entertaining campfire programs take place each night during the summer.

Idaho state parks charge a $2.00 per vehicle entrance fee. For more information on Massacre Rocks, call (208) 548–2672. You can find some other trail remnants by taking exit 33 and heading north to Eagle Rock Road. Turn left, drive 0.9 mile, and look for a rock cairn on the right-hand side of the

A skirmish between emigrants and Indians in 1862 gave Massacre Rocks its name.

road. Turn right at the cairn, look for a place to park near the top of the bluffs, and walk down toward the river.

American Falls Reservoir, just east of Massacre Rocks, is the largest reservoir on the Snake River and a favorite recreation spot for all of eastern Idaho. Fishing, boating, water skiing, and sailboarding are popular at the reservoir. The American Falls Marina offers camping, boat rentals, sailboarding lessons, and a dockside cafe.

West of Massacre Rocks, **Register Rock** was a major Oregon Trail campground. A shelter and fence guard a large basalt boulder on which visiting emigrants signed their names as early as 1849, and many of the signatures are still legible. Nearby, you can see where J. J. Hansen, a seven-year-old emigrant boy, carved an Indian's head on a smaller rock in 1866. In 1908, after he had become a professional sculptor, Hansen returned, carved a preacher's head, and dated the rock again.

Bonanza Bar, a gold camp, was established near here in 1878. The park at Register Rock offers picnic tables and shady relief from the Idaho desert. It's considered part of Massacre Rocks State Park, so the $2.00 fee applies. Register Road leads west from the Massacre Rocks area past Register Rock and back to the interstate; there's no need to backtrack.

Once the pioneers crossed the Raft River, near what is now the small farming community of Yale, they faced what amounted to their last chance to decide on their final destination. Raft River marked the last jumping-off spot for the California Trail. Many emigrants reportedly didn't make up their mind until reaching this point!

War Eagle Outfitter & Guides leads wagon and horseback adventures on the California Trail between Massacre Rocks and the City of Rocks. Riders traverse the Raft River Valley, crossing the California Trail in several places and enjoying outstanding big-sky scenery the whole route. Outfitter Ken Jafek also leads horseback camping trips to the Independence Lakes on nearby Cache Peak, the prominent mountain near Burley. For more information, call (208) 645–2455 or write War Eagle Outfitter & Guides, P.O. Box 1158, Malta, ID 83342.

Near Raft River, I–86 turns into I–84. Continue west on the interstate to Twin Falls, a good overnight stopping place, or detour via US 30 and see the Bureau of Land Management's fine **Milner Interpretive Area.** To do so, take exit 208 off the interstate at Burley. Drive south over the Snake River and turn right on Bedke Boulevard. This road leads to US 30, which again parallels the trail. West of Burley, watch for signs pointing to the interpretive area, which also offers picnicking, camping, and boat access.

Although it was not an Oregon Trail site, a rapid named Caldron Linn played a notable chapter in the history of western expansion. Near present-day Murtaugh, this was a narrow chute where the Snake River descended 40 feet into a violent, churning pool. Wilson Price Hunt's party of Astorians traveled through the area in 1811 and had already lost a man and a canoe upstream when they came upon the swirling waters. Seeing no end to the torrent, they decided to abandon river travel.

Historical accounts differ as to whether Caldron Linn was known to emigrants on the Oregon Trail. But several artifacts including an ax head, beaver trap, and a musket stock from the Hunt expedition may be seen at the Idaho Historical Museum in Boise. If you're traveling on US 30, stop in Murtaugh to ask directions to Caldron Linn. Or from I–84, take exit 188 and head south then east on Valley Road for about 4 miles. Turn south (right) on Murtaugh Road and follow it to the canyon, watching for signs. If you reach the bridge, you've gone too far.

ROCK CREEK STAGE STATION

As increasing numbers of pioneers passed over the Oregon Trail, smart entrepreneurs saw opportunities to provide goods and services to the emigrants. One such man, James Bascom, built the **Rock Creek Stage Station** southeast of Twin Falls in 1864. A year later, he added a log store, which still stands as the oldest building in south-central Idaho.

Rock Creek was a welcome sight to the emigrants, a good source of water and grass after a long, arid stretch across the Snake River Plain. The stage station also marked the intersection of the Oregon Trail, Ben Holladay's Overland Stage route, and the Kelton Road from Utah. For years, Rock Creek Station served as a popular emigrant campsite and transportation and commercial hub of south-central Idaho, much of which wasn't permanently settled until the late nineteenth century.

Soon after the stage station and store were built, the U.S. Army established Camp Reed to protect emigrants passing through the area. In 1875, Herman Stricker purchased the site. Today, visitors can still see the old log store, two stone cellars, and Stricker's 1900 home. (Tours of the latter are generally given from 1:00 to 5:00 P.M. on Sunday April to October or by appointment; call (208) 423–4000.) One of the stone cellars served as the area's first jail. A small, fenced cemetery 0.8 mile west of the Rock Creek Station contains several emigrant graves.

Rock Creek Station, also known as Stricker Ranch, can be reached by driving 5 miles south of Hansen, a small town along US 30, then 1 mile west. After visiting the ranch, consider driving on south into Rock Creek Canyon and the southernmost section of the Sawtooth National Forest. These "South Hills," as they're known locally, offer good camping, hiking, picnicking, and horseback riding.

Heading toward Twin Falls, consider a side trip to **Shoshone Falls**, well

CITY OF ROCKS
AND CRATERS OF THE MOON

The emigrants who turned southwest at Raft River soon came upon an amazing place not far from where Hudspeth's Cutoff joined the California Trail. Even in pioneer times, the area was known as the City of Rocks with its towering granite columns, some reaching 60 feet into the sky. Today, the City of Rocks National Reserve is one of the nation's premier rock climbing sites, and its remoteness also attracts hikers, stargazers, photographers, sightseers, hunters, and campers.

One of the City's most famous attractions is (yet another) Register Rock, where emigrants wrote their names with axle grease. This is located at the first Y intersection in the basin. Other notable formations include the Twin Sisters, Bath Rock, and Treasure Rock. These were all of great interest to the emigrants, and many described City of Rocks in their journals. Margaret Frink, who visited in July 1850, wrote this: "During the afternoon, we passed through a stone village composed of huge, isolated rocks of various and singular shapes, some resembling cottages, others steeples and domes. It is called City of Rocks, but I think the name Pyramid City more suitable. It is a sublime, strange and wonderful scene—one of nature's most interesting works."

To get to the City of Rocks, take exit 216 (Declo) off of I–84. Follow ID 77 south to Connor. From Connor, take the Elba-Almo Highway to the City of Rocks. The last few miles are on gravel road that can be impassible in wet weather or during the spring runoff season. For more information, call the City of Rocks National Reserve at (208) 824–5519. The Albion

Mountains en route to the City of Rocks are popular with hikers and hang-gliders.

After the Indian encounters of 1862, quite a few emigrants leaving Fort Hall took another trail alternative. This route, earlier used by fur traders, became known as Goodale's Cutoff after Timothy Goodale guided a large emigrant party across in 1862. But with its long fields of lava, Goodale's Cutoff was no easy road. J. C. Merrill wrote in 1864 that "at one place, we were obliged to drive over a huge rock just a little wider than the wagon. Had we gone a foot to the right or to the left, we would have rolled over."

Goodale's Cutoff passed near what is now one of Idaho's most fascinating natural areas, Craters of the Moon National Monument. Here, a strange and beautiful variety of lava flows and other volcanic features invite up-close inspection. Visitors can pitch a tent or park their trailer in a lava campground, hike to the top of a cinder cone, or explore an accessible section of officially designated wilderness. Most of the volcanic activity took place a mere 15,000 years ago, with eruptions occurring as recently as 2,000 years ago—a relative blip in geologic time.

Spring and fall are the best times to visit Craters of the Moon; summer is usually just too hot. In late May or early June, if the previous months have been wet enough, the black lava flows erupt with colorful wildflowers. Those who do visit during summer can beat the heat by exploring the Cave Area, a series of lava tubes. Wear sturdy shoes and bring a flashlight. For those seeking a quick tour, a 7-mile loop drive around the monument is an easy way to get acquainted with Craters' curiosities. Many hiking trails also begin along the loop road, and most are quite short.

Craters of the Moon is a considerable but delightful side trip from the Oregon Trail. The monument is 18 miles west of Arco on US 93/26 and can be reached either by taking US 26 northwest from Blackfoot or US 93 northeast from Twin Falls. Either way, the monument is about one-and-a-half hours away. For more information on Craters of the Moon, call (208) 527–3257. ▲

marked by signs on US 30. Although this 212-foot waterfall on the Snake River was 5 miles from the Oregon Trail, many travelers heard its roar and some hiked over to see the cascade for themselves. Shoshone Falls, sometimes called "the Niagara of the West," actually are 30 feet higher than Niagara Falls, but irrigation and hydropower demands have reduced the flow to a mere shadow of its former glory. Nevertheless, the city of Twin Falls maintains Shoshone Falls and adjacent Dierkes Lake as a park, and it is a popular spot for all kinds of outdoor fun. The falls are still an impressive sight, especially during spring runoff in April and May.

Twin Falls itself, a city of about 35,000 people, is a community rooted in agriculture but growing as a regional retail and business center. This part of Idaho is known as the Magic Valley in honor of the irrigation projects that turned a desert into some of the world's most productive farmland. Located on the major north-south axis of US 93 and near I–84, Twin Falls accommodates a lot of tourist traffic, accounting for the city's high density of motels and restaurants.

Much of Twin Falls' activity is concentrated around the College of Southern Idaho, a two-year school that serves as the region's educational and cultural capital. CSI's beautiful campus includes the Herrett Museum, with the biggest planetarium in Idaho, an art gallery, simulated rainforest, and an outstanding collection of pre-Columbian artifacts. The Twin Falls Municipal Band, one of the nation's oldest, plays each Thursday evening during the summer at City Park on Shoshone Street near downtown.

The Perrine Bridge spanning the Snake River north of Twin Falls is another top attraction, affording great views of the Snake River Canyon; it was near here that daredevil Evel Knievel tried to leap the chasm on his rocket-powered motorcycle in 1974. The canyon is home to two beautiful golf courses (Canyon Springs, reached via the south side, is public) and Centennial Waterfront Park. This is one of the easiest places along the trail to sample some quick whitewater action; Idaho Guide Service at (208) 734–4998 offers raft trips most days in the summer right from Centennial Park. You'll see lots of bird life and thrill to several rapids toward the end of the short trip. Gentler trips upriver to Pillar Falls are offered, too.

SUN VALLEY/KETCHUM AND THE SAWTOOTH NATIONAL RECREATION AREA

In the 1930s, railroad executive Averell Harriman dispatched Austrian Count Felix Schaffgotsch to find the perfect American setting for a winter resort in the European tradition. The result was Sun Valley, America's first destination ski resort.

Since then, Sun Valley/Ketchum has remained a favorite playground of the rich and famous, largely because Idahoans, while friendly, tend to grant other folks their privacy. The resort towns also serve as gateways to the Sawtooth National Forest, Challis National Forest, and Sawtooth National Recreation Area, all of which offer abundant solitude and recreational possibilities.

Ketchum is the nerve center of the Sun Valley area. This small, cosmopolitan town offers lodging, nightlife, boutiques, art galleries, and sports-oriented shops where the young-at-heart can rent everything from mountain bikes to fly fishing gear (and get free advice on where to play). The Sun Valley and Elkhorn resort complexes have their own selection of shopping, restaurants, and recreation. Whatever your sport, you are sure to find somewhere to enjoy it in the Sun Valley/Ketchum area, although prices can be steep for some activities. To economize, simply take advantage of the area's outstanding network of paved trails, all within gawking distance of Sun Valley's fabulous homes.

Sun Valley is best known for its skiing, but summer visitors can also ride the chair lift to the top of Baldy, its main mountain. From on top, hikers and mountain bikers look across what seems like an endless vista of mountain ranges. Many other hiking and cycling opportunities can be

A 45-mile trip south from Twin Falls lands the wanderer in Nevada, where the border town of Jackpot offers gambling, semi-big-name entertainment, and great deals on food and lodging designed to lure visitors into the casinos. The formula is working: Parking lots in this town are filled with vehicles bearing license plates from as far afield as Alberta and Montana. Savvy Idahoans fill up on cheap food and skip the slots.

For more info on Twin Falls–area activities and recreation, stop at the local visitor center just south of the Perrine Bridge, call (800) 255-8946, or see the Web site at www.rideidaho.com.

The area just north of the Perrine Bridge was traversed by the **Oregon Trail North Alternate,** which passed just a few hundred feet from the canyon rim. This mostly undeveloped area offers the traveler a good idea of what the emigrants were experiencing as their wagons rolled across southern Idaho, often during the dog days of summer in 90° or 100°F heat. John Fremont, who explored and mapped the West in the early 1840s, had this to say about found along Trail Creek Road east of Sun Valley and ID 75 north of Ketchum.

Ernest Hemingway spent his last years in Ketchum, and a memorial to the author sits along Trail Creek just northeast of the Sun Valley golf course (on the right side of Trail Creek Road). Visitors can also see "Papa's" grave in the Ketchum cemetery, or cast a line into Silver Creek, one of his favorite fishing spots.

North of Ketchum, ID 75 winds into the Sawtooth National Recreation Area. A visitor center about 8 miles north of Ketchum has information on trails and other opportunities, as well as free auto-tape tours that can be borrowed and played to describe the area's features and history. North of the visitor center, the highway soon climbs to the top of Galena Summit. A turnout just past the summit has a great panoramic view of the Saw-tooth Mountains and the headwaters of the Salmon River. Most folks would say the heart of the SNRA is Redfish Lake. Situated at the base of the Sawtooths near the town of Stanley, Redfish is a beloved site for hiking (try the Bench Lakes trail on the west side), boating, camping, and horseback riding.

The town of Stanley is known for its lively summer nightlife and several special events, including the Sawtooth Mountain Mama Arts and Crafts Fair, usually held the third week of July. Northeast of Stanley, ID 75 becomes the Salmon River Scenic Route. Attractions along this stretch include whitewater rafting, fishing, camping, and soaking at Sunbeam Hot Springs. Also consider a visit to the Land of the Yankee Fork State Park, including the old gold towns of Custer and Bonanza.

Sun Valley and Ketchum are 84 miles north of Twin Falls, and Stanley is another 60 miles northwest. For more information on Sun Valley/Ketchum, contact the Chamber of Commerce at (800) 634–3347. The Stanley Chamber of Commerce may be reached at (800) 878–7950, and the Sawtooth National Recreation Area's phone number is (208) 727–5013. ◆

what would become Idaho: "Water, though good and plenty, is difficult to reach as the river is hemmed in by high and vertical rocks and many of the streams are without water in the dry season. Grass is only to be found at the marked ramping places and barely sufficient to keep strong animals from starvation. Game, there is none. The road is very rough by volcanic rocks detrimental to wagons and carts. In sage bushes consists the only fuel. Lucky that by all these hardships the traveler is not harassed by the Indians, who are peaceable and harmless."

Before they could leave what is now Twin Falls, the emigrants had to get across Rock Creek. This was no easy feat, for while the creek itself was only about 20 feet wide, the canyon walls were steep and rocky. The crossing was finally accomplished near what is now the Amalgamated Sugar Factory, and the pioneers pushed westward.

From Twin Falls, the Oregon Trail stayed south of the Snake River. Modern travelers can, too, by taking US 30 (Addison Avenue) west out of town.

This is the Thousand Springs Scenic Route, and it leads to the Hagerman Valley, one of Idaho's best-kept secrets.

THOUSAND SPRINGS

Eighteen miles past the Rock Creek crossing, the trail returned to the Snake River at Kanaka Rapids. The rapids were also known as **Fremont's Fishing Falls,** after John Fremont publicized them following his 1843 exploration. Here, the pioneers traded with Indians, for whom this was an important salmon fishery.

West of Twin Falls, US 30 stays out of sight of the river through the towns of Filer and Buhl. Filer is home of the Twin Falls County Fair and Rodeo, held early each September, and Buhl boasts the world's largest commercial trout farm, Clear Springs. Past Buhl, the road zigzags north, then east, then north again, all the while getting closer to the canyon. After a few final descending bends, the **Thousand Springs** are in view. And although there are far fewer springs today than in emigrant times, the white water gushing from the black canyon walls is as enchanting as ever.

Where does the water come from? Some originates in eastern Idaho, where the Big Lost River and several other waterways abruptly sink into the

Water gushes from the black volcanic rock that forms the cliff walls above the Snake River at Thousand Springs.

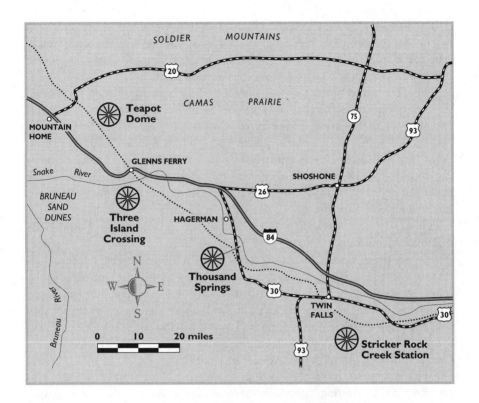

ground. From there, the water moves ever so slowly—possibly just 10 feet a day—through the underground Snake River aquifer, one of the largest groundwater systems in the world. Rain, snowmelt, and irrigation runoff add to the aquifer before the springs finally burst forth into the canyon.

In 1911, an Arizona company built a 400-foot-long flume along the north canyon wall to capture the water and produce electricity. At one time, the Thousand Springs plant produced about 20 percent of Idaho Power's electric load. Today, however, the plant's output fills a far smaller fraction of the utility's demands.

Around 1852, a road on the north side of the Snake River came into use. Some emigrants who decided to cross forded the river, but most used a ferry. After years of service to emigrant and local traffic, Payne's Ferry broke away and sank 3 miles downstream. Present-day Hagerman also was the site of Camp Reed No. 2, another temporary military post established to protect pioneer traffic.

Minnie Miller, a Utah businesswoman, owned an island in the Snake River during much of the first half of the twentieth century and used it to develop one of the nation's top Guernsey cattle herds. Today, the land is owned by The Nature Conservancy and is the site of an outstanding arts festival held in late September each year. There's also good hiking and canoeing nearly year-round. Call (208) 837–4505 for more information and directions to the preserve, which must be accessed via the canyon's north side.

The Thousand Springs signal entry into the Hagerman Valley. Hagerman consistently posts the highest temperatures in Idaho, and the mild year-round climate attracts recreationists and retirees. Top attractions include several commercial hot springs, some with private baths, and a number of good fishing holes (try the Oster Lakes, Anderson Ponds, or Billingsley Creek). Visitors can tour a state or national fish hatchery, see artists in action at the Snake River Pottery west of town on the old Bliss Grade, or take a float trip down the Snake River. But first, take a short detour from US 30 to see (and perhaps hike along) some outstanding Oregon Trail ruts in **Hagerman Fossil Beds National Monument.**

To get there, take the left turn (signed for Bell Rapids) just before US 30 crosses the Snake River. From here, it's 3 miles to the monument's Snake River overlook and—across the road—the start of the 3-mile, one-way Emigrant Trail, which parallels the Oregon Trail. Carry water and watch for rattlesnakes and scorpions on this path. The trails wind up at an Oregon Trail overlook area 1.7 miles by road from the Snake River overlook. Here, there's a shorter trail with glimpses of the emigrants' path.

The Hagerman fossil beds were discovered by a local farmer in 1928. The Smithsonian Institution conducted several expeditions to the site and unearthed 130 skulls and 15 skeletons of an early, zebra-like horse. Other fossils found here preserved early forms of camel, peccary, beaver, turtle, and freshwater fish. Stop by the monument's visitor center along State Street in Hagerman for interpretive exhibits and information on ranger-led programs and field trips to the site.

West of Thousand Springs, the emigrants found another good site for trading with the Indians at **Upper Salmon Falls.** Writing of the area's beauty, Fremont called it "one of those places that the traveler turns again and again to fix in his memory." US 30 climbs out of the Hagerman Valley to Bliss, a small community near I–84. From Bliss, a 7-mile backtrack east on I–84 to the Tuttle exit leads to Malad Gorge State Park, another site on the Oregon Trail North Alternate. Park staff here found remnants of the emigrant trail while cleaning up a local garbage dump. A short path leads from a parking lot to the deep, scenic gorge over the Malad River, which at just 2.5 miles long has sometimes been called the world's shortest river.

From Bliss, continue west on I–84 to Glenns Ferry, site of one of the Oregon Trail's toughest river crossings.

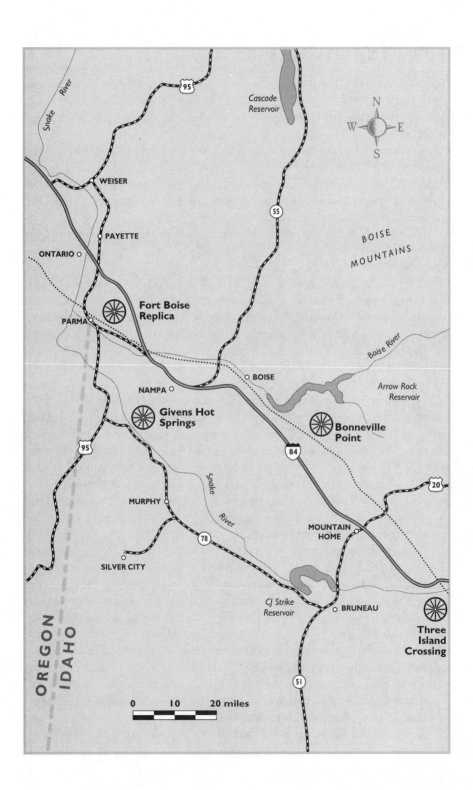

THREE ISLAND CROSSING

Near present-day Glenns Ferry, the emigrants faced another difficult choice. They could attempt the **Three Island Crossing** to a shorter, easier route north of the Snake River, or they could stay on the dry, rough Oregon Trail South Alternate.

Crossing the river meant contending with its formidable width, deep channels, and swift currents, but about half the emigrants decided to try. Today, the site is part of Three Island Crossing State Park, where a re-enactment staged the second Saturday each August features exact replicas of wagons, pack trains, and period clothing.

History shows that the emigrants actually used two different routes to cross the river here. One crossing that could be made without swimming or floating was called Three Island Ford. Two Island Crossing, a mile upstream, was more difficult and dangerous because wagons had to be floated across the Snake. (This crossing actually has three islands in sight, but only the southernmost and middle islands were used.) Most emigrants believed these separate crossings were the same, which is how the area became known as Three Island Crossing.

Crossing the river took considerable preparation and time. Men would swim to the opposite side of the river, then use ropes to pull the wagons across. Wagons and carts often capsized; livestock sometimes drowned. Few emigrants who passed here failed to mention the crossing in their diaries. P. V. Crawford, who emigrated in 1851, said the ordeal took the better part of three days. On July 31, he wrote: "This day we spent in arranging for and crossing the river. We accomplished this by corking two wagons and lashing them together. By this means we were able to ferry over a wagon and its load at each trip. By noon we had our boat ready and began operations, but found it slow business, but succeeded in getting over safely, but not the same day, for we had to lay by on account of wind. Leaving part of our camping on each side of the river, here we had both sides to guard."

Narcissa Whitman gave a detailed description of her party's crossing, which included loading packs atop the tallest horses in an effort to keep possessions dry. "Husband had considerable difficulty in crossing the cart," she wrote. "Both cart and mules were turned upside down in the river and entangled in the harness. The mules would have drowned but for a desperate struggle to get them ashore. Then after putting two of the strongest horses before the cart, and two men swimming behind to steady it, they succeeded in getting it across. I once thought that crossing streams would be the most dreaded part of the journey. I can now cross the most difficult stream without the least fear." The Three Island Crossing passed into history in 1869 when Gus P. Glenn established a ferry a short distance above the crossing.

Three Island Crossing State Park is reached via exit 120 off of I–84.

This re-enactment of the Three Island Crossing looks tame compared to tales told by emigrants.

Drive south into Glenns Ferry and follow the signs. In 2000, the park opened the Oregon Trail History and Education Center, a new facility designed to explain the crossing. Its exhibits offer a good overview of trail travel, but its real strength is its sensitive look at how the migration affected area Native Americans, and how relations between the tribes and newer arrivals have changed over the years. Around the center, with modern photographic portraits and on video, are quotations from Idahoans of both tribal and European descent. By 2001, the center expects to have a genealogical library where visitors can research their own family's trail history. Future plans also call for a riverside re-creation of the Native American fishing village that once stood at this site.

It's possible to get a bird's-eye view of the crossing. Head east out of Glenns Ferry on Cleveland Avenue (off Commercial Street), cross the Snake River over a small bridge, then continue along the river on Rosevear Road. At the top of the bluffs, watch for a Bureau of Land Management sign that shows the way to the Three Island Crossing. From this point, it's about a mile to a cattleguard crossing on your right. Turn here and follow the road to the bluffs.

Three Island Crossing has a pleasant campground (including several teepees for rent). Other activities at the park include swimming, fishing, bicycling, and picnicking. Park admission is $2.00, while the interpretive center

SOUTHWEST IDAHO'S RIVER AND CANYON COUNTRY

For some, the Three Island Crossing proved too much. Cornelia A. Sharp, an 1852 emigrant, wrote on August 9 that her party "made several attempts to swim our cattle, but without success." The next day, they "abandoned the idea of crossing the river; gathered up our cattle, hitched up our teams and took the sand and sage for it."

The South Alternate was a rough road but it did offer some spectacular scenery, including sand dunes, canyons, rivers, and buttes. About 40 miles west of Glenns Ferry and reachable today via ID 78 from exit 112 or 114 off of I–84, Bruneau Dunes State Park boasts the largest single-structure sand dunes in North America, the tallest rising 470 feet from the ground. The state park offers excellent fishing, camping, and hiking. The Big Dune hike is an unforgettable experience, but it's best tackled early in the day before the sun gets too hot. Call (208) 366–7919 for more information.

After passing the sand dunes, the wagon trains rolled on toward the Bruneau River. Today's Bruneau Canyon is home to bighorn sheep and pronghorn antelope, and it may be viewed by hanging a left at the small town of Bruneau, then traveling 18 miles southeast on the signed road. The Bruneau, Owyhee, and Jarbidge Rivers, all in this area, feature scenic whitewater rafting through some of the most remote areas of America. Call the Idaho Outfitters and Guides Association at (208) 342–1438 for information on rafting, hunting, and packing trips in the region.

ID 78 west of Bruneau continues to parallel the South Alternate. C. J. Strike Reservoir harbors fine boating, water skiing, fishing, and camping. The Snake River Birds of Prey Natural Area stretches from Grandview to Murphy; see this book's Boise section for more information. Murphy, seat of vast Owyhee County, is possibly the nation's smallest county seat. It has just one general store, one parking meter (placed in front of the courthouse as a prank), and maybe fifty people. There are only about 8,500 people in all of Owyhee County, which at 7,643 square miles is bigger than New Jersey.

The worst tragedy on the Oregon Trail happened in this area, near Castle Creek about midway between Grandview and Murphy. During September 1860, the Elijah Otter (or Utter) party consisting of forty-four people, eight wagons, and more than fifty head of livestock, had a battle with more than one hundred Indians. During the fight, eleven emigrants and some twenty-five Indians were slain. Of the thirty-three emigrants who survived the battle, seventeen died or were killed soon after. This was the largest recorded confrontation between whites and Indians at any place along the trail.

Oregon-bound emigrants often stopped at what is now Givens Hot Springs to wash their clothes and camp. One traveler said the springs were "sufficiently hot to boil eggs." Milford and Martha Givens had seen the springs on their way west and later decided to return and settle in the area. Today, Givens Hot Springs remains in the family and is a popular place for soaking, swimming, and camping.

Toward the end of the Oregon Trail era, mining became big business throughout southwestern Idaho. Silver City was one of the territory's busiest boom towns. In fact, at one time the silver production from its more than 250 mines was surpassed only by the Comstock Lode in Nevada. Silver City remains home to just a few dozen people, but many buildings remain standing with only minimal commercial activity to detract from the near-ghost-town ambience. To visit Silver City, take the Silver City Road 5 miles southeast of Murphy. The 23-mile unimproved road takes about an hour to drive. It's rough going, but most vehicles can make it. ▲

costs an extra $3.00 for adults and $1.50 for children under twelve. Call Three Island Crossing State Park at (208) 366–2394 for more information.

Glenns Ferry has limited visitor services: a couple of cafes, one small motel, a bed and breakfast, and an RV park. Mountain Home, another 35 miles west on I–84, is the next major town, and it offers a wider range of lodging and restaurants. From Mountain Home, it's about a half-hour drive to Bonneville Point, which marked the end of the emigrants' trek through the great Idaho desert.

BONNEVILLE POINT

At **Bonneville Point,** the pioneers found a welcome sight that marked the end of their difficult trip across Idaho's dry and dusty plains. Captain B. L. E. Bonneville's party arrived here in May 1833 and, seeing the verdant valley below, called out "Les Bois, les bois, voyes les bois!" ("The trees, the trees, look at the trees!") For years afterward, this spot continued to delight weary emigrants. "When we arrived at the top we got a grand view of the Boise River Valley," Cecilia E. M. Adams wrote. "It is filled or covered with dry grass and a few trees immediately along the bank, the first we have seen in more than a month." Fremont wrote of his joy at seeing the Boise River, "a beautiful rapid stream, with clear mountain water" and said he was "delighted this afternoon to make a pleasant camp under fine old trees again."

Bonneville Point was about 1,450 miles from the trailhead in Independence, Missouri. The emigrants had now completed about three-quarters of their journey. This—combined with the valley view—was cause to celebrate, even though some rough terrain still lie ahead. "You doubtless will think I regret taking this long and tiresome trip," Elizabeth Wood wrote in August 1851, "But no, I have a great desire to see Oregon."

To reach Bonneville Point, take exit 64 off of I–84 and follow the signs north. There's an interpretive kiosk, and a long stretch of excellent wagon ruts may be seen nearby. From Bonneville Point, the wagon trains rolled into the valley, just south of what is now Lucky Peak Reservoir, a popular recreation

A kiosk marks the historic view of Bonneville Point, Idaho.

area. The Bureau of Land Management has placed interpretive plaques along a bluff overlooking the area where the trail entered Boise. To get there, take ID 21 off of I–84, then turn left on Lake Forest Road. Look toward the edge of the bluffs for the markers, which were to be accessible by late 2000.

In 1863, an Army cavalry post called **Fort Boise** was built to protect both the emigrants and gold miners who were flooding into the region. The city of Boise grew up around the fort, and the community became an important stop during later years of travel on the Oregon Trail. The fort was deactivated in 1913, but several buildings are still in use as a Veterans Administration medical center. An old cemetery with about 200 graves dating from the 1860s and 1870s is behind the medical center. A city park is nearby.

Another Fort Boise was built much earlier by the Hudson's Bay Company about 5 miles northwest of present-day Parma. Nothing remains of the original fort, but a replica may be seen in a Parma park.

FORT BOISE

The British Hudson's Bay Company built Fort Boise in 1834, partially in retaliation for the American presence Nathaniel Wyeth had erected at Fort Hall. Fort Boise was situated on the east bank of the Snake River about 8 miles north of the mouth of the Boise River. Although it was built as a fur trading

A marker denotes the original site of Fort Boise near Parma, Idaho.

BOISE ATTRACTIONS

Survey after recent survey has dubbed Idaho's capital city, Boise, as one of the nation's most desirable places to live. The Boise metro area, by far Idaho's largest, was the fourth-fastest-growing region in the United States during the 1990s, and the rapid recent growth has meant big increases in traffic, real estate prices, and espresso carts. Yet despite the urbanization, Boise—with a metropolitan-area population of about 400,000—retains a lot of small-town charm and friendliness. Add a university and recreational opportunities galore, and it's easy to understand why Boise is booming.

For the visitor, many top attractions are found in a surprisingly compact area between the state capitol and Boise State University. Julia Davis Park includes a zoo, the Boise Art Museum, and the Idaho Historical Museum, with its fascinating displays on the Oregon Trail and other aspects of Idaho's past. The Boise Tour Train also departs from Julia Davis Park, offering citywide views from an 1890s-style locomotive. The Discovery Center of Idaho, in the same vicinity, features hands-on educational exhibits for children and adults.

About 20 miles long, the Boise River Greenbelt welcomes cyclists, joggers, power walkers, in-line skaters, and just-plain strollers, while tubers often float the river. (Rafts and inner tubes can be rented at Barber Park on the city's east side, while bike and skate rentals are available at Wheels-R-Fun at Thirteenth Street and Shoreline Drive near downtown.) Boise's summer is full of special events. The Boise River Festival, held late each June, features a nighttime river parade with lighted floats. The Western Idaho Fair in nearby Garden City runs the end of each August with big-name entertainment and carnival rides. Once college football season starts, the BSU Broncos play in what may be the world's only stadium with blue artificial turf.

Boise's arts and entertainment scene has ballooned with its growing population. Big-name pop and country music concerts usually take place at the Idaho Center in nearby Nampa, while lots of nightclubs offer local live music. The Idaho Shakespeare Festival performs all summer long in an open-air theater off Warm Springs Road. Go to The Flicks at Sixth and Myrtle for the latest in international and independent films and an adjacent cafe. Les Bois Park features parimutuel horse racing each May through August.

During the 1860s, more gold was mined from the mountains northeast of Boise than from all of Alaska. Idaho City, 22 miles from Boise via ID 21, was once the largest city in the Northwest and a wild mining town to boot. Legend has it that only 28 of the 200 people buried in the town's Boot Hill died a natural death. Idaho City today is heavily tourist oriented, with a number of places to eat and stay overnight. The neighboring Boise National Forest is full of great mountain vistas and campgrounds.

For more information on Boise-area attractions, contact the Boise Convention and Visitors Bureau at (800) 635–5240 or see www.boise.org on the Internet. ♠

post, Fort Boise later switched its emphasis to serving the emigrants, and it was a welcome outpost after 300 miles of dry travel from Fort Hall.

Fort Boise was managed for its first decade by Francois Payette, a successful French-Canadian fur trapper. Payette was well liked by the emigrants; one visitor described him as "exceedingly polite, courteous, and hospitable." An 1845 report on the post spoke of "two acres under cultivation . . . 1,991 sheep, 73 pigs, 17 horses, and 27 meat cattle." But when the emigrants started to arrive, they would sometimes completely deplete the fort's stores of flour, tea, coffee, and other staples.

Near Fort Boise, one pioneer band set off on an especially ill-conceived trail cutoff. Stephen H. L. Meek, leading an 1845 emigrant party headed by Captain Elijah White, convinced many of its members to join him in trying a new way to the Willamette—a route that would avoid the Blue Mountains but which had never been traveled by wagons before. Historians say even Meek probably didn't know the way, but between 150 and 200 wagons followed him anyway, possibly thinking that Meek was as smart as his brother, Joe, one of the West's best guides.

It was a big mistake. The route along the Malheur River offered little grass for the livestock, and it was murder on the animals' feet. The emigrants sometimes went days without water. Fever struck the party and some children died. To top it all off, the travelers were lost, and Meek finally had to go on ahead to find a rescue party. Writing in *The Oregon Trail Revisited*, Gregory Franzwa noted that was probably a good idea on Meek's part— "the thoroughly disillusioned emigrants would have blown his brains out had he stayed in camp another day."

Meek found a knowledgeable mountain man named Black Harris at the Columbia River, and Harris agreed to lead the rescue. He found the starving pioneers near the mouth of Tygh Creek and led them down the Deschutes River to the Columbia and to safety. Of nearly 500 who started out with Meek, more than 75 people had died.

In 1853, flooding extensively damaged Fort Boise, and historians indicate that attempts to rebuild—if any—were probably futile due to mounting tensions with the Indians. Troubles in the area culminated with the 1854 Ward Massacre, in which eighteen emigrants (out of a party of twenty) died. Hudson's Bay Company abandoned Fort Boise in 1855. Today, the land serves as a state wildlife management area. No signs of the fort remain, but its approximate location is marked by a striking, British-influenced monument that features a stately lion's head atop a pedestal.

The people of Parma have built a Fort Boise replica in their town, 5 miles southeast of the original fort site. It is open only from 1:00 to 3:00 P.M. Friday, Saturday, and Sunday during June, July, and August, but you can call (208) 722–7608 or (208) 722–5945 for an appointment to see it at other times.

Parma remembers its role in trail history late each May with the Old Fort Boise Days celebration.

The replica was built to the old fort's exact dimensions, although cosmetic changes were made to accommodate modern building codes. In addition to the emigrant story, the Fort Boise replica has artifacts and displays from later years in which southwest Idaho was permanently settled. One room features a desk built in 1891 by a boy whose family was traveling to Oregon when their money ran out and they decided to stay. Another exhibit tells how Parma is the only Idaho town to have produced two of the state's governors: Clarence Baldridge, a Republican, and Ben Ross, a Democrat. Visitors may also view a video on Fort Boise history.

A statue and historical marker on the replica lawn tell the story of Marie Dorian, an Iowa Indian who came to the area with Wilson Price Hunt's party of Astorians in 1811. (Dorian had, in fact, excused herself briefly on that trip to give birth to a boy somewhere near present-day North Powder, Oregon.) Three years later, Marie and her two children were the sole survivors of a mid-January battle with Bannock Indians at a nearby fur trading post. They set out with two horses on a 200-mile retreat through deep snow and were finally rescued by a Columbia River band of Walla Walla Indians in April.

The park adjacent to the fort replica includes a small campground with showers and a dump station, as well as shady picnic spots and a playground. To get to Parma, leave I-84 at exit 26, drive south over the interstate, and follow US 20/26 to Parma, 13 miles northwest. To see the original fort site, continue north on US 20/26, watching for the Sportsman's Access sign just before mile-post 50. From there, it's 3.5 miles back to the Hudson's Bay Company marker.

Near old Fort Boise, the emigrants crossed the Snake River and entered what is now Oregon. Modern travelers can continue northwest via I-84 or US 20/26, which enters Oregon near Nyssa and Keeney Pass.

Lodgings, campgrounds, and restaurants listed below are a representative sampling of what is available. Listing in these pages does not imply endorsement, nor is this a complete listing of all reputable businesses. For more complete listings, contact the visitor information bureau or chamber of commerce in each town. Room rates were accurate as of summer 2000, but are subject to change.

LODGING

MONTPELIER, IDAHO

Best Western Clover Creek Inn, (208) 847–1782, 243 North Fourth Street, $46–$89.

Budget Motel, (208) 847–1273, 240 North Fourth Street, $20–$35.

Fisher Inn, (208) 847–1772, 401 Boise Street, $30–$50.

Park Motel, (208) 847–1911, 745 Washington, $35–$50.

Soda Springs, Idaho

Caribou Lodge & Motel, (208) 547–3377, 110 West Second South, $25–$50.
J-R Inn, (208) 547–3366, 179 West Second South, $32–$44.
Lakeview Motel, (208) 547–4351, 341 West Second South, $25–$50.
Trail Motel, (208) 547–0240, 213 East 200 South, $22–$35.

Lava Hot Springs, Idaho

Home Hotel and Motel, (208) 776–5507, 305 Emerson, $30–$90.
Lava Spa Motel, (208) 776–5589, 359 East Main, $45–$110.
Lava Hot Springs Inn, (208) 776–5830, 94 East Portneuf Avenue, $60–$185.
Riverside Inn & Hot Springs, (208) 776–5504, 255 Portneuf Avenue, $60–$110.
Royal Hotel Bed & Breakfast, (208) 776–5216, 11 East Main, $77–$99.

Pocatello, Idaho

Best Western Cotton Tree Inn, (208) 237–7650, 1415 Bench Road, $66–$96.
Cavanaugh's Pocatello Hotel, (208) 233–2200, 1555 Pocatello Creek Road, $62–$89.
Days Inn, (208) 237–0020, 133 West Burnside Avenue (Chubbuck), $40–$50.
Motel 6, (208) 237–7880, 291 West Burnside Avenue (Chubbuck), $38–$46.
Pine Ridge Inn, (208) 237–3100, 4333 Yellowstone, $35–$60.
Thunderbird Motel, (208) 232–6330, 1415 South Fifth Avenue, $32–$45.

American Falls, Idaho

Falls Motel, (208) 226–9658, 411 Lincoln. $30–$60.
Hillview Motel, (208) 226–5151, I–86 exit 40, $34–$48.

Rupert, Idaho

Flamingo Lodge Motel, (208) 436–4321, 406 East Eighth Street, $30–$50.

Burley, Idaho

Best Western Burley Inn, (208) 678–3501, 800 North Overland Avenue, $60–$70.
Budget Motel, (208) 678–2200, 900 North Overland Avenue, $39–$69.
Parish Motel, (208) 678–5505, 721 East Main, $25–$50.

Twin Falls, Idaho

Amber Inn Motel, (208) 825–5200, I–84 exit 182 (Eden), $30–$45.
AmeriTel Inn, (208) 736–8000, 1377 Blue Lakes Boulevard North, $85–$125.
Best Western Cavanaugh's Canyon Springs Hotel, (208) 734–5000, 1357 Blue Lakes Boulevard North, $90–$100.
Comfort Inn, (208) 734–7494, 1893 Canyon Springs Road, $67–$109.
Monterey Motor Inn, (208) 733–5151, 433 Addison Avenue West, $30–$65.
Super 8 Motel, (800) 843–1991, 1261 Blue Lakes Boulevard North, $50–$60.

BUHL, IDAHO

Oregon Trail Motel, (208) 543–8814, 510 South Broadway (US 30), $28–$42.

Siesta Motel, (208) 543–6427, 629 South Broadway, $30–$40.

HAGERMAN, IDAHO

Hagerman Valley Inn, (208) 837–6196, State and Hagerman Streets, $37–$50.

Rock Lodge Resort, (208) 837–4822, 17940 US 30, $45–$75.

BLISS, IDAHO

Amber Inn, (208) 352–4441, I–84 exit 141, $29–$46.

GLENNS FERRY, IDAHO

Great Basin Bed and Breakfast, (208) 366–7124, $55 and up.

Redford Motel, (208) 366–2421, I–84 exit 120, $27–$60.

MOUNTAIN HOME, IDAHO

Best Western Foothills Motor Inn, (208) 587–8477, 1080 US 20, $50–$125.

Motel Thunderbird, (208) 587–7927, 910 Sunset Strip (US 30), $28–$65.

Sleep Inn, (208) 587–9743, 1180 US 20, $45–$80.

Towne Center Motel, (208) 587–3373, 410 North Second East, $24–$40.

BOISE, IDAHO

Best Western Safari Motor Inn, (208) 344–6556, 1070 Grove Street, $50–$62.

Boise Comfort Inn, (208) 336–0077, 2526 Airport Way, $50–$70.

The Grove Hotel, (208) 333–8000, 254 South Capitol Boulevard, $120–$160.

Holiday Inn Boise Airport, (208) 344–8365, 3300 Vista Avenue, $65–$95.

Idaho Heritage Inn Bed & Breakfast, (208) 342–8066, 109 West Idaho, $60–$105.

Rodeway Inn, (208) 376–2700, 1115 North Curtis Road, $65–$100.

Shilo Inn Boise Riverside, (208) 344–3521, 3031 Main Street, $65–$115.

MERIDIAN, IDAHO

Knotty Pine Motel, (208) 888–2727, 1423 East First Street, $39–$45.

NAMPA, IDAHO

Desert Inn, (208) 467–1161, 115 Ninth Avenue South, $34–$48.

Nampa Super 8 Motel, (208) 467–2888, 624 Nampa Boulevard, $42–$72.

Shilo Inn Nampa Suites, (208) 465–3250, 1401 Shilo Drive, $59–$109.

Starlite Motel, (208) 466–9244, 320 Eleventh Avenue North, $30–$43.

CALDWELL, IDAHO

Best Inn & Suites, (208) 454–2222, 901 Specht Avenue, $49–$120.

Holiday Motel, (208) 453–1056, 512 Frontage Road, $27.

Sundowner Motel, (208) 459–1585, 1002 Arthur, $32–$42.

Wild Rose Manor Bed & Breakfast, (208) 454–3331, 5800 Oasis Road, $120.

PARMA, IDAHO
Court Motel, (208) 722–5579, 712 Grove Street, $43.

PAYETTE, IDAHO
Elm Hollow Bed & Breakfast, (208) 452–6491, 4900 US 95, $45–$50.

CAMPING

MONTPELIER, IDAHO
Bear Lake State Park, (208) 945–2790, 20 miles south on US 89; follow signs.
Montpelier KOA, (208) 847–0863, 2 miles east on US 89.

SODA SPRINGS, IDAHO
Dike Lake, (208) 529–1020, 11 miles north on ID 34. Primitive sites.

LAVA HOT SPRINGS, IDAHO
Cottonwood Family Campground, (208) 776–5295, US 30.
Lava Mobile Estates RV Park, (208) 776–5345, 10255 East Old Oregon Trail Road.
Monty's Lava Ranch Inn RV Camping, (208) 776–9917, 9611 US 30.

POCATELLO, IDAHO
Cowboy RV Park, (208) 232–4587, 845 Barton Road.
Pocatello KOA, (208) 233–6851, 9815 W. Pocatello Creek Road.

AMERICAN FALLS, IDAHO
Indian Springs Swimming and RV, (208) 226–2174, 3 miles west on ID 37.
Massacre Rocks State Park, (208) 548–2672, 10 miles west on I–86.

BURLEY, IDAHO
4 Families RV Park, (208) 678–2200, 900 North Overland.
Snake River RV Park, (208) 654–2133, I–84 exit 216 (Declo).
Travel Stop 216, (208) 654–2133, I–84 exit 216 (Declo).

HAZELTON, IDAHO
Greenwood RV Park, (208) 829–5735, I–84 exit 194.

TWIN FALLS, IDAHO
Andersons Camp and RV Park, (208) 825–9800, I–84 exit 182 (Eden)
Oregon Trail Campground & Family Fun Center, (208) 733–0853, 2733 Kimberly Road.
Twin Falls–Jerome KOA, (208) 324–4169, I–84 exit 173.

Several Forest Service campgrounds are located in the Sawtooth National Forest south of Twin Falls. Call (208) 737–3200 for information.

HAGERMAN, IDAHO

Banbury Hot Springs, (208) 543–4098, between Buhl and Hagerman on US 30.
Miracle Hot Springs, (208) 543–6002, between Buhl and Hagerman on US 30.
Rock Lodge Resort, (208) 837–4822, 1 mile north on US 30.
Sligar's 1000 Springs Resort, (208) 837–4987, between Buhl and Hagerman on US 30.
Sportsman's River Resort, (208) 837–6202, between Buhl and Hagerman on US 30.

GLENNS FERRY, IDAHO

Three Island Crossing State Park, (208) 366–2394, I–84 exit 120; follow signs.
Trails West RV Park, (208) 366–2002, 510 North Bannock.

MOUNTAIN HOME, IDAHO

Bruneau Dunes State Park, (208) 366–7919, 18 miles south on ID 51; 2 miles east on ID 78.
Mountain Home KOA, (208) 587–5111, 220 East Tenth North.

BOISE, IDAHO

Americana RV Park, (208) 344–5733, 3600 Americana Terrace.
Fiesta RV Park, (208) 375–8207, 11101 Fairview Avenue.
On the River RV Park, (208) 375–7432, 6000 North Glenwood.
Several Forest Service campgrounds are located in the Boise National Forest near Boise. Call (208) 364–4100 for information.

MERIDIAN, IDAHO

The Playground Sports & RV Park, (208) 887–1022, 1780 East Overland Road.

MELBA, IDAHO

Givens Hot Springs, (208) 495–2437, 11 miles southeast of Marsing on ID 78.

CALDWELL, IDAHO

Caldwell Campground & RV Park, (208) 454–0279, I–84 exit 26.

PARMA, IDAHO

Old Fort Boise Park, (208) 722–5138, city park along US 20/26.

FRUITLAND, IDAHO

Neat Retreat, (208) 452–4324, 2701 Alder.

PAYETTE, IDAHO

Lazy River RV Park, (208) 642–9667, 4 miles north on US 95.

RESTAURANTS

MONTPELIER, IDAHO

Butch Cassidy's Restaurant & Saloon, (208) 847–3501, 230 North Fourth Street. Steaks, seafood, and prime rib.

Ranch Hand Cafe, (208) 847–1180, 2 miles north on US 30. Hearty meals at rustic truck stop.

SODA SPRINGS, IDAHO

Betty's Cafe, (208) 547–4802, west of town on US 30.

Ender's Cafe & Hotel, (208) 547–4980, 76 South Main. Salad bar, daily specials.

Stockman's Bar & Tee Bone Grill, (208) 547–9955, 96 South Main.

LAVA HOT SPRINGS, IDAHO

Royal Hotel, (208) 776–5216, 11 East Main. Specialty is pizza.

Ye Olde Chuckwagon Restaurant, (208) 776–5626, 211 East Main. Seafood, homemade pies.

POCATELLO, IDAHO

Buddy's, (208) 233–1172, 626 East Lewis. Idaho State University favorite serves pizza, pasta.

Continental Bistro, (208) 233–4433, 140 South Main Street. Fine dining with patio seating.

Cowboy Cafe, (208) 232–9404, 3256 US 30. Hearty food, open twenty-four hours weekends.

Frontier Pies, (208) 237–5900, 1205 Yellowstone Avenue. Popular regional chain restaurant.

Grecian Key, (208) 235–3922, 314 North Main. Greek food prepared tableside.

Mama Inez, (208) 234–7674, 390 Yellowstone Avenue. Authentic Tex-Mex food.

Portneuf River Grille, (208) 478–8418, 230 West Bonneville. Upscale dining.

Remo's, (208) 233–1710, 160 West Cedar. Fresh pasta and seafood, steaks, extensive wine list, outdoor dining in summer.

AMERICAN FALLS, IDAHO

Melina's Mexican Food, (208) 226–5919, 616 Fort Hall Avenue.

Melody Lanes Bowl Cafe, (208) 226–2815, 152 Harrison. Local favorite for lunch.

RUPERT, IDAHO

The Wayside, (208) 436–4800, ID 24 and I–84.

BURLEY, IDAHO

Cancun Mexican Restaurant, (208) 678–8695, 262 Overland Avenue.

China First Restaurant, (208) 678–7937, 1242 Overland. Chinese, American, and Vietnamese food.

Price's Cafe, (208) 678–5149, 2444 Overland Avenue. Home cooking, smorgasbord.

HEYBURN, IDAHO

Connor's Cafe, (208) 678–9367, I–84 exit 208. Fresh baked goods. Open twenty-four hours.

HANSEN, IDAHO

Crossroads Café, (208) 423–9671, US 30.

South Hills Saloon & Restaurant, (208) 423–9050, US 30.

TWIN FALLS, IDAHO

The Buffalo Cafe, (208) 734–0271, 218 Fourth Avenue West. Locally popular for breakfast and lunch.

Creekside Steakhouse, (208) 733–1511, 233 Fifth Avenue South.

Depot Grill, (208) 733–0710, 545 Shoshone Street South. Home cooking and smorgasbords.

La Casita, (208) 734–7974, 111 South Park Avenue. Mexican food, fast service.

Peking Restaurant, (208) 733–4813, 824 Blue Lakes Boulevard North. Variety of Chinese specialties.

Rock Creek, (208) 734–4154, 200 Addison Avenue West. Steaks, seafood, salad bar.

Uptown Bistro, (208) 733–0900, 117 Main Avenue East. Casual fine dining, sidewalk seating.

Vimarn Thai Cuisine, (208) 735–8333, 837 Poleline Road.

BUHL, IDAHO

Fay's Place, (208) 543–6272, 1000 Burley Avenue. American and Mexican food.

Linda's Family Dining, (208) 543–2060, 631 Broadway Avenue South. Home cooking and daily specials.

HAGERMAN, IDAHO

Little Bitt Cafe, (208) 837–6359, 160 South State. Home cooking.

Snake River Grill, (208) 837–6227, State and Hagerman. Wide menu.

BLISS, IDAHO

Oxbow Cafe, (208) 352–4250, US 30.

GLENNS FERRY, IDAHO

Carmela Vineyards Restaurant, (208) 366–2539, 795 West Madison. Creative food, wide menu.

Hanson's Cafe, (208) 366–9983, 201 East First Avenue. Home cooking.

MOUNTAIN HOME, IDAHO

Carlos' Mexican Restaurant, (208) 587–2966, 1525 American Legion Boulevard. Casual family dining.

Charlie's Top Hat Barbecue, (208) 587–9223, 145 North Second East.

Rattlesnake Station, (208) 587–3651, 135 Bitterbrush. Steakhouse and more.

Stoney's Desert Inn, (208) 587–9931, 2 miles east of I–84 at exit 90. Favorite with locals and truckers.

BOISE, IDAHO

Brick Oven Beanery, (208) 342–3456, Eighth and Main. Home cooking at lunch and dinner.

Cottonwood Grille, (208) 333–9800, 913 West River Street. Upscale dining near Greenbelt.

Desert Sage, (208) 333–8400, 750 West Idaho Street. Creative cuisine in upscale atmosphere.

Golden Star, (208) 336–0191, 1142 North Orchard. Cantonese food at lunch and dinner.

Grove Street Place, (208) 426–9990, 612 Grove Street. Three creative restaurants in one.

Joe's All-American Grill, (208) 344–4146, 100 South Sixth Street. Ribs and burgers.

Louie's, (208) 344–5200, 620 West Boise. An Idaho favorite, specializing in pizza and Italian food.

Noodles, (208) 342–9300, 800 West Idaho Street. Pizza, pasta, more.

Onati-The Basque Restaurant, (208) 343–6464, 3544 Chinden Boulevard. Basque specialties served family-style.

NAMPA, IDAHO

El Charro, (208) 467–5804, 1701 First Street. Inexpensive traditional Mexican food.

House of Kim, (208) 466–3237, 1226 First Street. Korean and Szechwan cuisine.

Little Kitchen, (208) 467–9677, 1224 First Street South. Home cooking.

Say You Say Me, (208) 466–2728, 820 Nampa-Caldwell Boulevard. Big omelettes and sandwiches. Breakfast and lunch only.

CALDWELL, IDAHO

Cattleman's Cafe, (208) 454–1785, 1900 East Chicago. Here's the beef.

Mancino's Pizza, (208) 459–7556, 2404 East Cleveland Boulevard.

PARMA, IDAHO

Fort Boise Cafe, (208) 722–7026, 102 Third Street.

PAYETTE, IDAHO

Keystone Pizza, (208) 642–9333, 17 South Eighth.

Overlook at Keeney Pass near Vale, Oregon.

TRAIL'S END: OREGON

"Friday, Oct. 27: Arrived at Oregon City at the falls of the Willamette. Saturday, Oct. 28: Went to work."

—Emigrant James Nesmith, 1843

THE MALHEUR VALLEY

*W*hen they crossed into what is now Oregon, the emigrants had already traveled 1,510 miles and had more than 400 miles—or about another month on the road—left to go. Ahead of them lay the most varied terrain of their trip: more stark desert, lofty mountains, cool forests, and raging rivers. Modern-day Oregon presents the same shifting visual panorama, but while the pioneers viewed it as one last frustrating stretch to their final destination, today's travelers can sit back, relax, and enjoy the ride across this scenic state.

The first notable trail landmark inside Oregon is at **Keeney Pass,** sometimes known as Lytle Pass. Here, a half-mile of deeply worn ruts may be seen through the pass. To get there, take OR 201 south from Nyssa to Enterprise Avenue. Turn west (right) and continue to Lytle Boulevard. Drive north toward Vale and watch for the Bureau of Land Management sign marking Keeney Pass Historic Site. A trail from the parking lot leads to an overlook from which you can see a full day's travel, from the Snake River crossing near Fort Boise to the Malheur River near Vale.

It's about 6 miles from Keeney Pass to Vale. Nearing town, watch for the sign pointing the way to the pioneer grave of John D. Henderson, who is buried below the gravel road that parallels Lytle Boulevard to its west. The monument marking his grave says that he died of thirst in 1852, unaware he was within sight of the river. But local historians contend that is not true, and that he actually died of black measles. In any case, a blacksmith from Henderson's party chiseled his name on a rock that still stands below the more recently erected monument.

Vale is an agricultural town of about 1,500 people who strongly recognize their Oregon Trail roots. About twenty murals depict the area's history, many focusing on the Oregon Trail. Some of the best include "The New Arrivals"

John D. Henderson grave near Vale, Oregon. Note original 1852 grave marker below monument.

outside the Malheur Drug Store, "Journaling" at the Vale Library, and "Hot Springs" at the Red Garter Ice Cream Saloon. Wilcox Horse & Buggy offers narrated, hour-long horse-drawn tours of the murals for $10 per person. The tours begin at 8:00 P.M. every Friday in June, July, and August and at 7:00 P.M. in September. They leave from the Rhinehart Stone Museum at 255 Main Street South, one of the oldest buildings in eastern Oregon. Reservations are requested for groups of six or more; call (888) TRY–VALE. If you're up for more trail-related activities, Wilcox Horse & Buggy also runs Vale's Historical Tours, which can help set up old-time photo sessions, bed-and-breakfast lodging, and chuck wagon dinners for large groups. Finally, the Oregon Trail Travelers, a Washington-based re-enactors group, visits Vale the second Saturday of September each year for the Circle Your Wagons event in Wadleigh Park. The public is welcome to view the re-enactors' living-history camp.

The Malheur River runs south of Vale, and its name means "unlucky" in French. Indeed, this is where the travelers following Stephen Meek left on their ill-fated trek across uncharted territory to avoid the Blue Mountains. There's no easy road paralleling the main trail toward Farewell Bend, so it's best to backtrack 16 miles on US 20/26 to Ontario and I–84. En route, watch for the scenic vista roadside pullout affording a good view of Malheur Butte, a volcanic formation visible even from the interstate.

In Ontario, consider a stop at the Four Rivers Cultural Center and Museum at 676 Southwest Fifth Avenue. This very well done interpretive center tells of all the major population groups who settled this "Treasure Valley": Paiute Indians, Basques, Mexicans, and Japanese-Americans. The story of the latter is especially fascinating: When Japanese-Americans living on the West Coast were sent to internment camps during World War II, the then-mayor of Ontario, Elmo Smith, put out the word that the "Nisei" were welcome to settle and work in his area instead. The center is open from 10:00 A.M. to 6:00 P.M. mountain time Monday through Saturday and from noon to 6:00 P.M. Sunday April through November. The rest of the year, it's open from 10:00 A.M. to 5:00 P.M. Monday through Saturday and from noon to 4:00 P.M. Sunday. Admission is $4.00 for those ages fifteen to sixty-four and $3.00 for seniors sixty-five and older and children ages six to fourteen.

Ontario is a good place to get more information for the rest of your trek through Oregon. The Four Rivers Cultural Center shares its quarters with the local chamber of commerce; there's also an Oregon welcome center at the Ontario rest area on I–84, along with the first of many excellent trail interpretive kiosks along the interstate in Oregon. Either way, pick up a copy of the excellent brochure *The Oregon Trail: Transforming the West,* which lists fifty major and minor trail access points and interpretive sites throughout Oregon. A $2.50 booklet, *The Oregon Trail Then & Now,* gives in-depth itineraries for tracing the trail all across the state, too. Most points are covered in this book, but the state book goes into more specifics. Be aware that Vale and Ontario are on mountain time, while the Pacific time zone starts about 20 miles west, just before Farewell Bend.

FAREWELL BEND

After traveling about 25 dry, dusty miles north from the Malheur River near present-day Vale, the emigrants once again arrived at the Snake River. This would be their last view of the river they had followed for more than 330 miles, so the area became known as **Farewell Bend,** and it was an important landmark for the emigrants. Today, the site is occupied by a popular Oregon state park.

Farewell Bend is at exit 353 off of I–84, and travelers get a great view of it from the highway. Interpretation at the park itself is somewhat limited, but there are good trail ruts nearby and the park does have good boating, fishing, and camping opportunities (including two covered "camper wagons," which sleep up to four people for $27; reserve by calling (800) 452–5687). It's a magnificent spot to sleep under the stars, too, since light pollution is nearly non-

Farewell Bend is where emigrants left the Snake River to begin their trek across Oregon.

HELLS CANYON

At Hells Canyon, the Snake River has carved the deepest gorge in North America—7,993 feet. The great depth comes courtesy of the river's neighbor to the east: Idaho's Seven Devils Mountain Range. The Hells Canyon National Recreation Area straddles the canyon and includes parts of the Wallowa Whitman National Forest in Oregon and the Nez Perce and Payette National Forests of Idaho.

Three power dams—Brownlee, Oxbow, and Hells Canyon—and their reservoirs lead downriver to the canyon. When Congress created the recreation area in 1975, it saved some of the best whitewater rapids in the United States by protecting 67 miles of the Snake River. Congress also set aside 215,000 acres as the Hells Canyon Wilderness, with an outstanding network of trails open only to hikers and horseback riders.

Abundant in fish, wildlife, and geologic splendor, Hells Canyon is a sight to see.

Sturgeon up to 12 feet long swim the depths of the Snake River. Elk, mule deer, bighorn sheep, cougar, bobcat, bear, and smaller mammals patrol the mountainsides. Many outfitters offer float, jet boat, or whitewater trips through the canyon. For a list, contact the Hells Canyon National Recreation Area headquarters in Clarkston, Washington, at (509) 758–0616. Private rafters and jet-boaters may also ply the area, but a Forest Service permit is required before launching. (The number for private boat trip reservations is (509–758–1957.)

Hells Canyon can be accessed via I–84 exit 356 between Ontario and Huntington (which feeds into US 95 at Weiser, then ID 71 at Cambridge); via OR 86 (which takes off east from I–84 exit 302 at Baker City); or by way of OR 82 from La Grande to Joseph. From Joseph, it is possible to go to Hat Point, a 6,982-foot canyon overlook on Forest Service Road 4240 via Imnaha. This steep, narrow, and rough road is not recommended for trailers or large RVs. ▲

existent. Look for interpretive programs almost every evening May through September in the A Loop amphitheater.

"We descended to the Snake River—here a fine-looking stream with a large body of water and a fine current; although we hear the roar and see below us the commencement of rapids where it enters among the hills," John Fremont wrote on his visit in 1843. "It forms here a deep bay, with a low sand island in the midst; and its course among the mountains is agreeably exchanged for black volcanic rock." The rapids noted by Fremont have been swallowed up by the Hells Canyon Dam downriver.

Just across from Farewell Bend is a point called Olds Ferry, established at the time of the Idaho gold rush to link the Oregon and Idaho sides of the Snake River above Hells Canyon. Late Oregon Trail emigrants may have used the ferry after taking an extended detour on Goodale's Cutoff (which ended for most emigrants near Bonneville Point). The nearby sand dunes and bad-lands are somewhat reminiscent of those near Scottsbluff, Nebraska.

To view the Oregon Trail ruts, head north from Farewell Bend State Park toward the town of Huntington on US 30. The remnants appear intermittently on the left side of the road, along with a small iron cross that marks the site where several emigrants were possibly killed by Indians in 1860. The traveler can return to I–84 via exit 345 at Huntington, an old railroad town. Most Huntington residents now work in the nearby lime quarry and cement plant.

Farewell Bend has one of only a few state park campgrounds in Oregon open year-round. For more information on the park, call (541) 869–2365. From Huntington, it's a 40-mile drive to Baker City, home of the National Historic Oregon Trail Interpretive Center at Flagstaff Hill.

FLAGSTAFF HILL

After leaving Farewell Bend, the emigrants had to travel through **Burnt River Canyon,** which proved a significant obstacle. It often took wagon trains five or six days just to negotiate the climb out of the canyon. Although it wasn't as steep as some other areas along the trail, the twisting canyon crossed several ravines. Food was scarce for both humans and livestock, which further depleted everyone's strength. Emigrant James Nesmith called the canyon "the roughest country I ever saw."

Today, I–84 takes the same narrow path. The Weatherby rest area just past Farewell Bend offers interpretation of the area, along with a small stone shelter that bears a plaque commemorating RATTLESNAKE SPRINGS—OLD OREGON TRAIL 1843–1857.

About 6 miles northwest of present-day Durkee, the trail leaves what is now the interstate and heads for the area known as Virtue Flat. To rejoin the trail, modern travelers must continue on I–84 to Baker City and take exit 302 to OR 86. From here, head 5 miles east to the Bureau of Land Management's National Oregon Trail Interpretive Center at **Flagstaff Hill.** If there's one "must-see" interpretive center along the Oregon Trail, this is it. There's something for everybody, from senior citizens who may remember their own grandparents' tales of trail travel, to youngsters who are asked to help "pack the wagon" for the trip west.

Upon entering the center, continue straight ahead. On both sides of a 100-foot walkway, dioramas offer a glimpse of what life was like on the Oregon Trail. Hired hands set the wagons a-rolling. A woman weeps at her baby's grave. Another young child teases a nanny goat and muses aloud "I wonder if I'll go to school in Oregon." Indians on a bluff warily survey the swelling emigration as it passes beneath them.

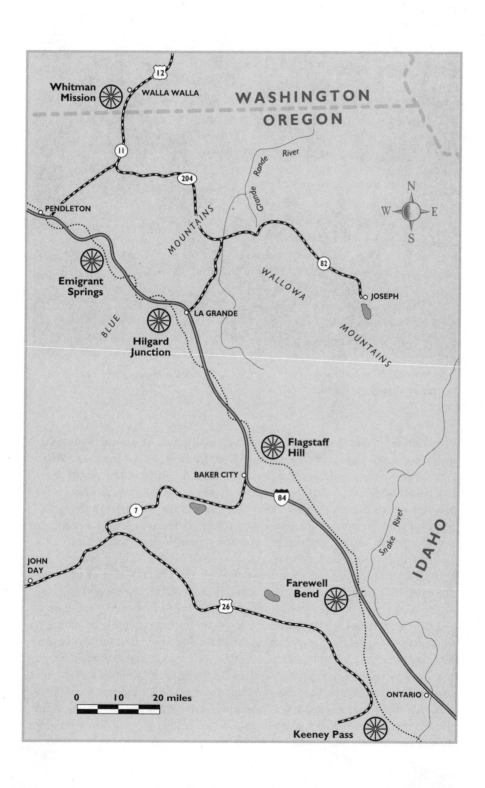

The National Historic Oregon Trail Interpretive Center has many exhibits that give insight into emigrant life along the trail.

From large windows at the end of this display, visitors have a 15-mile view of the trail as it descended Flagstaff Hill and rolled toward the Blue Mountains, now plainly visible in the distance to the right. (The mountainous region straight ahead is Elkhorn Ridge, considered part of the Blues.) The trail crossed this scene from the left through a draw and on over the alkali flat to the right.

From this viewpoint, the displays continue, each examining new aspects of the emigration as the wagons roll ever westward. Videos and exhibits show how the trains organized, how women and children fared along the way, how the travelers accomplished their most difficult river crossings, and what they did when they finally reached their destination. Beautiful photos and paintings of sites along the trail are interspersed with quotations from emigrant diaries.

Other activities at the interpretive center include a network of hiking trails that lead down to the wagon ruts. The total distance is about 2 miles, depending on which route is taken, and hikers are encouraged to walk early in the day, if possible, when it's still fairly cool. (Summer daytime temperatures in eastern Oregon frequently surpass 90° or even 100°F.) Pioneer encampment and lode mine living-history sites operate outside on a seasonal basis during the summer, and other special presentations are held on occasion in the indoor theater and outdoor amphitheater.

The interpretive center is open daily from 9:00 A.M. to 6:00 P.M. April through October and from 9:00 A.M. to 4:00 P.M. November through March except Christmas and New Year's Day. Admission is $5.00 for adults and $3.50 for seniors and kids ages six to seventeen. Special annual events include "A Taste of the Trail" living-history festival the last Saturday in July and a holiday open house the first Friday in December. For more information, call the center at (541) 523–1843.

One former trail landmark that is now long gone was the Lone Pine, which stood about 5 miles north of present-day Baker City on a branch of the Powder River. It was indeed the only tree for miles, and the earliest emigrant parties camped near it—until someone cut it down for firewood. Fremont, arriving in 1843, wrote that "on arriving at the river, we found a fine tall pine stretched on the ground, which had been felled by some inconsiderate emigrant ax. It had been a beacon on the road for many years past." In *The Oregon Trail Revisited*, Gregory Franzwa reported that the mayor of Baker City planted another tree at the site in 1945, but it did not survive.

Baker City got its start when gold was discovered in 1861 by miners who were seeking the mythical Blue Bucket mine. The Armstrong nugget, weighing eighty ounces, was unearthed nearby and is now displayed at the U.S. National Bank. The gold rush was responsible for much of the ornate architecture in Baker City, which boasts more than 135 buildings on the National Register of Historic Places. Maps and brochures for self-guided walking or driving tours are available from the Baker County Visitor and Convention Bureau at 490 Campbell Street. (Call 800–523-1235 or see the Web site at www.bakercity.com for information in advance.) You can stay at one of the most notable buildings: the Geiser Grand Hotel, built in 1889 and restored in the 1990s to its former glory. Even if you don't sleep here, stop in for a look and maybe a meal in the dining room or saloon.

The Oregon Trail Regional Museum at Campbell and Grove Streets has several notable exhibits, but none quite as fascinating as its collection of rocks, minerals, and semi-precious stones including many unusual "picture" cabochons. Also have a look at the Oregon Trail map and emigrant's guide painted on the front of York's General Store at 1549 Campbell Street. The Sumpter Valley Railroad, 22 miles west of Baker City on OR 7, travels through the historic gold mining district and a wildlife sanctuary begun after dredging left the land ill-suited for farming. The powder-rich Anthony Lakes region 35 miles northwest of Baker City is a favorite with local snow skiers.

THE BLUE MOUNTAINS

La Grande, a 40-mile drive from Baker City, is another charming eastern Oregon town. Set in the spacious Grande Ronde Valley (locally called "the Valley

THE WALLOWA MOUNTAINS

With their 10,000-foot peaks and rugged terrain, Oregon's Wallowa Mountains and Eagle Cap Wilderness have earned the nickname "the Switzerland of America." The Nez Perce Indians once called these lands home; now they are beloved by vacationers, artists, and outdoors enthusiasts.

The Wallowas can be reached via OR 82 out of La Grande. It's a 62-mile drive to Enterprise, the Wallowa County seat, and another 6 miles to Joseph (named for Chief Joseph, leader of the Nez Perce). Joseph is packed with art galleries and shops. Valley Bronze, a local foundry, serves sculptors worldwide. South of Joseph, forest-lined, 4-mile-long Wallowa Lake State Park is one of Oregon's largest, busiest, and most beautiful. Services and activities offered include a marina and cabins, campgrounds, water sports, a go-cart track, horseback riding, llama treks, and hiking trails. Campground reservations, still something of a rarity in the inland Northwest, are a must at Wallowa Lake during the summer. Call Reservations Northwest at (800) 452–5687. Many other campgrounds and backpacking opportunities exist throughout the 2.3 million-acre Wallowa-Whitman National Forest and Eagle Cap Wilderness.

A tramway—one of the nation's steepest and longest—climbs to the 8,200-foot level on Mount Howard. From this vantage point, visitors can see the Eagle Cap Wilderness, the rim of Hells Canyon, and Idaho's Seven Devils Mountains. The tram runs daily June through September. Call (541) 432–5331 for current hours and rates.

Joseph has many annual special events including a vintage car cruise in June, Chief Joseph Days Rodeo (one of the top events of its kind) in July, and a "rattlesnake and bear feed" and "brews and blues festival," both in August. The Wallowa County Museum in downtown Joseph has exhibits on the area's rich history. For more information, visit the Wallowa County Chamber of Commerce at 107 Southwest First Street in Enterprise, call (800) 585–4121, or see the Web site at www.wallowacountychamber.com. ♦

of Peace"), La Grande looks northeast to the Wallowa Mountains and west to the Blue Mountains. "Oh, if the Grande Ronde was west of the Cascade Mountains, how soon it would be taken up," emigrant Elizabeth Dixon Smith wrote in 1847. Elizabeth Wood, another traveler, called the area "one of Nature's beauty spots." Indeed, by the late 1850s when much of the good Willamette Valley land was taken up, some pioneers decided to backtrack to the Grande Ronde, where land was still plentiful. La Grande's Birnie Park once served as an emigrant campground. It's located on the south side of town at Gekeler Lane and B Avenue, which parallels the path taken by the emigrants. In addition to picnic tables and a playground, Birnie Park showcases several ceramic totem-style monuments completed by artists Tom Dimond and Don Gray in 1993 to commemorate the trail sesquicentennial.

Totem–style Oregon Trail monuments at Birnie Park in La Grande, Oregon.

La Grande's annual events include an Oregon Trail Days celebration in mid-August that features such activities as an old-time fiddling contest and a quilt show. Stop by the La Grande/Union County Visitors and Conventions Bureau at 1912 Fourth Street, call (800) 848–9969, or see the Web site at www.visitlagrande.com for more information or a self-guiding brochure to area Oregon Trail sites. La Grande is also home to Eastern Oregon University and serves as gateway to the many recreational areas in the Blue and Wallowa Mountains. From here, the emigrants headed west into the Blue Mountains—and hoped they'd make it across before the snow fell.

West of LaGrande, I–84 quickly accesses **Hilgard Junction State Park** on the Grande Ronde River. It takes about fifteen minutes to make the drive today; in the 1840s, emigrants often needed ten days to complete the same steep trip. Some historians (and a state interpretive panel at the park) say that this was probably an emigrant campground; others feel that the Pioneer Springs 1.5 miles northwest was the more likely site. But it was from this general area that the pioneers began their ascent of the Blue Mountains.

Although it's possible to zip over the Blues from La Grande to Pendleton in about an hour, this beautiful, heavily forested area has a way of holding visitors captive. The emigrants were enthralled, too, by the tall conifer trees and the bracing air so unlike the desert heat they'd endured all summer. "Indeed, I do not know as I was ever so much affected by any scenery in my life," Narcissa Whitman wrote in 1836, comparing the area to her eastern home. "The singing of birds, the echo of voices of my fellow travelers as they went scattered through the woods, all had a strong resemblance to bygone days." True, the terrain meant a long, tough climb. But firewood was no longer scarce, and the abundance of game, berries, and other edible wild plants meant delicious additions to the emigrants' meals.

Most travelers arrived at the Blues in late August or early September, before the heavy snows. Others weren't so fortunate. "While in the valley (the Grande Ronde), the snow fell to the depth of three feet, and on the Blue Mountains it was five feet deep," wrote F. A. Chenoweth, who made the trip in 1849. "The road over the mountains . . . difficult in good weather, was now utterly impassible with wagons. Our only alternative was to leave wagons, teams, and other property, and make our way across on foot."

The **Blue Mountain Crossing** interpretive area is a good spot to stretch your legs and enjoy some trail history. Open from 8:00 A.M. to 8:00 P.M. Memorial Day weekend through Labor Day weekend, the site includes a half-mile, paved path along trail depressions, with interpretive panels along the way. Two spur loops can extend the hike a bit longer over more moderate terrain. Rest rooms, drinking water, and a picnic area are available at the trailhead. To get there, take exit 248 and follow the signs 3 miles to the park. Admission is $5.00 per vehicle.

The small town of Meacham, at exit 234, was named for emigrant Harvey Meacham, one of several pioneers buried in the area. In July 1923, President Warren Harding stopped here to commemorate the Oregon Trail's eightieth anniversary and drew a crowd of more than 12,000 people. A monument on the south edge of town memorializes all the unknown dead of the Oregon Trail.

Emigrant Springs State Park, 3 miles northwest of Meacham at exit 234, marks the site where missionary Jason Lee discovered a good source of water in 1834. From that time on, the springs became a major campground for the travelers, and travelers can still camp there today. Five miles farther west, the trail wound straight through what is now the Deadman Pass rest area. Deadman Pass didn't get its name until the Bannock War several decades after the Oregon Trail heyday. A foot trail from the rest area leads to a short stretch of wagon ruts. Look for the sign near the eastbound rest area exit (which is accessible via an interstate underpass from the westbound rest area). A road from the westbound area leads to a beautiful overlook of Squaw Creek Canyon.

After Deadman Pass, the emigrants left what is now I–84 to head down the mountain in a northwest direction. Many pioneer diarists mentioned the sweeping view of the Umatilla Valley and, in those days, Mount Hood, Mount Adams, and Mount Saint Helens. "The sight from this mountain top is one to

The view looking north from the Squaw Creek overlook in the Blue Mountains.

be remembered," John Minto wrote in 1844. "It affects me as did my first sight of the ocean, or again, my first sight of the seemingly boundless treeless plains before we saw the Platte River." The valley view is still there, but modern dust and smog have unfortunately obscured the Cascade peaks.

The trail divided below, with one branch pressing westward across the Columbia Plateau and the other heading north to the Whitman Mission. Although a few obstacles remained, the emigrants had put one of their biggest worries—the Blue Mountains—behind them.

THE NATIVE PERSPECTIVE

The Oregon Trail had an unmistakable impact on Native Americans. During the migration's earliest years, contacts between the whites and the natives were mostly beneficial to both sides. But as traffic increased, disease outbreaks and ecological depredations became rampant. The **Tamastslikt Cultural Institute** near Pendleton is the only native-owned interpretive center along the Oregon Trail; as such, it's one of the best places to learn more about how the trail changed Indians' lives.

Pronounced Tuh-MUST-slikt, which means "interpreter" in the Walla Walla language, the museum has impressive exhibits laid out in a circular fashion. The "We Were" displays tell about the traditional culture of the Walla Walla, Cayuse, and Umatilla tribes, and how it was altered by westward expansion. The "We Are" and "We Will Be" sections show how the tribes are striving to preserve their traditions. Multimedia presentations in several theaters delve deeper into the tribes' stories and culture, and future plans call for more living-history programs. Before you leave, have a snack in the Kinship Café and take a peek at the gift shop, which features native-made art and crafts and Pendleton woolen goods. Tamastslikt is open from 9:00 A.M. to 5:00 P.M. daily except Thanksgiving, Christmas, and New Year's Day. Admission is $6.00 for adults, $4.00 for seniors ages fifty-five and older, and $4.00 for children and teens. Call (541) 966–9748 for more information.

Pendleton, with 15,000 people, is the biggest city in eastern Oregon. At one time, it had thirty-two saloons and eighteen bordellos and was considered the entertainment capital of the Northwest. Today, Pendleton is best known for its woolen mills and the famous Pendleton Round-Up, a festival of rodeos, parades, and pageantry held the second week in September.

Pendleton Underground Tours, based at 37 Southwest Emigrant downtown, offers two different guided tours of underground tunnels and businesses built by Chinese immigrants in the late nineteenth century. Attractions include the Shamrock Cardroom, a laundry, meat market, and brothel. Reservations are required; call (541) 276–0730 for more information.

The Pendleton Woolen Mills at 1307 Southeast Court Place also offers tours Monday through Friday. The Round-Up Hall of Fame on the Round-Up Grounds showcases Western and Indian memorabilia, photographs, and artifacts, as does the Umatilla County Historical Society Museum at 108 Southwest Frazer. For sleep or a meal, consider that Pendleton has the largest concentration of restaurants and motels within the next 125 miles. Call the Pendleton chamber at (800) 547–8911 or see the Web site at www.pendleton-oregon.org for more information on area events and attractions.

The opening of Tamastslikt means it's no longer necessary to head farther north to learn the story of the **Whitman Mission,** where the cultural clash came to a head in 1847. Still, the National Park Service site at the mission is a worthy side trip for travelers who have a few extra hours. In November 1834, the Reverend Samuel Parker traveled around New York State asking for missionaries to go west with him the following spring. In Wheeling, New York, Marcus Whitman—a country doctor for twelve years—agreed to make the trip. Together, they got as far as the Green River, where Whitman decided to return to the States to prepare for a trip the following year—a trip designed to establish a mission for the natives.

The next spring, Whitman set off anew. With him were two things that would forever alter the course of American history: a wagon, which he was determined to take all the way west, and his bride, Narcissa Prentiss Whitman. She, too, had heard Parker's speech two autumns before and had long yearned to make the trip. Narcissa made it all the way, and with Eliza Spalding—another missionary's wife—was the first white woman to cross the continent overland. The wagon was converted to a cart in Idaho and later traveled as far as Fort Boise, farther than any other wheeled vehicle before it. These successes inspired many frontier families to try the trip themselves.

Together, the Whitmans founded Waiilatpu, "Place of the Rye Grass," on the banks of the Walla Walla River. For the next decade, they would serve as missionaries, teachers, and friends to the Cayuse Indians. Their efforts brought only limited success and were destined to end in tragedy. In the meantime, however, the mission served as an important station on the Oregon Trail during the emigration's first few years. Travelers stopped for rest, supplies, medical treatment, and the Whitmans' hospitality. The mission was the birthplace of Alice Clarissa Whitman, born three months after the Whitmans' arrival. Sadly, the baby drowned in the Walla Walla just two years later.

Whitman thought that for his mission to succeed, he needed to change the Cayuse's nomadic ways. He encouraged them to farm, but few went along. The Cayuse were also indifferent to religious books, worship, and school. By 1842, reports of the mission's troubles caused Methodist officials back in the United States to order Waiilatpu closed. But Whitman, convinced the mission should stay open, made a midwinter ride back east to plead his case. Impressed by his commitment, the officials changed their minds.

Still, the cultural differences remained and—with the coming of ever more whites—deepened. In 1847, emigrants brought a measles epidemic that spread rapidly among the Cayuse, who had no resistance to the disease. Soon, half the tribe was dead. When Dr. Whitman's medicine helped whites but not Indians, many Cayuse believed they were being poisoned to make way for the pioneers. On November 29, 1847, a band of Cayuse attacked the mission and killed the Whitmans and eleven others.

Like Tamastslikt, the Whitman Mission shows the collision between the native people of the West and those who pursued religious zeal and America's "manifest destiny." A small interpretive center tells the sad story from both sides. On one hand, the Whitmans were genuinely interested in the Cayuse and their welfare. On the other hand, they could not understand the centuries-old Cayuse practice of hunting and gathering on seasonal rounds. What seemed like aimless wandering to whites was the Cayuse's way of honoring the creator and the food they'd been provided.

Other sites at the Whitman Mission include a great grave in which the massacre victims were buried and an excavated area where early mission buildings are outlined. Visitors can get a good view of the entire grounds by taking the short, steep walk to the Whitman Memorial Shaft. From the top, you can see all of Waiilatpu, as well as the Blue Mountains, still stretching northward. Living-history demonstrations featuring pioneer and Indian crafts are given on summer weekends.

Whitman Mission is open daily from 8:00 A.M. to 6:00 P.M. June through August and from 8:00 A.M. to 4:30 P.M. the rest of the year. Admission is $2.00 per person for ages eighteen and up. To find the site, take OR 11 from Pendelton about 45 miles north to Walla Walla. The mission is 7 miles west of town on US 12. Call (509) 522–6360 for more information.

Walla Walla, meaning "many waters" or "small rapid stream," grew up in the wake of the Whitman Mission and is now a thriving city of 26,000. Its sights include the Fort Walla Walla Museum Complex, with its exhibits on pioneer and agricultural life; and Pioneer Park, which features duck ponds, an exotic bird display, a playground, swimming pool, and tennis courts. Although primarily an agricultural and regional retail and service center, Walla Walla and its neighbor, College Place, are home to three colleges: Whitman College and Walla Walla College (both four-year schools) and the two-year Walla Walla Community College.

Walla Walla has an abundance of lodging and restaurants, although camping in the area is somewhat limited. Annual events include the Walla Walla Balloon Stampede, ethnic heritage festivals, horse shows, and a mountain man rendezvous. For more information, contact the Walla Walla Valley Chamber of Commerce at (509) 525–0850.

The monument of Whitman Mission commemorates the collision of the native people of the West and those who pursued religious zeal and America's "manifest destiny."

From Whitman Mission and Walla Walla, travelers can either return to Pendleton and parallel the Oregon Trail across the Columbia Plateau or save a little time by continuing west on US 12 to US 730, which winds along the Columbia River to I–82 (which, in turn, connects with I–84 just a few miles south).

THE COLUMBIA PLATEAU

West of Pendleton, the arid climate and wide open spaces are reminiscent of southern Idaho. Here, the Oregon Trail moves farther away from the modern interstate than it has in many miles. But one site that is fairly close to I–84 is the **Umatilla River Crossing** at Echo, accessible via exit 193.

The U.S. government established the Umatilla Indian Agency in 1851 to oversee the Cayuse, Umatilla, and Walla Walla tribes. The agency was destroyed during the Yakama Indian wars of 1855. Later, the Oregon Mounted Volunteers established Fort Henrietta on the site, but it was abandoned after raids attributed to the Indians, and then burned to prevent Indian occupation. Further settlement in the area was delayed until the gold rush of 1858, when the federal government stationed more troops in the area.

Today's town of Echo has about 500 residents. The town took its name from the daughter of its co-founder, J. H. Koontz. A small park sits near where the emigrants forded the Umatilla River. It has an informative historical display and several campsites and is home to the Fort Henrietta Days celebration each September. Echo is remarkably well attuned to its Oregon Trail history for such a small town, and City Hall can provide visitors with friendly advice and several informative brochures including a map of area trail sites and a flyer detailing the emigrant route from Pendleton to Arlington.

After crossing the Umatilla, the pioneers traveled through (and often took the mid-day "nooning" break) at **Echo Meadows,** where several stretches of ruts still exist. To get there, drive 5.5 miles west of Echo on OR 320, then a half-mile north on the gravel road. Another 25 miles west, the emigrants arrived at **Well Springs,** one of the few reliable sources of water on the dry stretch across the plateau.

Other traces of the trail still exist through **Fourmile Canyon** southeast of Arlington; near **McDonald Ford**, where the emigrants crossed the John Day River; and at several other locations across the Columbia Plateau. But one of the very finest remnants is just west of the town of Biggs, right off I–84. Get off the interstate at exit 104 and head west on US 30. The ruts are well marked on the road's south side, and they are definitely worth a stop and maybe a picture or two. It was here that the emigrants, who had been traversing the plateau to the south, got their first view of the Columbia River.

Stay on US 30 to reach the Deschutes River Recreation Area. The original crossing was flooded by the construction of The Dalles Dam, but in its day, it was a dangerous ford. Oregon Trail ruts may still be seen climbing the hill on the river's west side. An Oregon state park, the Deschutes River Recreation Area is a favorite for fishing, picnicking, and camping. The Deschutes also is known for great rafting along its stretches farther south near Bend.

In this area, the Oregon Trail converges with another of America's great historic trails: the route of the Lewis and Clark Expedition, which traveled down the Columbia in 1805 and back again the following year after wintering at Fort Clatsop near present-day Astoria on the Pacific Ocean. For more information, you might want to consult *Traveling the Lewis & Clark Trail*, also by this author and available from The Globe Pequot Press.

US 30 dead-ends 7 miles from Biggs at Celilo, a sacred Indian fishing ground inundated by The Dalles Dam. From here, it's a short drive to the town of The Dalles.

THE DALLES

Until 1846, **The Dalles** was—in a sense—the end of the Oregon Trail, or at least the overland portion of it. At the time, emigrants could continue their journey only by floating down the Columbia River. Dams have turned today's Columbia into one big series of reservoirs, but in the nineteenth century it was a river of treacherous rapids. Maneuvering rafts and livestock down the broad, swift river was quite difficult, to say the least. In fact, The Dalles got its unusual name from French trappers who called the area "les dalles," or "the trough," because of its once-wild character.

A park at Sixth and Union Streets in The Dalles bears a monument marking "The End of the Oregon Trail." Actually, emigrants choosing to brave the river would start their float at Chenoweth Creek, a protected harbor just west of The Dalles where rafts could be built and boats loaded.

The Dalles also was the site of an important Methodist mission started by Daniel Lee in 1838. This is where survivors of Stephen Meek's cutoff were taken and treated after their foolish trek in 1845. Until its closing in 1847, the mission also served other emigrants who stopped here to camp and resupply.

The Dalles Visitor and Convention Bureau at 901 East Second Street (800–255–3385; www.thedalleschamber.com) has maps that detail self-guiding walking tours through the city's historic areas. A free train runs from town to The Dalles Dam, which offers daily tours in the summer. Other attractions include the Original Wasco County Courthouse at 410 West Second Place and the Fort Dalles Museum, at Fifteenth and Garrison Streets in the last remaining building of a fort built in 1850 to protect emigrant traffic. Like Vale in eastern Oregon, The Dalles has quite a few murals, including the 70-foot-high, Oregon Trail–themed "Decision at The Dalles" by Don Crook at the corner of Second and Federal Streets downtown.

The Dalles is the gateway to the Columbia Gorge, recognized as an official national scenic area. This is a land of stunning waterfalls, varied recreational opportunities, fine restaurants, fun festivals, and roadside fruit stands. See the Columbia Gorge section for more information on things to see and do. But start here at the **Columbia Gorge Discovery Center/Wasco County Historical Museum** just west of The Dalles at exit 82. This superb interpretive facility explains the geological, human, and natural history of this unusual region. There's a lot to tell: When it was first created by the Oregon territorial legislature, Wasco County stretched from the Cascades to the Continental Divide in Wyoming; from 1854 to 1859, it was probably the largest organized county in the United States. Before that, of course, the area was a major meeting and fishing grounds for many Native American tribes. The Discovery Center portion of the building includes great forest dioramas and the chance to "try" sailboarding (on a video monitor, anyway). The center's excellent gift shop includes many Oregon Trail books and fine craft items; there's a small restaurant—the Basalt Rock Café—on the premises, too. Outdoors, the grounds include walking paths, living-history displays, and striking views of the Gorge. The center is open daily from 10:00 A.M. to 6:00 P.M. Admission is $6.50 for adults, $5.50 for senior citizens, and $3.00 for children ages six to sixteen. Call (541) 296–8600 for more information.

Beginning in 1846, the emigrants had to make a choice. They could take the river, or they could continue overland on the Barlow Road. Today's travelers face the same decision. Those in a hurry should probably opt for the river route, which parallels I-84. If time isn't a concern, consider the Barlow Road, which winds across the south shoulder of majestic Mount Hood. Either way is quite scenic!

DOWN THE COLUMBIA

By the time they reached The Dalles, the emigrants were tired, broke, and more than ready to stop traveling. But they had one last hurdle to clear: the mighty **Columbia River.** Even after the Barlow Road was opened in 1846, late-arriving emigrants would sometimes find that way closed by snow. Then as before, the river remained the only option for getting to Oregon City.

People often spent days waiting to float down the Columbia. Some travelers built their own rafts out of timber scattered near the river. Others opted to pay for a ride, but the price could be high—up to $50 or $100 per wagon, an exorbitant amount of money back then, particularly for emigrants who had been on the road for months. Livestock were often traded in lieu of cash payments.

At what is now the town of Cascade Locks, a prehistoric landslide had clogged the Columbia with piles of rocks, and most emigrants had to leave the

CRATER LAKE NATIONAL PARK AND SOUTHWEST OREGON

Crater Lake National Park, about 250 miles south of The Dalles, is one of Oregon's top scenic attractions. This once was the site of 12,000-foot Mount Mazama, a volcano, but eruptions about 6,850 years ago emptied the magma chamber beneath the mountain and caused the mountaintop to collapse, creating the depression which now cradles Crater Lake.

Crater Lake is America's deepest lake and one of its bluest. Its beauty is further enhanced by spectacular lava cliffs and forested slopes that rim the shore. Crater Lake is also a haven for wildlife. Bears, bald eagles, elk, mule deer, and more than 200 species of birds are among the species living in the national park.

The Rim Drive, a 35-mile circuit around the lake, offers several wonderful views including those at the Sinnott Memorial (outside the visitor center) and Cloudcap. More than 100 miles of hiking trails are also available. A 5-mile round-trip hike reaches Mount Scott, the park's highest point at 8,926 feet, nearly 2,000 feet above the lake. A 1.1-mile trail leads to the boat landing at Cleetwood Cove, launching point for the Crater Lake boat tours. These two-hour trips include information on Crater Lake's geologic and natural history; cost is $12.00 for adults and $7.00 for those under age twelve.

No license is required to fish at Crater Lake, and anglers might catch rainbow trout or kokanee salmon. Swimming is also permitted, but beware—the water is only 50°F! Crater Lake National Park has two first-come, first-served campgrounds with no hookups.

Bend, Oregon, is the largest town along US 97 en route to Crater Lake. Bend has been booming lately, thanks to its scenic setting near the Cascade Mountains and an influx of residents from the West's bigger cities. Just south of Bend, the High Desert Museum is one of the finest in the West, its indoor exhibits supplemented by more than twenty acres of outdoor trails. Visitors can see feeding time at the porcupine pen, stroll by an old settler's cabin, and learn about birds of prey.

Southwest of Crater Lake, the town of Ashland is home to one of America's premier theater companies, the Tony Award–winning Oregon Shakespeare Festival. Operating from mid-February through October, the festival annually performs a variety of plays ranging from Shakespeare's works to those of contemporary dramatists. Ashland is also known for its abundant art galleries, antiques dealers, and boutique shopping.

For more information on these areas, contact Crater Lake National Park at (541) 594–2211, the Bend Chamber of Commerce at (541) 382–3221, or the Ashland Chamber of Commerce at (541) 482–3486. ♠

river for a portage of 3 to 5 miles. Wagons that had been disassembled for the float were now rebuilt and repacked, then taken apart again once the cascades were past. Boats were typically floated right over the rapids and hauled ashore by Indians hired to help the process.

Samuel Parker, who emigrated to Oregon in 1845, wrote of arriving at the portage with an ill daughter. "I put my sick girl in a blanket and pack her and only rested once that day," he recalled. Larger craft such as steamboats could try to ply the rapids fully loaded, but it was a dangerous practice. Still, this was the last point of hardship for those who concluded their trip west via the Columbia River route. From here, all was smooth sailing.

Today, the *Sternwheeler Columbia Gorge* offers riverboat sight-seeing rides three times daily mid-June to September, with departures at 10:00 A.M., 12:30 P.M., and 3:00 P.M. One cruise daily (usually the 12:30 trip) focuses on Oregon Trail history. Cost is $12.95 for adults and $7.95 for children. Take exit 44 off of I–84 East. The company also does summertime dinner-dance and champagne brunch cruises in the Gorge; from October through April, it moves downriver to Portland for similar offerings. Call (541) 374–8428 in Cascade Locks or (503) 223–3928 in Portland for more information.

Many emigrants on the river route stopped at **Fort Vancouver**, established by the Hudson's Bay Company in 1824. This represented a bold move by the HBC, which hoped to secure Britain's claim to Oregon by moving its Northwest headquarters inland from the mouth of the Columbia. That may have been the case had the fort not been run by John McLoughlin, a kind-hearted Canadian who welcomed emigrants to Fort Vancouver and gave them supplies, often on credit.

By 1846, Britain's hopes of claiming Oregon were dashed when the territory was divided along the forty-ninth parallel (the current U.S.–Canada boundary), not the Columbia River, as the British had hoped. Fort Vancouver was on American soil. McLoughlin retired and moved to Oregon City, became an American citizen, and continued his charitable ways. Today, he is revered as "the Father of Oregon."

Fort Vancouver is now a national historic site. Stop first at the visitor center to view a fifteen-minute video on the fort's history and see exhibits showcasing many artifacts from the past. Then proceed down the hill to the fort's grounds, where the stockade and several major buildings have been reconstructed on their original locations. Visitors are welcome from 9:00 A.M. to 5:00 P.M. daily March through October and from 8:00 A.M. to 4:00 P.M. the rest of the year, with guided tours on the hour. There are often living-history demonstrations in the blacksmith's shop, carpenter's shop, and kitchen. Admission is $2.00 per person or $4.00 for a family; it's sometimes waived in the off-season. This is the site of a gala Fourth of July celebration often called one of the Northwest's best. For more information about Fort Vancouver, call (360) 696–7655.

Fort Vancouver sits near an area known as Officers' Row, a stately promenade of Victorian homes that once served as residences for the U.S. Army post established near the site in 1849. The houses are now occupied by shops and professional offices. Marshall House, at 1310 Officers' Row, was named for General George C. Marshall, architect of the post–World War II recovery plan. A tour of the house includes a video on the history of Officers' Row and of Vancouver's role in the military since 1850. Horse-and-buggy rides are available in the area, too. Other historical sites include the Pearson Air Museum at 1105 East Fifth Street; the Clark County Historical Museum at 1511 Main Street; and Covington House, an 1846 log cabin that once served as a schoolhouse. It is located at 4201 Main Street.

Vancouver, the oldest city in Washington State, has a population of about 130,000. It sits right across the river from Portland and within easy reach of many outdoor attractions including Vancouver Lake, Battleground Lake State Park, Paradise Point State Park, the Ridgefield National Wildlife Refuge, and Mount Saint Helens National Volcanic Monument. Get a shopping fix at the Vancouver Mall, with more than 115 shops, restaurants, and theaters; or attend August's Clark County Fair, one of the nation's ten largest. For more information on Vancouver, contact the Vancouver/Clark County Visitor and Convention Bureau at (800) 377–7084.

Travelers who didn't stop at Fort Vancouver floated on to the mouth of

The rugged beauty of the Columbia River Gorge near The Dalles is still impressive today.

THE COLUMBIA RIVER GORGE AND MOUNT HOOD

What's your pleasure? Hiking? Sailboarding? Dining? Scenic drives? The 80-mile-long Columbia River Gorge National Scenic Area has all these and a lot more, all within easy reach of I-84 (for fast-laners) and WA 14 (for those who like to dawdle).

Hood River, a town of about 5,000 people, is the sailboarding capital of the world, and it sometimes seems every other car in town is piled high with sailboards, mountain bikes, kayaks, and other recreational gear. This is also big bungee jumping territory, and a local group called the Dangerous Sports Club is always on the lookout for new ways to risk life and limb. But Hood River has another side, too: It is home to an astounding array of great restaurants, ranging from the elegant (and expensive) Columbia River Court Dining Room in the Columbia Gorge Hotel to the Whitecap Brewpub, home of Full Sail Ales, traditional and unusual bar food, and live entertainment.

Hood River is also a jumping-off spot for Mount Hood, highest point in Oregon at 11,235 feet. The 1.1 million-acre Mount Hood National Forest offers more than 100 campgrounds and more than 1,000 miles of hiking trails. Timberline, one of three ski areas at Mount Hood and a favorite training area for Olympic athletes, actually offers skiing well into summer at an elevation of 8,500 feet.

The Mount Hood Railroad transports passengers from Hood River to Parkdale (44 miles) on excursions April through mid-December. The train, built in 1906, offers views of Oregon's famous fruit orchards, towering Mount Hood and Mount Adams, and the beautiful Hood River Valley. Kids ride free on their birthday with proof of age. There also are brunch trains and murder mystery dinner trains, among other special events. Reservations are recommended; call (541) 386–3556 for more information.

Washington State also borders the Gorge, and boasts several great attractions of its own. The Maryhill Museum of Art near the Biggs Junction includes work by the French sculptor Auguste Rodin and an extensive collection of Native American baskets and artifacts. The museum was named for Mary Hill, wife of lawyer Sam Hill, who also built the nearby replica of England's famous Stonehenge.

Bonneville Dam has visitor centers on both its Washington and Oregon sides. The Washington center features views of the dam's generators and turbines; the Oregon side shows the workings of the Bonneville Locks. Both sides have fish-viewing areas from which trout and salmon can be seen negotiating the dam's fish ladders. Near the Washington side of the dam, the town of Stevenson has several good restaurants and the Columbia Gorge Interpretive Center. The latter is worth a stop for its impressive multi-projector slide show, which tells how the Gorge was formed.

Carson Mineral Hot Springs Resort at the tiny town of Carson, Washington, offers very reasonable lodging and inviting creature comforts, including 126°F natural mineral baths, massages, RV hookups (tent campers are welcome, too), and a restaurant. Folks have been flocking here for more than a century, and the baths are supposed to be good for whatever ails you. Call (509) 427–8292.

Waterfalls may be the Gorge's most popular draw. A few cascades, including lovely Multnomah Falls, may be briefly glimpsed from the interstate. But to really appreciate the falls, leave the freeway near Bonneville for the Columbia River Scenic Highway, which runs 22 miles between Ainsworth State Park and Troutdale. The highway was begun in 1913 and passes by Bridal Veil, Horsetail, and Mult-nomah Falls, among others. Many Gorge waterfall areas offer hiking opportunities, including the popular Eagle Creek Trail to Punch Bowl Falls and the Larch Mountain hike at Multnomah Falls. Stop at Crown Point and its Vista House for a great view of the Gorge and information on the area's history.

For more information on the Columbia River Gorge, call The Dalles Convention & Visitors Bureau at (800) 255–3385 or the Hood River County Chamber of Commerce at (800) 366–3530. For information on Mount Hood, call (888) 622–4822. ♠

the Willamette and, from there, on to Oregon City. To reach Oregon City today, take I–84 west to I–205, the beltway that circles Portland. Head south on I–205. Oregon City is at exits 8, 9, and 10.

THE BARLOW ROAD

Most early emigrants made it successfully down the Columbia River. But others lost their possessions, even their lives, in its raging rapids. Others were incensed by the high tolls charged by boatmen on the Columbia. Here they were, so close to the Willamette Valley and yet so far away. Could there be another route . . . a land passage around the great Mount Hood?

In 1845, two pioneer leaders—Samuel K. Barlow and Joel Palmer—decided to find out, and the result became known as the Barlow Road. Historians say Palmer intended to float down the Columbia until he heard the two ferry boats were engaged for at least ten days. He then learned Barlow had already set off to find a route around the mountain. Palmer chased Barlow down, their parties camped together at Tygh Valley, then they set off to find the last link in the overland route.

It was tough going. Each day, members of the party would move out in advance to clear brush and timber, while Palmer, Barlow, and a few other men went still farther ahead to try to find the pass over the Cascades. It was October, and they were racing against time. The sun set earlier each evening, and the nights were bitterly cold. Food supplies dwindled, and the travelers were growing ever more weary.

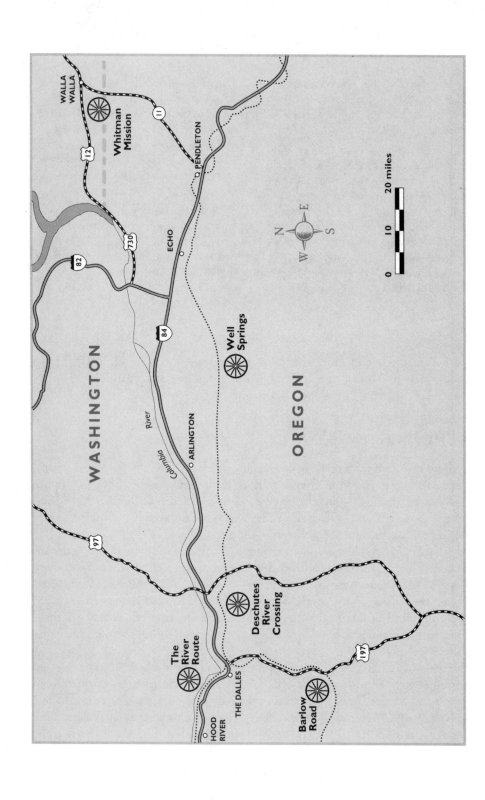

By climbing Mount Hood, Palmer finally found the pass they were seeking, through Summit Meadows and the Zigzag River watershed. But snow was threatening, and the travelers decided to cache supplies at a place just east of the pass they called Fort Deposit and move on by pack team to the Willamette Valley.

Soon after reaching his destination, Barlow approached the Oregon provisional legislature, saying he would clear and maintain the road over the Cascades if officials would allow him to collect tolls. The deal was made, and the Barlow Road officially opened in time for the fall emigration season of 1846. That autumn, an estimated 145 wagons and nearly 1,000 people used the road that Barlow, Palmer, and their men had hacked out just the year before.

Barlow Road tolls amounted to $5.00 per wagon and 10 cents a head for livestock, much cheaper than passage down the Columbia River. But the trip was not for the faint of heart. "Toward noon, our roads became intolerable," Esther McMillan Hanna wrote in 1853. "I never could have imagined such roads nor could I describe it for it beggars description! Over roots and branches, fallen trees and logs, over streams, through sloughs and marshes, up hill and down—in short, everything that could possibly make it intolerable."

Today's traveler can view the Barlow Road much as it was in emigrant

Views from the Barlow Road show 11,235-foot Mount Hood and its glaciers.

times. The Forest Service has done little to alter the route, meaning that it is as bumpy as Hanna described it. In the interest of time (and to preserve passengers' nerves and dental fillings), you'll probably want to traverse only part of the Barlow Road. The rest of the time, you can stay on well-maintained blacktop roads that skirt south of Mount Hood.

To get there, take US 197 south from The Dalles to Tygh Valley, a distance of 31 miles past fruit orchards and grain fields. You might want to stop at the Forest Service office in Dufur, 13 miles south of The Dalles, for a detailed Mount Hood National Forest map. (You can also call ahead for information at (541) 467–2291, or write the Dufur Ranger Station, 780 Northeast Court Street, Dufur, OR 97021.) Continue on to Tygh Valley, then follow the signs to Wamic. Bear left into Wamic at the Y intersection just before town. Follow the Barlow Road signs onto Forest Road 48. The road travels into, then out of, then back into Mount Hood National Forest. Finally, watch for a small brown sign indicating the **Old Barlow Road.** Turn left and take FR 170 a mile back to FR 3530.

Barlow's tollgate was in this vicinity, and the Forest Service has restored this area via selective clearing to resemble how it looked in the mid-nineteenth century. Some of the ponderosa pine trees here are hundreds of years old. You can follow FR 3530 as long as you want; there are several bailing-out points back to the main highways that you can identify via the detailed forest map. Travelers with low-clearance cars may want to turn around at the cattleguard almost 1.5 miles in; the ruts just past here were very deep in 2000. Summertime travelers on FR 3530 will find interpretive panels telling stories of the route, but these are removed in the winter. If you don't want to brave even part of the Barlow Road, continue on FR 48 to OR 35. Drive south on OR 35 to US 26, then turn west toward Sandy.

Many emigrant parties camped east of Barlow's tollgate, and it became quite a dumping ground as the travelers sought to lighten their wagon loads before crossing the mountain. The next day, they'd press on as many as 18 miles to the White River. This same stretch can be followed closely today, but at a pace of just 10 to 15 miles per hour. A few primitive campgrounds are scattered along the way.

Near White River Station, travelers can continue on the Barlow Road or cut over to FR 48. The latter soon reaches OR 35, the Mount Hood loop road from Hood River, which in turn soon merges with US 26. FR 3531, 2 miles west of the White River East Snow Park on US 26, is the road to the **Pioneer Woman's Grave,** easily one of the most affecting sites along the Oregon Trail. The grave marks the burial site of a woman who died on the Barlow Road, and it has gradually developed into a mound of boulders and stones placed by passersby. It's impossible to view this monument and not feel sorry for this unknown woman who came so close to her destination before finally succumbing

Looking up Laurel Hill today, it appears much like it did when the emigrants struggled up its grade.

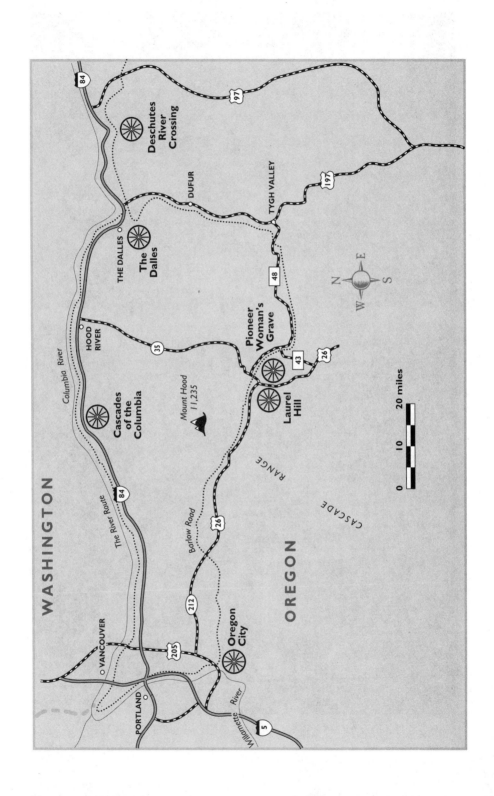

to the trail's rigors. Barlow Pass and a good hiking segment of the old emigrant road are located near the grave, as is a trailhead for the Pacific Crest Trail.

Laurel Hill was loudly cursed by all who came upon it, and some travelers thought it was the most difficult passage of the entire trip. After returning to US 26 from FR 3531, watch for a turnout about 6 miles west on the left-hand side. This is the trailhead to Laurel Hill, which actually consisted of two chutes for a combined vertical drop of more than 300 feet and a grade of about 60 percent.

Standing at the bottom or the top of the scree-covered chute, it is hard to imagine how the travelers made it down this unbelievably steep slope. The round-trip hike up and back can easily be done in a half-hour today. Not so in the nineteenth century. Some emigrants took their vehicles apart and slid them down the grade. Others dragged felled trees behind the wagons as brakes. Still other travelers used long ropes, one end tied to the wagon, the other wound around a sturdy tree. They would then let out the rope ever so slowly, praying it would not break. For decades after trail travel ended, it was possible to see rope burns on several tree stumps along Laurel Hill, but the last of the stumps so marked reportedly rotted away in the 1970s.

A replica of the most recent Barlow Road tollgate (used from 1879 to 1915) stands about 5 miles west of Laurel Hill, along with a pleasant picnic grove and Forest Service campground built during the 1930s by the Civilian Conservation Corps. From here, the travelers rolled on west across the Sandy River. Many stopped for final rest and rations at the Phillip Foster Farm on Eagle Creek, now privately owned. Finally, they arrived at Oregon City, the end of the Oregon Trail.

OREGON CITY

By all rights, **Oregon City** should probably be called McLoughlin after John McLoughlin, the man who did more than any other to ensure the success of this town and, indeed, all of Oregon. From his base at Fort Vancouver, McLoughlin directed the building of several cabins at the falls of the Willamette River in the late 1820s. They were soon burned by Indians, but McLoughlin responded by building a sawmill and flour mill in 1832. Settlers continued to trickle in over the next decade, and in 1843 they named Oregon City—which McLoughlin had named—the seat of their new provisional government.

Trail history looms large in Oregon City, but nowhere so big as at the **End of the Oregon Trail Interpretive Center,** accessible via exit 10 off I–205. The center features three 50-foot-high covered-wagon-shaped buildings, which are experienced through an hour-long "guided show." Visitors begin in a room outfitted like a trail provisioner's depot in Independence, Missouri, but filled

PORTLAND ATTRACTIONS

With its views of the Cascades and plentiful parks, Portland is a city uncommonly blessed by nature. But Portland is more than just a pretty face. It is home to a progressive populace, an active arts scene, and loads of activities. Mix these with a keenly developed sense of humor: Former Mayor Bud Clark was possibly best known for the "Expose Yourself to Art" poster, which featured his honor in a trenchcoat flashing a statue.

Naturally, many Portland-area people spend their free time fleeing town to the slopes of Mount Hood or the beaches of the windswept Oregon Coast. But anyone deciding to stay and explore the city itself has plenty of options from which to choose. Portland is a city of parks, with 4,700-acre Forest Park on the west side leading the way. This beautiful spot boasts hiking trails and picnic grounds with spectacular views of the city. It is also close to Washington Park, home of the Metro Washington Park Zoo, the World Forestry Center, and an impressive Japanese Garden. Others seeking reflection may want to visit The Grotto, a religious sanctuary and botanical garden at Northeast Eighty-fifth Avenue and Sandy Boulevard.

Weekends between March and December, the Portland Saturday Market beneath the Burnside Bridge offers wares from more than 250 artists, craftspeople, and fresh produce sellers. Food to eat on the premises and a wide array of entertainment are also available, and the market is open Sunday as well as Saturday.

Portland's appreciation of its past can be seen at the Oregon History Center at 1230 Southwest Park Avenue (where several trail-era treasures are showcased) and by the James F. Bybee House, built in 1858 and restored to reflect life in Oregon in those heady post-trail days. The Bybee house is in Howell Territorial Park on Sauvie Island, a rural refuge just north of Portland. Other museums include the recently expanded Oregon Art Institute at 1219 Southwest Park Avenue, the Children's Museum at 3037 Southwest Second Avenue, the American Advertising Museum at 9 Northwest Second Avenue, and the Oregon Museum of Science and Industry (OMSI) at 1945 Southeast Water Avenue.

Portland's arts and entertainment scene is really tough to beat. A constant stream of live popular musical acts parades through such venues as the Rose Garden Arena, Crystal Ballroom, Aladdin Theater, Roseland Theater, and innumerable small clubs. Chamber Music Northwest plays several times weekly during the summer, and outdoor jazz festivals abound during the warm months.

Special events in Portland include the Rose Festival, which takes place annually each June and lasts several weeks. Activities include parades, an air show, a hot air balloon festival, and much more. Downtown Portland is known for its public gathering places and eclectic architecture: Don't miss Pioneer Courthouse Square or Michael Graves' pastel Portland Building. The heart of the city also has a wealth of unusual shopping (or browsing) opportunities including Powell's Books, which takes up an entire city block, and Nike Town, an unabashed monument to the famous shoe manufacturer based in nearby Beaverton. What's more, Oregon has no sales tax, which means shopping in the Beaver State saves several pennies on each dollar.

For more information on Portland-area attractions, call the Portland Oregon Visitors Association at (877) 678–5263 or see its Web site at www.travelportland.com. The state also maintains an "Oregon Welcome Center" at exit 308 off of I–5 near the Oregon-Washington border. ●

PORTLAND TRAVEL TIPS

Portland International Airport (PDX) is served by Air BC, Alaska, America West, American, Canadian Regional, Delta, Continental, Harbor Air, Hawaiian Air, Horizon Air, Northwest, Reno Air, Skywest, Southwest, TWA, and United. All major auto rental companies have offices here, too. Amtrak serves Portland's Union Station at 800 Northwest Sixth Avenue; Greyhound is at 550 Northwest Sixth Avenue.

Portland has excellent public transportation via buses (Tri-Met) and light rail (MAX), with passengers riding free in "Fareless Square" (most of the downtown area and Lloyd Center) and for $1.10 to most other destinations. The MAX trains will run all the way to the airport by fall 2001. For schedules and other information, visit the Tri-Met office at Pioneer Courthouse Square, Portland's main downtown gathering place at Broadway and Yamhill, or call (503) 238–7433. Look for the colorful Cultural Bus (#63), which hits many of Portland's high spots including the Oregon Zoo, Oregon Museum of Science & Industry, the Portland Art Museum, Tom McCall Waterfront Park, and more. ▲

with many items—such as a fiddle and family Bible—actually taken west by emigrants. With this backdrop, a costumed interpreter gives visitors an overview of the trail. Everyone travels into another theater for a twenty-minute multimedia presentation that traces the stories of three typical emigrants and their relief at reaching Oregon City.

Before or after the show, take time to check out the exhibits and living-history demonstrations. Interesting artifacts include a tree limb from Laurel Hill, still scarred by rope indentations. Visitors can register their own ancestors who traveled the Oregon Trail; different families are regularly showcased in a pioneer family spotlight exhibit.

The center is located on Abernethy Green at Abernethy and Washington Streets—the very spot where many emigrants, too poor to afford a room, camped upon reaching Oregon City. It's open from 9:00 A.M. to 5:00 P.M. Monday through Saturday and 10:00 A.M. to 5:00 P.M. on Sunday from late May through mid-September, and from 9:00 A.M. to 5:00 P.M. Monday through Saturday and 10:00 A.M. to 5:00 P.M. on Sunday the rest of the year. The tour costs $5.50 for teens and adults, $4.50 for seniors sixty-five and over, and $3.00 for children ages five to twelve. (Younger children are admitted free, but toddlers and preschool-age kids are apt to squirm through the shows.) Tours are time-specific (with shows every forty-five minutes or so in summer), and the center recommends tickets be purchased in advance at Ticketmaster locations or at the interpretive center's ticket kiosk at 1726 Washington Street. There is no admission charge to the Abernethy & Co. museum store. Most

The End of the Oregon Trail Interpretive Center entrance, Oregon City, Oregon.

summers, the center grounds also serve as the site of an Oregon Trail pageant and other special events. For current schedule and ticket information, call (503) 657–9336.

Next, tour the restored **McLoughlin House National Historic Site** at 713 Center Street, where McLoughlin and his wife, Marguerite, lived after his retirement. (The house, originally built closer to Willamette Falls, was moved when development threatened it in the twentieth century.) The McLoughlins continued the tradition of hospitality they'd started at Fort Vancouver, opening their home to newly arrived emigrants, the needy, and the sick. The home is filled with beautiful period furniture, and the tour guides tell entertaining tales of McLoughlin's fascinating life. The house is open for tours from 10:00 A.M. to 4:00 P.M. Tuesday through Saturday and 1:00 to 4:00 P.M. on Sunday except major holidays and during the month of January, when it is closed. Admission is $4.00 for adults, $3.00 for seniors, and $2.00 for students ages six through seventeen. Call (503) 656–5146 for more information.

By the mid-1840s, Oregon City was a thriving little town with all the comforts the emigrants had known back in "the States." And although the travelers had spent five to six months on the road by the time they reached Oregon City, few took much time to rest upon getting here. Most newcomers spent the winter at Oregon City, then fanned out come springtime across the

A trail-side plaque marks the end of the trail in Oregon City.

Treasures from the trail at the End of the Oregon Trail Interpretive Center, Oregon City, Oregon.

Willamette Valley and beyond.

Americans have always been a restless breed, ever ready to move for fresh land, opportunity, or the mere thrill of going somewhere new. But here in Oregon, the restless young republic had moved as far west as it could go. Now the emigrants faced the challenges of staying put and of building new lives for themselves.

Industrious James Nesmith, quoted at the beginning of this chapter, became Oregon's first senator. Rachel Fisher Mills experienced the deaths of her husband and the youngest of their four children en route to Oregon, but here she remarried and had a second family. And Ezra Meeker, who traveled west as a young man in 1852, later retraced his route eastward, marking the way with monuments and asking all he met to remember and preserve the Oregon Trail and the brave emigrants who made the greatest peacetime migration in human history. It is unlikely this nation will ever forget.

Lodgings, campgrounds, and restaurants listed below are a representative sampling of what is available. Listing in these pages does not imply endorsement, nor is this a complete listing of all reputable businesses. For more complete listings, contact the visitor information bureau or chamber of commerce in each town. Room rates were accurate as of summer 2000, but are subject to change.

LODGING

VALE, OREGON
1900 Sears & Roebuck Home Bed & Breakfast, (541) 473–9636, 484 North Tenth Street, $60–$85.

ONTARIO, OREGON
Holiday Motor Inn, (541) 889–9188, 615 East Idaho Avenue, $45–$70.

Oregon Trail Motel, (541) 889–8633, 92 East Idaho Avenue, $30–$55.

Ontario Best Western Inn & Suites, (541) 889–2600, 251 Goodfellow Street, $60–$70.

Holiday Inn-Ontario, (541) 889–8621, 1249 Tapadera Avenue, $75–$85.

HUNTINGTON, OREGON
Farewell Bend Motor Inn, (541) 869–2211, I–84 exit 353, $43.

BAKER CITY, OREGON
Best Western Sunridge Inn, (541) 523–6444, 1 Sunridge Lane, $65–$80.

Eldorado Inn, (541) 523–6494, 695 Campbell Street, $40–$51.

Geiser Grand Hotel, (541) 523–1889, 1996 Main Street, $80–$90.

Oregon Trail Motel, (541) 523–5844, 211 Bridge Street, $36–$44.

Super 8, (541) 523–8282, 250 Campbell Street, $50–$80.

LA GRANDE, OREGON

Howard Johnson, (541) 963–7195, 2612 Island Avenue, $68–$88.
Quail Run Motor Inn, (541) 963–3400, 2400 Adams Avenue, $27–$32.
Stang Manor Bed & Breakfast, (541) 963–2400, 1612 Walnut Street, $85–$100.
Super 8, (541) 963–8080, 2407 East "R" Avenue, $50–$70.
Travelodge, (541) 963–7116, 2215 East Adams Avenue, $32–$64.

MILTON-FREEWATER, OREGON

Morgan Inn, (541) 938–5547, 104 North Columbia (OR 11), $40 and up.

WALLA WALLA, WASHINGTON

Budget Inn, (509) 529–4410, 305 North Second Avenue, $50–$75.
Green Gables Inn Bed & Breakfast, (509) 525–5501, 922 Bonsella, $95–$125.
Hawthorn Inn & Suites, (509) 525–2522, 520 North Second Avenue, $70–$110.
Walla Walla Travelodge, (509) 529–4940, 421 East Main, $52–$75.

PENDLETON, OREGON

Best Western Pendleton Inn, (541) 276–2135, 400 Southeast Nye Avenue, $70–$90.
Chaparral Motel, (541) 276–8654, 620 Southwest Tutuilla, $44–$62.
Red Lion Hotel, (541) 276–6111, 304 Southeast Nye Avenue, $70–$80.
7 Inn, (541) 276–4711, I–84 exit 202, $40–$50.
Wildhorse Resort Motel, (541) 276–0355, 72779 OR 331, $55–$120.

UMATILLA, OREGON

Desert River Inn, (541) 922–1000, 705 Willamette Avenue, $45–$75.
Tillicum Motor Inn, (541) 922–3236, 1481 Sixth Street, $35–$45.

HERMISTON, OREGON

Economy Inn of Hermiston, (541) 567–5516, 835 North First, $40–$75.
Oxford Suites, (541) 564–8000, 1050 North First Street, $60 to $110.

BOARDMAN, OREGON

Dodge City Inn, (541) 481–2451, First and Front Streets, $41–$45.
EconoLodge, (541) 481–2375, 105 Front Street Southwest, $50–$80.

ARLINGTON, OREGON

Village Inn Motel, (541) 454–2646, Cottonwood and Beech Streets, $42–$48.

BIGGS, OREGON

Riviera Motel, (541) 739–2501, 91484 Biggs Rufus Highway, $55–$75.

THE DALLES, OREGON

American Hospitality Inn, (541) 296–9111, 200 West Second Street, $40–$50.

Best Western River City Inn, (541) 296–9107, 112 West Second Street, $50–$90.

Columbia House B&B, (541) 298–4686, 525 East Seventh Street, $85–$95.

The Inn at The Dalles, (541) 296–1167, 3550 Southeast Frontage Road, $30–$65.

Quality Inn–Columbia River Gorge, (541) 298–5161, 2114 West Sixth Street, $50–$95.

Shilo Inn, (541) 298–5502, 3223 Bret Clodfelter Way, $70–$90.

Super 8 Motel, (541) 296–6888, 609 Cherry Heights Road, $55–$75.

Windrider Inn, (541) 296–2607, 200 West Fourth Street, $40–$50.

HOOD RIVER, OREGON

Best Western Hood River Inn, (541) 386–2200, 1108 East Marina Way, $80–$110.

Comfort Suites, (541) 308–1000, 2625 Cascade Avenue, $110–$160.

Hood River Hotel, (541) 386–1900, 102 Oak Avenue, $50–$155.

Love's Riverview Lodge, (541) 386–8719, 1505 Oak Avenue, $70–$75.

Meredith Gorge Motel, (541) 386–1515, 4300 Westcliff Drive, $55–$75.

Vagabond Lodge, (541) 386–2992, 4070 Westcliff Drive, $52–$82.

BINGEN, WASHINGTON

Bingen School Inn, (509) 493–3363, Humboldt and Cedar Streets, $14 (hostel).

CASCADE LOCKS, OREGON

Best Western Columbia River Inn, (541) 374–8777, 735 Wanapa Street, $60–$125.

Bridge of the Gods Motel, (541) 374–8628, US 30, $40–$65.

Cascade Motel, (541) 374–8750, 300 Forest Lane, $40–$52.

STEVENSON, WASHINGTON

EconoLodge, (509) 427–5628, 40 Northeast Second Street, $65–$70.

Skamania Lodge, (509) 427–7700, west on WA 14. $240.

TROUTDALE, OREGON

McMenamins Edgefield, (503) 669–8610, 2126 Southwest Halsey Street, $85–$125.

Motel 6, (503) 665–2254, I–84 exit 17, $39–$50.

Phoenix Inn, (503) 669–6500, 477 Northwest Phoenix Drive, $70–$90.

VANCOUVER, WASHINGTON

Best Inn & Suites, (360) 256–7044, 221 Northeast Chkalov Drive, $65–$75.

Best Western Ferryman's Inn, (360) 574–2151, 7901 Northeast Sixth Avenue, $55–$70.

Homewood Suites Hotel, (360) 750–1100, 701 Southeast Columbia Shores Boulevard, $100–$120.

Salmon Creek Motel, (360) 573–0751, 11901 Northeast WA 99, $50–$58.

Shilo Inn Downtown Vancouver, (360) 696–0411, 401 East Thirteenth Street, $65–$95.

GREATER PORTLAND, OREGON

Best Western Sunnyside Inn, (503) 652–1500, I–205 exit 14 (Clackamas), $60–$70.

Chestnut Tree Inn, (503) 255–4444, 9699 Southeast Stark (I–205 exit 21A), $48–$58.

Days Inn City Center, (503) 221–1611, 1414 Southwest Sixth Avenue, $80–$110.

Governor Hotel, (503) 224–3400, 611 Southwest Tenth, $135–$165.

Hawthorn Inn & Suites, (503) 233–7933, 431 Northeast Multnomah, $90–$120.

Hostelling International–Portland, (503) 236–3380, 3031 Southeast Hawthorne Boulevard, $15.

Red Lion Hotel/Coliseum, (503) 235–8311, 1225 North Thunderbird Way, $50–$110.

Sweetbrier Inn, (503) 692–5800, 7125 Southwest Nyberg (Tualatin), $80–$120.

MOUNT HOOD, OREGON

Brightwood Guest House Bed & Breakfast, (503) 622–5783, 64725 East Barlow Trail Road, $125.

Huckleberry Inn, (503) 272–3325, Government Camp Business Loop, $60–$150.

Mount Hood Inn, (503) 272–3205, 87450 East Government Camp Road, $135–$165.

Timberline Lodge, (503) 272–3311, 6 miles north of Government Camp, $65–$200.

OREGON CITY, OREGON

Ainsworth House Bed & Breakfast, (503) 655–5172, 19130 Lot Whitcomb Drive, $70–$100.

Budget Inn, (503) 656–1955, 19240 Southeast McLoughlin Boulevard, $35–$85.

Hydrangea Bed & Breakfast, (503) 650–4421, 716 Center Street, $60–$75.

Lewis Motel, (503) 656–7052, 18710 South OR 99 East, $50–$85.

Rivershore Hotel, (503) 655–6141, 1900 Clackamette Drive, $65–$125.

CAMPING

VALE, OREGON

Prospector RV Park, (541) 473–3879, 511 North Eleventh Street.

ONTARIO, OREGON

Country Campground, (541) 889–6042, 660 Sugar Avenue.

HUNTINGTON, OREGON

Farewell Bend State Park, (541) 869–2365, I–84 exit 353.

BAKER CITY, OREGON

Baker City Motel & RV Park, (541) 523–6381, 880 Elm Street.

Mountain View Holiday Trav-L-Park, (541) 523–4824, 2845 Hughes Lane.

Oregon Trails West RV Park, (541) 523–3236, 42534 North Cedar Road (exit 302).

LA GRANDE, OREGON

Hilgard Junction State Recreation Area, 9 miles west on I-84.

LaGrande RV Resort, (541) 962-0909, 2632 Bearco Loop Road.

Hot Lake RV Resort, (541) 963-5253, 65182 Hot Lake Lane.

MEACHAM, OREGON

Emigrant Springs State Park, (541) 983-2277, I-84 exit 234.

WALLA WALLA, WASHINGTON

Fort Walla Walla Campground, (509) 527-3770, west on Dalles Military Road.

PENDLETON, OREGON

Brooke RV Park, (541) 276-5353, 5 Northeast Eighth Street.

Mountain View RV Park, (541) 276-1041, 1375 Southeast Third Street.

Stotlar RV Park, (541) 276-0734, 15 Southeast Eleventh Street.

Wildhorse Resort & RV Park, (541) 966-1646, 72781 OR 331.

ECHO, OREGON

Fort Henrietta RV Park, (541) 376-8411, 10 West Main Street.

UMATILLA, OREGON

Hat Rock Campground, (541) 567-4188, east on US 730 across from Hat Rock State Park.

BOARDMAN, OREGON

Boardman Marina & RV Park, (541) 481-7217, I-84 exit 164.

BIGGS, OREGON

Maryhill State Park, (509) 773-5007, I-84 exit 104, across the Columbia River in Washington.

Deschutes River State Recreation Area, (541) 739-2322, west on US 30. Primitive sites.

THE DALLES, OREGON

Horsethief Lake State Park, (509) 767-1159, I-84 exit 87, across the Columbia River in Washington. Primitive sites.

Memaloose State Park, (541) 374-8811, along I-84 (westbound access only).

HOOD RIVER, OREGON

Sunset RV Park, (541) 386-6098, 2300 West Cascade Avenue.

Toll Bridge Park, (541) 386-6323, 17 miles south on OR 35.

Tucker Park, (541) 386-4477, 4 miles south on OR 281.

Viento State Park, (541) 374-8811, 8 miles west along I-84.

Numerous Forest Service campgrounds are located in the Mount Hood National Forest south of Hood River. Call (503) 352-6002 for information.

CASCADE LOCKS, OREGON

Bridge of the Gods RV Park, (541) 374–8628, 630 Wanapa Street.

Cascade Locks KOA, (541) 374–8668, 2 miles east on Forest Lane.

Marina Park, (541) 374–8619, on the Columbia River.

BONNEVILLE, OREGON

Ainsworth State Park, (503) 695–2261, 8 miles west on I–84.

Eagle Creek, (503) 695–2276, eastbound access only off of I–84.

PORTLAND, OREGON

Jantzen Beach RV Park, (503) 289–7626, 1503 North Hayden Island Drive.

Pheasant Ridge RV Park, (503) 682–7829, 8275 Southwest Elligsen Road (Wilsonville).

Reeder Beach Resort RV Park, (503) 621–3098, 26048 Northwest Reeder Road (Sauvie Island).

Trailer Park of Portland, (503) 692–0225, 6645 Southwest Nyberg Road (Tualatin).

MOUNT HOOD, OREGON

Mt. Hood Village, (503) 622–4011, 65000 East US 26 (Welches).

RESTAURANTS

VALE, OREGON

Red Garter Ice Cream Saloon, (541) 473–2294, 293 Washington Street West. Oregon Trail mural outside.

Riverside Inn, (541) 473–3640, 163 Short Street North. Breakfast anytime.

Starlite Cafe, (541) 473–2500, 152 Clark Street North.

ONTARIO, OREGON

Brewsky's Broiler, (541) 889–3700, 23 Southeast First Avenue. Casual dining with microbrews.

Casa Jaramillo, (541) 889–9258, 157 Southeast Second. Mexican food.

Cheyenne Social Club, (541) 889–3777, 111 Southwest First Street. Steaks, seafood.

Far East Restaurant, (541) 881–8888, 44 Northeast Third. Chinese and Japanese food.

HUNTINGTON, OREGON

Farewell Bend Restaurant & Lounge, (541) 869–2281, I–84 exit 353.

BAKER CITY, OREGON

Baker Truck Corral, (541) 523–4318, I–84 exit 304. Homestyle cooking, open twenty-four hours.

Barley Brown's Brewpub, (541) 523–4266, 2190 Main Street.

El Erradero, (541) 523–2327, 2100 Broadway Avenue. Authentic Mexican food.

Geiser Grand Hotel, (888) 434–7374, 1996 Main Street. Fine dining in historic hotel.

Haines Steak House, (541) 856–3639, 10 miles north on US 30. Closed Tuesday.

Oregon Trail Restaurant, (541) 523–5844, 211 Bridge Street. Home cooking.

Sumpter Junction, (541) 523–9437, 2 Sunridge Lane. American and Mexican food.

LA GRANDE, OREGON

Foley Station, (541) 963–7473, 1011 Adams Avenue. Fine dining.

Flying J Travel Plaza, (541) 963–9762, I–84 exit 265. Open twenty-four hours.

Mamacita's, (541) 963–6223, 110 Depot Street. Mexican food.

Nature's Pantry, (541) 963–7955, 1907 Fourth Street. Vegetarian deli.

Sydney's Delicacies & Delights, (541) 963–6500, 1115 Adams Avenue. Upscale casual cafe.

WALLA WALLA, WASHINGTON

The Homestead Restaurant, (509) 522–0345, 1528 Isaacs. Seafood, beef, and pasta.

Jacobi's Cafe, (509) 525–2677, 416 North Second Street. Italian, American, and vegetarian food.

Modern Restaurant, (509) 525–8662, 2200 Melrose. Cantonese and American dishes.

Paisano's, (509) 527–3511, 26 East Main Street. Creative Italian dining.

Red Apple, (509) 525–5113, 57 East Main. Steak and seafood.

PENDLETON, OREGON

Big John's Hometown Pizza, (541) 276–0550, 225 Southwest Ninth. Pizza, salad bar.

Cimmiyotti's, (541) 276–4314, 137 South Main. Italian and American fare.

Circle's Barbecue, (541) 276–9637, 210 Southeast Fifth. Steaks, prime rib, seafood.

The Hut, (541) 276–0756, 1400 Southwest Dorian. Steaks and seafood.

Kinship Café, (541) 966–9748, 72789 OR 331. At Tamastslikt Cultural Institute.

Lee's Cafe, (541) 276–5819, 205 Southwest Emigrant. Chinese and American food.

ECHO, OREGON

Echo Hotel Restaurant & Lounge, (541) 376–8354, Main and North Dupont Streets.

H & P Cafe, (541) 376–8573, 231 Main.

STANFIELD, OREGON

Stanfield Cafe, (541) 449–1321, 170 North Main.

UMATILLA, OREGON

Desert River Inn Restaurant, (541) 922–1100, 705 Willamette Avenue. Wide menu.

Nick's Italian Restaurant & Lounge, (541) 922–2572, 610 Sixth Street.

BOARDMAN, OREGON

C & D Drive-In and Bakery, (541) 481–4981, 103 North Main.

Pizza Corner, (541) 481–2550, 103 Southwest Front Street.

BIGGS, OREGON

Biggs Café, (541) 739–2395, Biggs Junction.

Jack's Fine Foods, (541) 739–2362, Biggs Junction. Steaks, daily specials.

THE DALLES, OREGON

Baldwin Saloon, (541) 296–5666, 205 Court Street. Dine in historic building.

Basalt Rock Café, (541) 296–8600. In the Columbia Gorge Discovery Center.

Casa El Miradoro, (541) 298–7388, 302 West Second Street. Mexican food.

Cousins Restaurant & Saloon, (541) 298–2771, 2114 West Sixth Street. In the Quality Inn.

Dave's Hometown Pizza, (541) 296–2281, 809 Chenowith Street. Pizza, chicken, pasta, microbrews.

O'Callahan's, (541) 298–8225, I–84 exit 87. Wide menu in the Shilo Inn.

Windseeker Restaurant & Portside Pub, (541) 298–7171, 1535 Bargeway Road. Riverside dining.

HOOD RIVER, OREGON

Bette's Place, (541) 386–1880, 416 Oak Street. Locally popular breakfast and lunch spot.

Big City Chicks, (541) 387–3811, Thirteenth at B Street. Seafood, many vegetarian dishes.

Columbia Gorge Hotel, (541) 386–5566, 4000 Westcliff Drive. Northwest cuisine, "famous farm breakfast." Reservations advised.

Full Sail Brewing Co., (541) 386–7329, 506 Columbia Street. Noted brew pub.

Mesquitery, (541) 386–2002, 1219 Twelfth Street. Variety of cuisines grilled over 100 percent Mesquite wood.

Sage's Café & Coffee House, (541) 386–9404, 202 Cascade. Sandwiches, quiche, and salads.

Santacroce's Italian Restaurant, (541) 354–2511, 4780 OR 35. Traditional Italian food.

CASCADE LOCKS, OREGON

Charburger Restaurant, (541) 374–8477, 745 Northwest Wa-Na-Pa. View of the Columbia River.

STEVENSON, WASHINGTON

Big River Grill, (509) 427–4888, WA 14. Creative food, casual setting.

Joe's El Rio Mexican Café, (509) 427–4479, WA 14. Closed Monday.

TROUTDALE, OREGON

McMenamins Edgefield, (503) 669–8610, 2126 Southwest Halsey Street. Brew pub.

Tad's Chicken 'n Dumplins, (503) 666–5337. On the Crown Point Highway with view of the Sandy River.

VANCOUVER, WASHINGTON

Billygan's Red Hot Roadhouse, (360) 573–2711, 13200 Northeast WA 99. Steaks, seafood, prime rib.

Fa Fa Gourmet Chinese Restaurant, (360) 260–1378, 11712 Fourth Plain Boulevard.

Hudson's Bar & Grill, (360) 816–6100, 7805 Northeast Greenwood Drive. Northwestern cuisine.

Sheldon's Café at the Grant House, (360) 699–1213, 1101 Officers' Row. Casual fine dining.

PORTLAND, OREGON

Atwater's Restaurant, (503) 275–3600, 111 Southwest Fifth Avenue. Great views atop U.S. Bank Tower.

Esparza's Tex-Mex Cafe, (503) 234–7909, 2725 Southeast Ankeny. Lunch and dinner. Closed Sunday and Monday.

Hamburger Mary's, (503) 223–0900, 239 South Broadway. Funky local favorite near theaters.

Jake's Grill, (503) 220–1850, 611 Southwest Tenth Street. Fine dining in the Governor Hotel.

Kells, (503) 227–4057, 112 Southwest Second Avenue. Irish pub and restaurant.

Macheezmo Mouse, (503) 228–3491, 723 Southwest Salmon and other locations. Authentic Mexican food.

Rustica, (503) 288–0990, 1700 Northeast Broadway. Italian food.

Shenanigan's on the Willamette, (503) 289–0966, 4575 North Channel (Swan Island). Seafood, Sunday brunch. River view dining.

Typhoon, (503) 224–8285, 400 Southwest Broadway. Upscale Thai in the Imperial Hotel.

OREGON CITY, OREGON

Elmer's, (503) 655–1837, 1837 Molalla Avenue. Family dining.

Friendship Restaurant, (503) 657–4507, 1003 North Main Street. Chinese restaurant.

River Shore Bar & Grill, (503) 655–5155, 1900 Clackamette Drive.

Shari's Restaurant, (503) 657–9183, 1926 Southeast McLoughlin Boulevard.

INDEX

ABOUT THE AUTHOR

Julie Fanselow was born in Illinois and grew up in Bethel Park, Pennsylvania. She earned a bachelor's degree in journalism at Ohio University, where she minored in history and political science. After ten years as a reporter and editor for daily newspapers in Ohio, Washington State, and Idaho, Fanselow turned to full-time freelance writing in 1991. The first edition of this book, published in 1993, won the best guidebook award from the National Association for Interpretation.

Fanselow's other travel guidebooks include *Traveling the Lewis & Clark Trail* and *Idaho Off the Beaten Path* (Globe Pequot), and the Lonely Planet guides to *Texas and British Columbia*. She is a regular contributor to *Sunset* magazine and co-founder of www.guidebookwriters.com, the leading online source of top travel-writing talent. Fanselow lives with her family near the Oregon Trail in Twin Falls, Idaho.